Wrong Woman at the Wrong Time... TURNT UP

BY D. HARVEY RAWLINGS

This book is a work of fiction. The names, characters, businesses, organizations, places, events and incidents either are the product of the author's sole imagination or used fictitiously. Any resemblance to actual persons, living or dead, events or locales is entirely coincidental.

Jacket Design by Darren Harvey Sr.
Cover Design: Darren Harvey Sr.
Cover Model: LaKendra Brooks

Contact the Author
www.dharveyrawlings.com

Comments on Facebook Page
D. Harvey Rawlings

Twitter & Amazon

Dedications:

Darren, love you buddy, you are the best and the most honest thing I have <u>ever</u> done in my life...you won't be able to read this novel for a few years but, regardless you inspire me to do my best. I hope I do for you as well...always enjoy yourself, Dad

Tracy, thank you for your love, hard work & support ... Mother Mary E...
Sharon...Gwen...Claudette...Dallas...Robert...Oswald... Shaffers...Angelic. Lakeya, Nicole, Dallas Jr, Kiee, Alexis. Dee Dee D, Darlena and Terrance; Carroll...Connie...Aunt Rena...Angelia (Na)...Kim...Cameron (RIP)...Gary...Christy... Faith

LaKendra B for your amazing photo, simply beautiful. Your image jumps off the cover...God's speed on your modeling career. The other two Sanderson Sisters: Nykisha, Takiyah (LOL)

Special Thanks to,
My loving grandmother, Elizabeth Smothers-Harvey, I wish you could see the man that I've become; I mean before this...I don't speak about this much but I miss you a lot...D

TO ALL THE READERS: GRATITUDE. I COULD NOT HAVE CONTINUED IN THIS POSITIVE DIRECTION WITHOUT THE HELP OF YOUR WORDS OF ENCOURAGEMENT AND YOUR PATRONAGE OR HONEST REVIEWS DIRECTLY FROM YOUR POINT OF VIEW...EACH ONE OF YOU HAS MY UTMOST THANKS FOR LETTING MY STORIES INTO YOUR FREE TIME.

I CANNOT SAY ENOUGH, D

CHAPTER 1

"I don't care I just want out of this shit right now. It's choking me," Tony Parker said into his Bluetooth to his girlfriend, Valerie Dupree. It's Saturday, morning around 2 AM. He's riding in his Escalade truck on his way back to his house in Bowie, Maryland. She's getting on his damn nerves, he thought. The more he talked to Valerie the more he pushed the gas pedal harder with his foot. She's been going on up in his damn ear since he pulled out of the parking lot at Maryland Live. But, this is something he's been used to hearing. He didn't even bother to pull the earpiece from his ear, like he usually does so he ain't got to hear that crap she's talking 'bout. He's already numb to her complaints. Really, he's putting on a show because he's got his sidepiece, Sharnia Burkefield over on the passenger side riding with him. He knows the more he goes in on Valerie the more Sharnia will eat it up. Then he knows it's going to be on tonight. She likes to feel special.

They are traveling through the night just exiting I95. He reached over and unsnapped the top of the tight jeans. He slid his hands down the opening of her jeans as far as he could maneuver. She giggled and wiggled like some immature teenager in her seat as he touched her. She has been listening to him talk on the phone. She enjoyed the way he disrespected Valerie and it is all because he wants to be with on her tonight.

It's about damn time that he got rid of his uppity, bitchy girlfriend and be with her, she thought. After all, she is the one he runs to whenever Valerie doesn't treat him right and that's all the time. She knows how to treat him and make him feel good. Damn good. She knows what a black man needs and doesn't have to be a black woman to pull it off.

The brothers love this white woman.

He's hers now or at least for tonight, but she's not stupid.

She knows she could be on the other end of that phone call just as quick. But, this time she plans to keep him and make him love her.

"Tony this can't be happening again. Look if I come over and get my things I'm not coming back this time. I mean it this time. You think you can kick me out every time you want to bring one of those whores you deal with on the side to our bed?" Valerie asked him snapping at him. "Yeah, you didn't think I knew you do that, did you? I'm not dumb."

How in the hell did she know that?

Tony Parker is always two up on the women he smashes. That's why they can't catch him. She must be reaching trying to get him off his game.

There's no way she could know that.

Tony noticed she isn't doing her usual thing like crying or begging to work out their relationship. It doesn't matter this is what he wants to do, cause he can't wait to get this broad home, so she can melt her ass all over him.

"You know Tony, I am too classy of a chick to be messing with you anyway. So yeah, I'll come over to get my things. I'll come by right now. Your bitch had better not be there when I get there. I don't want any shit," she said firmly. "Ugh, I am so damn tired of you," she screamed.

"Uh, uh. Tell you what Valerie. You come by tomorrow cause I don't want no shit either. Hell, I'm tired."

What's the point in messing up his night with ole' Nia, he thought? Hell, he raked in seven grand tonight at the black jack table and won back the three grand it took to get it. Hell, he's on a roll. He don't need no speed bumps.

She hung up on him without saying a word.

He knows she's being shady cause he just let her ass walk. She bet not come by his place, tonight.

His attention went back to his cellphone as he dialed another number.

"Yeah. Be there in few." Tony stated ending the call.

****

Later as Tony pulled up in front of his house. He blew his horn twice. Sharnia and he jumped out of his truck. The summer night felt warm as it hit them in their faces. Sharnia ran her hands all over the tight blouse she wore, caressing herself. She loved checking herself out in front of Tony like this because she knows how it sets him off. She wore it especially tight because she knows Tony likes to see her like that. When she glanced over at him, she saw him watching her licking his lips.

Once they walked into the house Sharnia went straight upstairs and disappeared down the hall into his master bedroom. Tony stayed on the first floor and went to the back of the house, into the sunroom. He went to the door which connected to the room and led outside to the deck.

He opened the door and walk out onto it. It was pitch dark on the deck with a few neighbors' lights shining slightly illuminating the backyard. Off to the edge of the deck a figure sat on one of the benches.

"You ready?" Tony asked.

"Um hmm," said the female who appeared in the dim light from the dark area of the deck.

Tony led the sexy framed woman in through the sunroom and upstairs they went. She wore a pair of tight hip hugging shorts and a wraparound tie bikini top. He watched her body sway as she walked down the hallway in front of him, through the door and into his bedroom.

"Sharnia baby, I asked my next-door neighbor, Marietta, if she could turn us up tonight. You mind?" He said to her slyly as he pulled on the strings of Marietta's bikini top.

He really didn't care if she answered or not. It's just a formality for Tony to ask her cause he's going to have what he wants to have anyway. This is his world and what he says goes or she can get the hell out.

He turned his back and walked over to the mini bar to pour himself a stiff drink straight with no chaser.

Sharnia sat up in Tony's bed staring at Marietta. She's someone Sharnia didn't know. She looks older to her. She wasn't expecting this but, she didn't want to make him mad by telling him no.

"That's what's up, Tony. You know how we get down…," Sharnia giggled trying to cover up how she really feels. She got rid of one trick now here's another. "It's time to get at it, Big Tony."

****

It's not that he didn't love Valerie anymore, it's nothing like that. She just couldn't keep up with the Tony Parker rule, sex, sex and more sex…and keep your damn mouth shut. Valerie would never have participated in something like what went down last night. He had Sharnia and Marietta in raw dog last night.

Lately since he and Sharnia's been doing their thing this has been his maneuvers. He's gotten used to being this way living in his own, created single world. In his world, the women in his life do what the hell he says. They keep their mouths shut and stop asking him for shit.

What good ole Deron trying to tell him for years; something about sacrifices? Well Big Tony can't do that. It gets in the way too much.

Chicks need to stop asking for time.

Stop asking for money.

Stop asking to move in.

Stop asking to get married.

Stop asking for children.

Just lie on your back, spread your legs and shut the hell up.

He tried to get Valerie to do this stuff but, she acts like she can't follow simple damn direction and here they are again; ain't together.

But, he does loves Valerie.

He'd never admit it verbally but, he does.

This playing hubby and wifey thing with Valerie is really trying to make him soft. She's been in his house too long. He should've never let her move in, he thought as he pounded the bedframe with his fist.

Shit, he's got to keep still in this bed.

He's too lost in his thoughts that he forgot Sharnia is still here. Marietta left an hour ago, just before he drifted off to sleep. But, she didn't have to go far.

Just out back and through the fence.

She lives with her sister in the house right outside of Tony's backyard. Deron calls them the 'booty sisters' cause both of them are too fine.

He has to admit it, Marietta isn't bad for a broad in her late forties. Hell, she and her sister don't look it anyway. He guessed it must be those damn Zumba classes she says she's always running off to attend. He thought she was just flipping him off. That shit really must work cause she was wiggling all that last night.

She gave little Sharnia a run for her money, that's why she's sleeping so sound.

He don't want to wake her. He don't feel like answering any of those questions he knows she would ask him.

What's wrong baby?

Are you hungry, baby?

You want some baby.

Anything I can do to make you feel good baby.

He just wanted to enjoy the spoils of them lying together in his bed in silence. Since she's here.

As Sharnia turned slightly, he started to feel a little guilty on how things went down with Valerie, which is surprising to him. She's been good to him. It's just that he can't be all that she wanted loyal or stable. Did he mention loyal? It's just too many fine women out here for him to settle on just this one. Hell, he's just about to turn thirty-one this year, been there, done that shit, with all that domestic married life trimmings.

What's the point of getting married again for all the trouble its worth?

Yeah Valerie is right she has that class and is hella fine. The day he met her he thought she was this chocolate dip in a five-six frame. She's real sexy with a World Star hip-hop beauty. She knows she's super-fine. She's got it going on like she's one of those girls in those videos on World Star hip-hop.com. But, there's more to being in this thing with him than that. Prince Georges County, Maryland has a whole lot of fine woman with class to settle down with. Those ones looking for the house with white picket fences and two point one kids with a dog.

Nah not, for Mr. Tony Parker.

He's post up in this seven hundred-thousand-dollar home and got all the trimmings and all alone.

He likes it like that.

A home worth seven hundred thousand dollars but, he got it for fewer than five; with the help of his realtor buddy, Erica Fontanne. They were always able to make good money on property together when they weren't punishing the sheets and it's just beginning.

Making money is something Tony likes to do on the side these days. They are about to take it to the next level and blow this real estate thing wide open before it flips down again. Damn DOW JONES.

It hasn't been easy either trying to make this dough with all these slick investments. He needs time to work all these figures and his contacts, like he do in peace. So, he needs a woman who's gonna ease his tension, not cause him headaches. Valerie caused him headaches. She was always planning too far ahead into the future and damn it she wanted a child. That's all she's been talking about for these last past few years. No more children.

How many more times can he explain this to a broad that he's been there, done that and ain't gonna do it no more. He's not setting himself up to be an alimony hoe for no broads, no more. His baby mama, Katrina hit him up with his son, Tony Jr. It hipped him to all the other gold diggin' chicks who are after his loot.

The more he thought about it though, the more he realized he didn't really learn all of that then. It wasn't until crack head Monica, his ex-wife, hit him up with alimony after they divorced. Monica all but tried to finish him off and then a few years ago, she came back with that fake ass paternity scare.

Another time he trusted some broad she bled him for over ten Gs and he never even hit it, not once.

She's definitely a viper.

That one owes him.

So of course, he don't want no marriages or no live-ins.

Most of all he don't-want-no-more-kids.

It's not that he doesn't love or appreciate his son, but Tony Jr. is the last Parker on this end. Let him carry on the legacy. Tony wants to spend his money while he's here. He can't take another eighteen-year hit. Not when Tony Jr.'s so close to releasing his pockets and his monetary link to his bitch-ass mother.

So, having Valerie try to trap him into a marriage with white picket fences and child support checks is not where he's heading. Never again.

When his boys, Deron and Bryan, were hanging with him tough, he guessed he could carry that game with Valerie as far as he wanted it to go. It was a blasé, blasé thing to do cause everybody was booed up going here and there.

All that went down changed a lot of things.

Tony's never experienced death before and especially not this close. That shit hurt like hell. The desire to want to change. The desire to want to be like them and especially wanting to be tied down again all went out the window.

Things just kept changing for the worse.

Although these past years it went on pretty good, at least for him, it's time to move on.

He used to be able to be single and be down with his girl at the same time. Like he always did but, things changed.

His boy Deron went Christian on him and he didn't have a running partner no more. They're still like brothers but, to be honest it's hard for Tony to get adjusted to Deron being so…holy. Or what Deron says having a spiritual cover. It's like having a brother you really don't have anything in common with; but because you *are* brothers you try to keep it going. No need to try to flip him back because his wife Dawn has him on lock down. But, who knows Deron might just want to get back out on the streets to party. He knows though Dawn's not letting up, ever.

Not what she went through to get him.

That was Cheresse's doing.

He all but begged, Deron not to mess with Cheresse. He knew up-close and personnel she was bad news. But, he wouldn't listen. He sniffed some of that booty and he was gone. Tony knew the allure. He'd been there before. That was one of the stupidest moments in his life. Maybe he should have told Deron the truth.

He didn't want to admit he was set-up by Cheresse.

"Tony what's on your mind baby?" Sharnia said to him seductively, jarring him from his muse.

That's a new one, he thought.

He didn't notice that she is up. He was trying to be still, but he's mad as hell. He isn't supposed to think about what these chicks felt once he's done with them. It must be some of Deron's halo rubbing off on him. He should've kept on moving when he and Deron had that fight. He knew that religious stuff would make him weak. He's got to get a drink, he thought. That's what he needs to start this day a nice glass of Patron on ice.

Shit. After all this is Saturday morning.

It's the freaking weekend.

It ain't that he's an atheist or something worst. he just ain't ready right now to attend church every Sunday singing hymns. He's still trying to have his fun and he likes his world just like it is right now.

At least he's got something right with what went down with his side thing, Sharnia. She's got something too that draws him to her Kim K tan hot body, but she's a little needy. Still she does what Captain Tony tells her. She fulfilled, as usual, all his expectation of her and with no complaints just like he wants. She's been his back and forth, run around girl for years; and she keeps that body just the way he likes it. She even shaves down south in the shape of the letter capital T for her big stud Tony.

It's increased in the number of times he's been with her the more Valerie nagged him. It's funny how things sort of went this way after that shit went down in Deron's office a few years back. Ever since then she's been willing to be his sex-toy again.

As much as he tries not to feel it, no woman actually can compare to Valerie. She's his class act three times over. He's tried so many times to purge her from his system but, he can't seem to do it. It was an instant attraction the night they met. They've been together ever since even though it's been rocky.

If he were to get married, she would be it.

It's the least he could do.

He shook his head to ward off the crazy thought as if a bee buzz around his head. What in the hell is he thinking? His thoughts are everywhere.

Sharnia, yeah, now that's the ticket. Quiet and obedient.

"You're not sleeping well baby?" She spoke again to get a response from him.

"Yeah, I slept okay. You hanging around or are you about to leave?"

Her body tensed up and stiffen. She knows what that line means. She's been with him too long not to. She doesn't like this part about him.

How ice cold he gets at the drop of a dime.

Tony and that damn ego.

Just literally hours ago, they were doing all these sexual things some which made her question her own logic. The way they turn it out last night was incredible. Both she and Marietta are nothing but, playthings to him and now he's bored again. Just that quick. He really wants her to leave but, he didn't want to ask her to do it, he wants her to say it. He's slick like that. He always seems to know what buttons to push to get a woman to do what he wants.

He didn't even think about the time and how early it is.

She's put up with him too long, tending to his every need. She's stuck hoping one day she will be his woman. There was a time when she wouldn't even talk to him because she knew how much of an ass he could be to women. But, he's been good to her. Or is it she enjoys his sex far more than she wants to admit and it's clouding her judgment?

He's all up in her mind constantly, every day, far more than any other black man she's dated or any man to be exact. She didn't want anybody else. She enjoys his power and besides she's seen a side of him nobody's seen. Deron all but warned her years ago, that she might want to let go of that little fling that happened with Tony.

But that just lit the fuse.

That just set her on fire.

She knew it took a lot for Deron to betray his friend with that bit of information. But, he was only looking out for her. It's all because Tony is unpredictable with women he said. He said she needed to stick with somebody that's going to treat her like she needed to be treat.

But she didn't listen.

She couldn't listen.

She knew what she would be getting when she wrapped her heart around Tony. At least she thought she did. She knew about the girlfriend, but they were on shaky ground; and that any day she would take her place. But, things were uncertain and she came to him before he left Valerie.

She should've waited. She played herself.

Instead, she entered into a hot bed of sex with him being the other woman and behind Deron's back. She rationalized this is her business. Even though he's her supervisor at work he can't supervise her life. She didn't mean for Tony to catch her literally with her panties down and her mind as well. No, she knew what she was doing and she knew eventually Valerie would be gone. This is what she's been wanting since they got together that first time.

As Sharnia got up out of the bed to go take a shower, she stroked Tony's chest.

She's never going to leave him alone.

He'll have to force her to leave. If she keeps on loving him with her fine body, it'll never happen.

He is hers.

"Hey, where you going?" he asked as he reached out to her playfully grabbing her arm.

"I'm going to take a shower so I can get out of your hair baby. I know you need some downtime to yourself."

He thought about it a moment before he responded to her looking at her.

He didn't really want to be alone. Not today.

Valerie isn't coming back here until later today to get her things. Even if she came by now Sharnia could wait in the other room. So, he don't need her to get out quick he thought. As she walked around his large bedroom he continued to watch her move like water in a Jacuzzi.

"Well I tell you what," he said getting up from the king-size bed and walking towards her. She could visibly see what he wants to do as she looked down at him. He made sure she seen him swinging. "Let's go in there the shower together and see if I can get you to handle this business right here. Might as well turn up the rest of the weekend and let me make love to you."

Sharnia giggled at his efforts to be romantic.

He don't want her to leave.

She has him.

****

Monday around noon, Dawn Stone put her house keys down on the foyer table once she entered the house through the front door. She stood in the foyer for a minute. It is quiet to her but she knows it shouldn't be, Deron should be here. Maybe he's sleeping she thought. After she didn't hear anything she decided to walk downstairs to the basement, his usual hangout.

"Deron baby are you here?" Dawn said as she walked through the basement of their home. She heard the TV loud as usual coming from the theater room. "Deron?" she called again, louder, but he didn't answer.

She began to worry as she hastily went to the closed door and opened it. Once inside she saw that he wasn't there and the TV blared loudly. She turned the TV off with the remote. She heard a flushing sound from the adjoining bathroom. Almost immediately, Deron emerged from the opened door.

"Hey baby," he said to her causally.

That's all he can say she thought?

It's twelve noon on a Monday and he's home from work again. She wouldn't have known is she hadn't called to speak to him and Sharnia told her he had gone home.

"Deron, are you sick or something? Why are you home? Why didn't you call me?"

"I just didn't feel like finishing the day. I think I'm coming down with something. I took off the rest of the week."

"You were off last week and some days before that. You know you're taking off a lot of days before the cookout we're throwing in a couple of weeks. Are you going to be ready for that? You seem fine. I mean you haven't been to the doctor yet. Is there something going on at work that I need to know about?"

"Dawn baby nothing's going on that you don't know about. I've just been feeling kind of blah these days and just needed some time to myself. I figure it's not fair to you that I just come home and retreat to my man cave leaving you with Jr. So this way I get a little Deron time and I'm all good when he gets home from the daycare."

"It's not really necessary. I told you that if you're tired from work at any time Jr. will be okay. I know it's not a habit and you have a heavy workload. I get it baby but you can't keep missing work like this. You're the Regional Manager now. You can't cut out days at a time like this, like you own the place. It just doesn't look right to the rest of the staff. You need to be there."

"I know," he said as he walked up to her, embraced and kissed her.

She's right he is missing quite a bit of days. Having gone from General Manager to Regional Manager in less than two years is something he didn't expect. But it happened. He can't start messing up now. He really don't know why he's doing what he's doing. Just all of a sudden these days he just can't seem to function or concentrate at work. Home has been a retreat for him.

He loves his family so much.

When he met Dawn, she was like his instant lifeline. After all that drama he went through with Cheresse, it's as if God just reached down and sent him this angel.

She has been so good to him beyond words.

He don't deserve her, not with what he's done.

As he went to sit back down Dawn looked at him. She knows something else is going on other than what he's giving to her as an excuse.

He's being too distance without really being distance.

She knows her husband, Deron Stone very well. She don't think it's another woman, they were passed all that. To this day, she can honestly say he's never lied to her since that time two years ago. It was a time when they were getting together and he wasn't honest with her. She felt the pain a little, remembering when he broke her trust in him. By the grace of God, she was able to see it through because she believed this man truly loves her. Yes, he did some really foul things, but he confessed to God.

He stuck by his apology and made them whole again.

She had to forgive him to move on with her life.

Then she had to move on from him to be with him again.

She could have continued to hold it over his head throughout their time together, but it would've just destroyed them in the end. He needed forgiveness.

When he declared his need for her, not his want, but his need for her to come back to him, she knew. She knew that Jesus had sent him through his trial and that he came out of it a new man. That's what her faith has taught her and what she believes in.

It's almost as if he needed to go through what he went through to be the perfect man for her and she's honored so much to be his perfect woman. The woman God has made her to be. Not perfect but, perfect for Deron.

She was able to restore her trust in him and it has been rough. Deron Jr. was the toughest part.

Raising another woman's child is not as comfortable as she's made it seem. But, they have been able to do it because she's been in Deron Jr.'s life since he was born.

She never had to deal with the mother ever and that's the blessing.

It's not as if she wanted to prevent the mother from being in his life, which was her choice not Dawn's. So to Deron Jr., she's his mother and to Dawn, he's her son.

No one will *ever* take that from her.

Once the adoption papers are completed at the end of the year, legally she will be his mother.

But, it won't matter either way.

Why did she wait this long to secure it?

Was it because she was trying to have one of her own? They're trying but, it hasn't happened yet. Nothing's wrong with neither one of them physically. According to the doctors it simply hasn't happened yet. For now, they will have Deron Jr. as their only child and she will be his mother. She said she was his mother the moment she said she would marry his father. She means it.

She has invested too much in this to see it rocked. So if Deron's going through something she's going to make sure he knows that she's here for him. He's the love of her life and she needs him, just like she knows he needs her.

Practically, a little over two years have moved on pretty fast through their time together.

She remembers the day when Deron came to her office declaring his love after so many months they had been apart. Even though she was, kept in the loop about his activities by Valerie and eventually Yolanda she'd given up hope that they would be together. Even to the fact that she would actually want to be with him again. It was a bitter pill to swallow.

The lies.

The betrayals. Cheresse. Audrey and Deron Jr.

Now they are living in this house together, married. A life they instantly built together before they knew they were going to work out completely.

It had to work.

She thought at times that maybe they got married too quickly. It must have been love at first sight she thought, when they first met. He looked like he had lost his world.

There was something about him which drawn her to him instantly and he seemed complex. It was a lot of tension there. She found out where all that tension was coming from. It was the woman he was dealing with at the time, Cheresse Bennett. That's a name that she hasn't thought about in years.

She guessed with all the strangeness Deron's exhibiting brought Dawn back to that time when she found out he was hiding something from her. The more she was with him the more it was clear to see. A place in time when Cheresse threatened everything and Dawn found out how treacherous Cheresse could really be.

She had never encountered anyone before or since as wicked as Cheresse. She was so many things and some things Dawn promised herself she would never call her. Cheresse tried her faith those days and especially that one day at her office building.

Cheresse showed up at Dawn's job unexpectedly. Dawn had her engagement ring on shining brightly on her finger. The one Deron just gave to her minutes before. Cheresse was witness to her happiness, which was poetic justice. But, that wasn't what Dawn wanted.

All she wanted is peace.

She wasn't trying to show Cheresse that she had won the man.

She wasn't competing for him that was all Cheresse.

She became a nuisance on that day more than she had ever been in Dawn's perspective.

The memory of it is right on the forefront of her mind. She flashed back to the day it happened...

---*"I should bust you in your face bitch." Cheresse said to Dawn as she walked behind Deron and her on the busy street.*

They'd just come out of Dawn's work place on their way to lunch. Deron had proposed to Dawn and of course, she'd accepted. They were going to talk and get their relationship back on track. It had been nine months since they broke up all because of Cheresse. Now she was back. Cheresse kept on with the torrents of loud cursing as arm in arm Deron and Dawn walked down M street NW. They were making their way toward the nearby parking garage where Dawn parked her car daily. It was rough. Dawn almost lost it a couple of times, but she allowed the Lord to keep her steady.

"Don't say anything Deron, it's alright," she reassured him.

Dawn just wanted to make it to her car because of the embarrassment of passersby's staring and starting to gawk at the three of them. This is just one more thing that made it hard to be with Deron, Cheresse's public displays. The first time it was at TGI Friday's. Several of the people at the other table were looking and listening to every word Cheresse said to her that night. She made every dirty word stick. She did it on purpose.

"Deron Stone," she yelled behind them. "All you do is play games. You're not going to do this to me. I want your bitch to hear this. You think I'm your whore at night while you parade her around in the public like she's your wife? I'm nobody's whore, damn it. I'm a bad bitch, you know it."

"Don't say anything Deron. You know she just wants us to stop," she said again.

"What did you say?" Cheresse said stepping up closer behind them. "You know I want fight you anyway. You think you're so holy but you're the whore. Stealing my man. Come on Dawn admit it you pregnant or something. That's the only reason why Deron's not saying anything. Whore bitch."

"Dawn I'm sorry I got to do something about this. Go on and get the car. I'm just going to talk to her."

"No! Ignore her," she demanded almost shaking. "That's your problem now you cater to her tantrums. I said that I'm good with this. Let's just get my car. I'll call back to the office and take the rest of the day off."

They got to the car and drove to the entrance of the garage. Cheresse was waiting there at the garage entrance when they pulled up. She instantly starting to act like a fool once she saw them. She got in front of their car and yelled at them through the front window shield looking like, a complete idiot.

Garage traffic started to back up and it became quite the spectacle. She started pounding on the hood of Dawn's car and continued to call Dawn completely out of her name.

Several times Deron attempted to get out of the car to deal with her and Dawn had to calm him down. Cheresse did leave once the garage attendant threatened to call the police. He told Dawn not to park there for a while. Cheresse's bull has caused him nothing but headaches and Dawn was right. Why does he keep feeding into that crap? So he didn't---

Cheresse had a lot of nerve on that day. It was another big pill to swallow but, she thought the one incident was going to be it.

The following month became the worst.

It wasn't just one thing it was everything she did.

Cheresse acted like a sixteen-year-old mean girl. The one, who didn't get to steal the high school jock she dreamed about from the nice girl who won him. Between the stalking, phone calls, vandalism and destruction to property, she didn't think it would stop. She was about to give up on Deron because it seemed Cheresse was intent on having him.

Once the police got involved it was a different story. Once she spent the weekend locked up at Prince Georges' Correctional Center, she started to change her tune. Cheresse was given a two-year probation to stay away and seek counseling. Deron began to be more of a liability to Cheresse. She started to go away, only slowly.

After the wedding Cheresse disappeared from their lives altogether. She must have known by then Dawn wasn't going to leave Deron, no matter what she does. It has been pure heaven not having to deal with that woman anymore.

Once they had cemented their relationship for the second time, Deron was hers forever. The question marks were gone. His old life was thrown in the trash.

God is so good.

So, what's going on with her husband now?

CHAPTER 2

Thursday morning, Tony walked into work feeling like he owned the place. Hell that's every morning. It didn't hurt his ego that the office he worked in is a suite in a building on Connecticut Avenue and 17th Street northwest. Everyone in the bank seems like they're on his tip. Washington Federal Security Bank has been his home for a short minute. Its more money and prestige here. Two years there now and he's been moving up. The World Bank was his stomping ground for more than seven years but he had to walk. There was no growth there like he wanted and plus he got into it with his former supervisor. Nobody questions Tony Parker's production. My money moves are tight he thought. Too much world politics they got going on there and it drove him crazy. He just wants to do business at a straight-laced, money lending, institution with just corporate greed on his side; not we are the damn world.

As he waited for the elevator, he thought about his fight with Valerie. It's been nearly three weeks and she hasn't call to beg him if she could come back home yet. That's not the usual way this thing goes down. He gets mad at her; she gets mad back at him, she says '*fuck him*', she packs her things and then leaves for no more than a week. Then she would call him and say she will give him another chance and that she's sorry. It's been like this for years. The same old routine and she puts up with it. Though she never caught him with any broads, she always accuses him of it.

What the hell's wrong with her now?

Tony didn't know why he kept Valerie in his life when he wanted to be free at the same time. Maybe it's because Bryan got married and that damn Deron chose to settle down too. He was caught up in the thrill of it all. Did he try to do it to follow the crowd or did he really love Valerie?

He boarded the elevator with the puzzling thought. Of course, he loves Valerie. She did a lot for him. Most of all she changed him for a little while. He didn't know whether it was for her good or his bad. But, somehow she changed him. Plus she's sexy as hell. He cares more now when he didn't really before. Part of him wanted her to leave but, the better part of him wanted her to come home. Damn, it's like being two people and he hated feeling like that. It made him seem weak. It made him consider other people's feelings before he said what he felt straight from the nine millimeter chamber.

Tony went straight to his office this morning.

Usually he stops and checks out what new piece of ass, the Temp agency sent this week. As far as he's concern he hopes they never permanently fill that slot. He likes the variety. He sat down at his desk and pulled out his cell phone. He checked his messages and texts, nothing. Valerie's playing hardball. He'll call her and he'll take the plunge in. That's right, Tony Parker the ever changing night rider will submit. He will change up the game and have Valerie back at the crib at the end of the day and in his bed.

Why? Because he loves the game and the chase.

He picked up the phone and dialed her office number. He knows she's at work now.

"Yes Tony?" Valerie said annoyingly when she answered the phone.

"Hey," he knows he has to be coy.

"Hey." She responded flatly and directly. "What do you want?"

"Oh that's how we are now?"

"That's how you made the situation. I'm only responding to how you want things. What did you tell me? Oh yeah, that what I wanted is so unrealistic these days, fairy tales. I needed to wake up. Well I'm finally waking up."

"Well you must have misread me."

Valerie paused and puffed a breath as she looked down at the phone in her office, like it is Tony she's looking at. She can't believe that he has the nerve to try and con her. Every time he wants to be out and about single running with the guys or whoever; he does something to break them up. Then when he realizes his mistakes, he calls her. No, not this time. There's no going back. Not this time.

"No I got it right."

She isn't going to come willingly.

He's going to have to try another angle. Up it a little.

Something that he knows will work on her.

"Look Valerie, I ain't gonna bullshit you. I called cause you know I miss you. You know. You been gone too long and I'm lonely."

"I think you're not used to the fact that I haven't come crawling back to you trying make peace. I'm done. I'm not going to be your second choice when you can't find some trash to lay up with. You won't marry me and you don't even want any more kids. This is a useless relationship to me. A relationship that only existed to serve your sexual pleasures. Well no thank you."

"I can't believe you just said that."

"Believe that. I love you Tony, but I don't love how you treat me. Its round and round and I'm not waiting on you, anymore."

"I can't believe you said that," he repeated.

He really couldn't. He ain't never heard her speak with this much punch before. She's really going beast mode this time. He wasn't sure if it's the fact she seems serious about not coming back or he's really missing her that made him break.

"...Please baby...I...I love you."

Tony brought in the big guns. Like any player whenever things don't work out in your favor you can always play the soft brother.

"I love you too Tony, but this rollercoaster relationship has to stop. I'm almost thirty. I'm trying to settle down for real. I've been in love with you from the first time you said something to me at Friday's. I knew I wanted to be with just you, but all you seemed to do is play around. I don't know with who, but I know you've done something."

"You gotta trust that I didn't. Please baby. I need you. You know how hard it is for me to say I'm sorry, but I am. I am damn sorry."

"It's embarrassing for me to keep moving my stuff in and out of your house. I don't want to keep doing that, is this for real? Are we going to get married? Am I going to get my child?"

"Yes."

He hopes he didn't answer that too fast. The real deal is he ain't too sure about the kid thing. He's already choking on the marriage thing. Been there done that. He just thought he should just take it day by day.

"You really mean it, Tony?"

"Yes, Valerie."

****

When an hour before lunchtime hit, Tony tore out of the bank like he stole some money from there. He had to purge his mind of that holy conversation he just had with Deron. He wants to do what he wants to do without all that Christianity blocking his fun. Like right now, all he wanted to do is grab a quick bite to eat, not kneel down and pray.

He's getting the jump on all the other quick workers who are thinking the same thing.

He's gonna to try out this new place on 13th and Penn.

Apparently, it's the newest, best place to eat lunch according to the people in his office. French style, American food by some French Chef to boot. This might get on the list to impress the ladies. Before he brings his potential bed partners to this place, he has to get the all clear first.

His MO is going to the best restaurants and drawing the women in with a little investment.

He promised Valerie a mouthful and he isn't sure he can deliver. It's hard to take off his player's cap when it's seems to fit so good every day. All you have to do to these broads is lie about everything and you're in between. Tell them everything they wanna hear and they will open their legs like you just brought them a house. It doesn't hurt to be a bad brother either.

Take for instant, Sharnia. She's the perfect example of a mindless, booty mattress, on legs. Her sleep number is 1000. All he has to do is blow her way. He could lay up on her, turn her out and kick her to the curb. However, he feels and she deals with it. How could he give up all that juicy behavior; it was like paradise; dripping baby?

Tony went to the ATM a block from the restaurant and then proceeded to the place. Walking up to the door, he placed his hand on the door handle. He was just about to pull on it to go in; when a woman walked up from the opposite direction and placed her hand on top of his.

"Tony Parker…I don't believe it," she said.

Tony remained calm and turned to look at her; never ever losing his cool.

"Phaedra McCoy, what's up with your sexy ass?" Tony said to her not hiding that he's literally licking his lips at her; while taking in her whole scenery. She hasn't changed from the last time they met up. She still got that cocoa deep skin to go along with that tight body.

She's got that fun park body.

"So, you're talking to me now, that's, a good sign."

"Why would you say that baby?"

"Well the last time we saw each other we were in a hotel suite, a few years ago; and it wasn't good. You cuss me out."

"Was that the last time we saw each, I didn't know that?" He tried to sound neutral.

Tony remembers that night.

There were a lot of things going on that night. He had setup a couple swap with, Phaedra, his boy Deron and her girl, Nelicia. It was going to be a freak fest to the ninth level. They had been toying with each other at work when they used to work together at the World Bank. They made big plans for that weekend. It was iffy. Phaedra knew she stacked high up. She knew how to play that body to punish a brutha's pockets and she was a tough shell to crack.

But he knew all it took was to dangle something she wanted in her face and she would bite the apple; Deron.

But, Deron was going through his shit with Dawn and didn't get down with the plan. He pissed Tony off really bad that night he thought he might punch Deron in his face. He was glad they got pass that stupid shit. They ain't supposed to let no thots bust up their friendship.

Not with all this booty out here.

Still Phaedra had him turning on his buddy.

He didn't want to admit it but, he was kind of jealous that Deron booked Cheresse, with his cash; but she played him out of his. She became obsessed with Deron and didn't give Tony a second look. He couldn't let his buddy fall in too deep for that gold digger. But, he also didn't like his ego taking that hit. No woman is supposed to be immune to Tony Parker and that thot, Cheresse, should have eaten out of his lap.

One of these days, Cheresse is going to give him a return on his money.

So, with his mounting anger dealing with that Tony reached his boiling point when Phaedra played hard to get. She knew how bad he wanted that booty. Instead, she wanted Deron to punish her. She was the one who suggested he bring a friend and even brought up Deron's name. He knew she was on him and he was cool with her slight interest in him.

Because he knew he was going to smash Phaedra first.

That was thing with Tony. He never minds sharing. He just got to be first. When he's not first it becomes a whole other ballgame and he tends to turn on everyone around him. He's like a pit-bull.

That's when he found out that Deron's his true friend.

Deron hung in those rounds like a real boxer. That brutha would probably die for Tony if he had too.

So, that's why he rides with him, always.

That's his damn brother.

Ain't nothing gonna change that.

Still, Phaedra got some stuff started. Cause right after Deron caught a case of the guilt's because he wanted to be with Dawn; he decided to leave the hotel. She left right after him. She never gave Tony none and she never came back to work either. He didn't know she had put in her two weeks prior to all that and decided not to work the two weeks left. That was some real raunchy shit she did trying to make him pay for her to get with some other nigga.

More wasted money.

Even though she was tasty he had forgotten about her, because she wasn't all like that in his mind. She played him too like Cheresse. It just made it harder for all those other broads he encountered afterwards. If he ever gets the opportunity to get that body he's gonna smash it like she killed somebody close to him.

Hell, Cheresse too if he gets that chance.

"That's all-in reruns, baby," Tony said playing it off, so he could stay in control. "I forgot about that. It was heavy that night, huh? Soap Opera drama ain't good for swapping."

"Yeah," she said evenly. "You look good. You been working out or something?"

"Ain't been no change in my plans. Just making my way like I do. I manage to hit the gym four days a week like usual. But you got it, believe that. Look, it's lunch time and I'm about to go in to grab me something..."

"You know I was about to do the same thing. I just had to run up on you and shock you. I knew you would be surprised. You know…," she paused to make sure he notices that she wants to continue. "Why don't we sit down and grab lunch together, so we can catch up. It's really good to see you, seriously."

Got her, he thought.

He felt he had her right where he wants her, now.

Now he's going to take her to Parker town, where the female inhabitants live only to serve him.

"Naw, I don't have the time. When I leave here, I gotta meet somebody. I can't miss this appointment. You know what I mean?"

"I really wanted to talk to you. You know I've been thinking about you lately. I regret the way things left off and I wanted to see what you were doing to see if we can't pick up where we left off."

"Here's my number."

He passed her a business card.

"My personal cell ain't changed, it's on there, oh yeah and a new office number. Call me tonight and we'll talk. "

"Well let's hook up tomorrow and I'll cook dinner at my place," she said urgently.

"Oh yeah, that's what's up. Let's hook it up," Tony said to her knowingly with a sly grin. He then faked looking at his watch. "Man, I don't even have time to go in here. Talk to you tonight."

Tony walked off and disappeared around the block. Phaedra stood at the entrance of the restaurant, watching him. When she saw, him turn the corner block she whipped out her cell phone and walked off as well.

"Hey, it's me… I think I got one… I use to know him… just saw him on the street and I know he'll do it but it'll take a little persuasion, I got that though… it might take a bit because he's not stupid… I can't believe how he just fell in my lap…yeah according to his card he's perfect, more than I thought yeah…I'm sure, I got it…okay bye."

Phaedra hung up the phone and continued walking down the block in the opposite direction.

****

There's no need to go out to lunch Valerie thought. There's no way she's going to eat after this call from Tony. All this time, years to be a matter of fact. The way that he's treated her she can't understand why she would risk being with him again. She knows deep down inside that he's not going to change, ever.

She has never been able to catch him but she knows he's been with other women. That's possibly the reason why she won't leave, hoping that she herself could be wrong.

She sat back in the high back chair at her desk in her office looking out of the window. She's more than this. She's more than she has allow herself to be in her personal life. But she couldn't help it she's so in love with Tony Parker that she would gladly accept any plea from him to come back to him.

She picked up her office phone and dialed on it.

"Hello," the female voice answered.

"So, I was thinking when did, I disconnect from my own life," Valerie stated. "I graduated college with honors, I'm an Admin Officer at a prestigious company making six figures and I'm only twenty-nine. I'm not mentioning the physical attributes are up to par. I'm dark and lovely. Why am I having problem with this man of mine? Dawn, what am I doing wrong? What should I do?"

"Why do you think it's you?" Dawn asked.

Dawn wasn't sure how she should answer so she reversed a question back at her. This is not the first-time Val has come to Yolanda or her for advice only to, in the end do the exact opposite of what is, suggested. Dawn has learned that it's best to just listen more and maybe guide her to a solution that she has in her mind all the time.

"Once again I'm going back to Tony."

"Oh really?" Dawn said surprisingly.

"Didn't Deron tell you?"

"No, he hasn't mentioned it."

"That's funny. About three weeks ago, we broke up. I was sure that Tony would've told him by now. I was sure he would be the first person he'd call to tell him we're back together."

"Well guys don't really talk like that and besides Deron's kinda been in his own zone lately. I think he's sick but he's not trying to admit it."

"Oh, I'm sorry what's going on?"

"He's just seems mopey lately and tired. He's missed quite a bit of work. I can't explain it."

"Wow, well I hope he feels better."

"So, you're back with Tony?"

"Just happened today. He called begging me for another chance and I of course told him no. Then he proposed to me."

"He proposed to you over the phone?"

"Not an official proposal but he wants to get married. I guess that will come later. For Tony that's a milestone. He also wants children."

Dawn paused before she spoke.

"Val the two of you just broke up with a three-week gap and now you're engaged. That doesn't make sense."

"I can't make sense out of it either because you know that Tony is a wild card, but I'm kinda wild too."

"So, what was all that talk about your life's disconnection?"

"I'm just wondering why I got to go through so much hell to be with the man I love. Yolanda didn't have that problem. You don't have that problem…"

"I don't think you want to use me as an example. Remember I had the year of hell and then some. I don't recommend my deal to anyone but we do what we do for what we think want…"

"But, Deron changed for you."

"He changed for God and I'm the gift he received for his choice. He's my gift because I always prayed for someone as loving as him. A little rusty in beginning but he's gold now," she giggled.

"Exactly. Why is that not me?"

"You have your own path. Don't look at me. You don't really know how all this came together," she warned. "Girl, relish in your achievements and know that you are too wonderful for words. If you're asking if there's something wrong with you the answer is no. You might be with the wrong man."

When Dawn said it, she wished she had held the wrong man part back but, this is one of her best friends. She can't let her fall to save face. Tony's not the right man for her period. He's as bad as Cheresse Bennett was to Deron.

That she has never shared with anyone before.

She knows from experience how easy it is to be a victim. You fall prey to a cheater, maybe an abuser, controller, just a rotten person overall. She's had a few in her day. You say you're not going to take anything from anyone but, when you don't know going in, it becomes a shocker. This is when your faith in that person is tested and your knowledge of yourself is revealed.

You find out how strong you can be.

"I just might be." Valerie said as she pondered what Dawn just said to her. Then she looked up and saw a man in her outer office doorway through the glass. She smiled at him. "Well, I'll catch up with you later girl."

"Okay Val. I think we need to talk about this further," Dawn said thinking she may have hurt her feelings, because Valerie is rushing to get off the phone.

"Anytime baby girl. I *gotta* go." Valerie said hurrying her off the phone. She motioned to the man who stood outside her office to come in. "Hi," she said happily and seductively. "This *is* a pleasant surprise."

"Ms. Dupree, it's nothing but pleasure when I come see you. It's been a while," the male visitor said as he came further into her office and stood in front of her desk.

"Nathan Collins. I don't believe it. What are you doing here in Washington, D.C.?"

"Isn't it obvious," he said coming around the desk, grabbing her hand and pulling her up to him. "Well let me give you the backstory. I just touched down at National. I grabbed a cab straight from there and this is the first place I came to, so I can be with you." He finished and kissed her.

CHAPTER 3

The next morning at National Airport, Audrey Butler waited patiently for her ride to pick her up. She's back in the Metropolitan area once again and that's something she didn't like. What is she doing here again? She gave the D.C. area up. She has made Los Angeles, California her home for the past two years and adding to the many years, she's already put in there.

There's nothing in DC for her.

DC is the city's where she was hurt once and where she hurt others by being vengeful and reckless. Then, she met Deron Stone. He was a one nightstand. Not really. Well yes. Well, it's complicated.

He was supposed to be Cheresse's man but that was complicated too. She thought she would never feel for a guy as quick as she did him or was it just that he was so nice. Although she never told him, she did have thoughts of them being together. She thought about using the baby he fathered with her to get him to be with her but, she didn't want that.

She doesn't ever want kids.

Besides once she found out about his real girlfriend, Dawn, she knew she wouldn't hook him.

Complicated.

She feels like she ruined his life by bringing him into her feud with her so-called best friend, Cheresse. Their off again on again friendship has ran over a lot of guys. One of them was bound to get knocked up. She got caught in the game. Abortion was never an option. She never purposely wanted to burden him with the responsibility but, she didn't want a baby, by-no-means; and she still doesn't. She won't be visiting Deron Jr this trip because she doesn't want to see him. She wants to stay out of his life.

She's only back in this area for Cheresse.

They're girlfriends, sisters. No matter what problem they have or what goes on between them.

No one knew this tragedy was going to happen to one of them. No one deserved this, not even Cheresse. Sisters since their childhood, Cheresse Bennett and she have been like along with their other friend, Renita Combs. Renita is married now with children. They've always manage to come together when one of them needed the other two.

There have also been distances between the three of them. Especially between Cheresse and her because they always have this thing with sleeping with each other's men, playing games.

Cheresse started it first.

She slept with Audrey's fiancée and it hurt Audrey to her core. It was dirty and she doesn't think she's gotten pass it yet.

She wished she could but, she can't.

Audrey started to notice that other people, many of their friends and family members started to catch onto their feud when they were together at joint family functions.

Especially that day five years ago, when the two of them were together at Cheresse's family cookout in North Carolina. They each took a dude but, were too busy pushing up on the one belonging to the other that they made a fool of themselves.

It was so obvious, that one of Cheresse's drunk female cousins asked the two of them about one of the guys.

She asked them if he was both their man.

It was an embarrassment to her because the drunk cousin was so loud with it that all the other people who were sitting near them heard it and bust out laughing.

They were, clowned on all day. They were the clowns.

Sometimes the revenge game does blind her to what is real. The fact that they're just laying up with guys who don't really give a damn about them.

Those guys used to catch onto the game quick.

Aside from all of that, she's trying to keep their sisterhood intact.

Looking back on the past though she regretted what happened the last time she last seen Cheresse. She was in town signing the papers to give full custody of her baby to Deron. This was something she had to do to make things right instead of what Cheresse suggested. She couldn't just keep the baby, move to Los Angles and make it hard for Deron to see the boy; all the same time trying to drain his pockets. Cheresse has always wanted to hurt him for some reason. It could be jealousy because he moved on to Dawn and didn't stay with Cheresse to deal with her mess.

It's her own fault anyway. When she had him she treated him like she didn't want him.

Cheresse stepped to her saying something about her being one of Deron's whore. Telling Audrey, she's the reason why Deron and she are not together. She told her she would do anything for Deron because Audrey's hooked what he has between his legs. That's when she got up in Cheresse's face. The argument between the two of them got too deep. Cheresse smacked her and the two of them fought in the bathroom of the law firm Cheresse works at. Audrey really cut loose on her leaving her with a bloody nose and walking out of the firm.

Cheresse likes to fight.

She's always jumping up to fight somebody and really can't fight. She didn't even return to the office to get her copies of the custody papers.

The law firm just mailed it to her weeks later.

What the ultimate kicker is that playing this crazy, childish revenge sex game with Cheresse got Audrey knocked up. Deron Stone's the first one Audrey's ever known Cheresse to get this crazy over in a long while. She went over the edge with not really wanting him and not really wanting to keep him. She likes dealing with multiple men for some reason. But, she wanted that safe haven he offered too. She played too many games. He was way too good to her. He knew it too. That's why he left her alone.

Deron was good to Audrey as well.

He never lied to her or misled her. When they hooked up to have sex, it was only supposed to be that. Damn it was good sex but, she should've been on the pill or made sure the condom didn't rip. She doesn't know why she lied and told him she was on the pill. But, it was just that heated and all that safe sex shit went out the window. She's learned her lesson because she could've caught a STD instead of getting pregnant.

He didn't even fault her much when she presented him with DJ. It took her a long time to admit to herself that she was pregnant and the delay cost.

Damn it because of this 'tit for tat' cycle they have fallen into. Not only did she ended up pregnant by a guy that didn't want her. She caught feelings for him too.

Nevertheless, the comfort to her of it all is Cheresse was deeply hurt. Deron didn't love her anymore either. He probably never did. It was just sex. He just got caught up in her sex. Like Audrey's fiancée said after she caught Cheresse and him in her bed. Cheresse seduced him with her sex. She did sexual things to him he said before they even got to the actual penetration.

She's good at that, even when they were teenagers.

It was still as much her ex's fault though as it was Cheresse's for being weak. He didn't have to do it. But, Cheresse is like family. She never should've done it. That's why she screws every man Cheresse gets a hold of, for revenge. The ultimate get back was Deron. Cheresse never got over that even though she says she doesn't care about it.

Now after all that drama Audrey is concerned about her friend. They are still so young with a whole life ahead of them. At twenty-seven, there's no room for speed bumps in their lives now. But here it is, possibly Cancer.

Well actually, Cheresse isn't sure about what it is. She's due to take some more tests. However, they saw something she said that freaked her out.

When Cheresse called after about a two years' absence and laid that in her lap Audrey cried for days. How could this be happening to her friend? She isn't the best person in the world; but, she certainly doesn't deserve this. The mere mention of the word relating it to one of them made Audrey crazy. That's why she came to DC as soon as she could.

She should be with her friend.

She continued to think to herself.

She didn't see the car coming up the curbside as she stood there. The sound of the horn blowing instantly jarred her and she saw Cheresse behind the driver's seat.

"Audrey," Cheresse said as she jumped out of the car and opened the trunk. Once Audrey came towards her with her luggage, they hugged each other for what seemed like a long time. Audrey really missed her and she fought hard not tear up as she stepped back and really looked at Cheresse. She has gotten so thin than she was a few years ago, which didn't seem to Audrey like a good sign at all. Her clothing looked loose on her.

"Che," Audrey said calling Cheresse by her childhood nickname. "It's so good to see you. You look good girl," she continued to say awkwardly.

"Girl, stop lying you know I've lost too much weight. You know I don't normally look like this. I'm a size two and still losing. I can't even eat anything. I don't have an appetite."

Audrey just waved her off. She isn't about to debate her right here at the pick-up and drop-off point when they could be on their way. It is true though. Cheresse used to have a body like a video vixen and now she's so skinny like some super model. But, she's not that tall.

She looks like she's almost anorexic. At least it's seems like it under those loose-fitting type clothes she's wearing.

She just knows that this must be hard on Cheresse.

Audrey wanted to burst out crying but she held it in. She just instantly started walking toward the passenger side and got in the front seat of the car. Once Cheresse got in the car, she began talking to Audrey again.

"You heard what I said Audrey? I can't eat a thing. I've been quit smoking. I don't know what's going on but I'm glad that you're here."

"I heard you, but your sister's here now and I will take care of you. You're gonna to be alright."

"Have you talked to Deron?"

Talk to, Deron why would she do that? What possible interest would she have in doing that? There's nothing to talk about. He would only do what he always does, try to be nice and try to get her bonding with the DJ. Didn't they all talk about this before and she made it perfectly clear that she didn't want to be a mother? Besides, she respects his marriage. She just can't call that man like that even if they do have a child together. It's not that easy.

As far as Audrey is concern, she was the surrogate to Deron and Dawn's baby and she never has to deal with it again. She ain't going to do it again either. She made damn sure that she would never have to go through labor again. Because right after she had the baby she had her, tubes tied and burn. If she could have gotten a hysterectomy, she would have done it. She *never wants a child*!

"There's no reason for me to talk to Deron, Cheresse."

"It is. Don't you want to know how your son's doing?"

"I don't have a son, Cheresse. I thought we talked all this out, you, Renita and me. He belongs to Deron and Dawn."

"I thought that by now you'd be interested in my nephew. After all, no one would blame you for not wanting a baby, but he's almost three now."

"So?"

"He should know his mother and his aunts now. Now before it's too late," Cheresse said and turned her head.

Audrey looked at Cheresse for a minute as she drove the car they're riding in. What is she trying to tell her she wonders? Is she going to die?

This thing is scaring her. Maybe she does need to reaffirm her life with her child. Maybe it is wrong for her to have given her child away completely to be, raised by another woman. What kind of mother is she? However, that's just it she never planned on being a mother.

Cheresse smiled as she took in the silence of Audrey quiet thoughts. Everything is working perfectly but it's just the first stage. She knows what she's thinking and she felt good about it. It's time that she learns who her boy is. Deron and that sneaky bitch Dawn shouldn't have taken him away from Audrey.

She only took in that boy just to keep Deron from her, Cheresse thought. Well now, she won't have either, anymore. *He is my man*, she thought. Deron is not going to get away with breaking her heart. He will know that Cheresse Bennett is the wrong bitch to fuck with right now.

"After I drop you off at my apartment Audrey, I'm going back to work. I have something I need to finish up. It'll only take an hour to do it. Then I'll come and get you for lunch around one 'o' clock."

****

Downtown on 19th NW, Cheresse had to literally, pull Audrey into her office late that afternoon. They met for lunch because Cheresse wanted to talk to her about something. Once she talked to her about what was on her mind, Audrey didn't want any part of it. They went straight to Cheresse's office and sat down in the two chairs that are in front of her desk. Again, Cheresse tried to persuade her to agree with what she suggested.

"I don't want to do that, Cheresse," Audrey said to her seriously.

"Audrey you owe it to your son. It's not right that Dawn is trying to claim your child, damn," Cheresse said trying to convince her.

"But I gave him to her. Deron is his father, so I don't see what the problem is."

"I don't know what the problem is with you getting back into your child's life. You're his blood mother. It's not fair that you deprive him of your side of the family and his Aunts, me and Renita."

"I told you that I'm not trying to be a mother. So there's no need to do this. Deron will take care of him."

"Well what about me? I won't have any kids; it's too late for me. I can at least spend some time with my nephew, what little time I got. You know Deron's not going to let me see him."

"Well it's because of what happened Che, damn. Deron is still a nice guy and I don't want to get in between the two of you. You did some foul stuff to him and Deron Jr's fine with the two of them. What is this really about Che?"

Cheresse dropped her head.

"It's because when you got pregnant with Deron's baby, I was real mad at you. I hated you and well, now it's like I wished, well…"

"What Che?"

"Well in some way I wished that it was me that got pregnant by Deron. I would have done anything to have his baby, because I realized that I love him."

"Aww Che, I'm sorry but I thought you were really playing with him for his money, you know like you do. I didn't know that. You know how you like to play games."

"I know how I was. I know what I did, but that was at first; people change. It's complicated, but right now I'm hurt. I don't want anybody but him."

"So what's my asking for my parental rights back going to do to help you with that other than hurt the two of them, especially Dawn?"

"That can't be help. Dawn will get over it. That bitch doesn't want DJ. At least I will have a part of Deron in my life and he'll be in my life; once you move back here."

"What? I'm not moving to DC. You know I don't do DC."

"I thought you were going to stay and take care of me."

"I thought you would eventually go back home to your mother and father."

"They're too old to do that. I'm staying right here. Besides," she said as she turned her head. "We don't get along no more. None of the family's talking to me and it's too personal to tell you about."

"I don't know Cheresse; I only took off three weeks leave of absence from my job. I was fortunate to get that. That was a stretch. I actually took leave without pay. I'm using some of the money in my 401K, so it worked out," she grabbed Cheresse's hand. "I'm going to be here to get through this thing with you okay?"

"Girl, you're going make me cry. You see why you have to get your custody back and move here."

"Cheresse, I signed papers. It's done," Audrey said to her frustrated.

Getting up from the chair Cheresse went to the file cabinet that is in her office and opened it. After thumbing through the files, she pulled out one and returned to where Audrey is sitting.

"You forgot that I helped you fill out your papers," she said opening the folder. "I kept a copy of what you submitted and was looking at it last month. You didn't sign two documents that were in the packet. I'm sure Deron and Dawn got the same package."

"Are you kidding? I know for sure that I signed all the paperwork that was there. I know it because the other Paralegal Specialist, Norma made sure that I did, before we were finished. She wouldn't notarize it until I did."

"That chick don't know what the hell she's doing. She's stupid as hell. I assure you some of the documents weren't signed. That transaction is not legal."

"What does this means?"

"It means that you can now file a petition for joint custody of your child. I am filing as we speak on your behalf. Isn't God good?" Cheresse said as she smiled.

Audrey just looked at Cheresse. What is, she doing she thought? Why all of a sudden is she so interested in bonding with Deron Jr. Cheresse has always been just like her, not wanting anything to do with kids. Even when Renita was having those twins, she would secretly comment to Audrey about how she's ruining her life.

Now all of a sudden she is Aunt of the year.

She probably hasn't seen those twins since they've been born. Something's not right.

****

Later on that night when Tony arrived at Phaedra's townhouse, he rang the doorbell. He already had it in his mind what he's gonna to do with her when she lets him in. He's gonna to make up for that blow time he had with her a few years ago; costing him all that money for that suite and the drinks.

As he waited for her to come to the door, he thought about her neighborhood and the fact that she seems to be doing good for herself. She didn't seem like she could manage those little bit of accounts that she was managing when she worked at the World Bank; let alone own a hair shop.

Phaedra McCoy is really, full of surprises.

Just like on cue Phaedra opened the door.

He looked at her like she's opening the door to a Victoria Secret's closet. She has on a sexy little item he knows very well from VS, a Baby Doll nightie.

It is just that too cause it isn't covering much; not even enough for a baby doll.

It's unlucky for the neighbors that it's so dark outside cause all he saw is ass when she turned around and walked back into her house. She is bold tonight and he knows he's going get just what he came here for, payment in full. Don't no thottie make him pay for a suite at a hotel, promises him some nectar and leaves him hard up.

Time to pay up *bitch*.

Neither one of them exchanged any words. She didn't say nothing when she opened the door and so he didn't say anything either. Tony knows a smash off when he senses one and this smells just like one. Oh and the smell. It is nothing but her straight up sex in the air and that went straight down to his third eye.

Once they got to the main upper level the living room, she stopped in the middle of the floor with her back to him. He just simply walked pass her, ran his hand on the back of her ass and sat down on the soft sofa.

He loves playing with his food before he eats it.

"So you not going say nothing to me Tony?" She asked trying to be coy.

"I said it. I rubbed you on your ass and sat down on the sofa. I'm just waiting for you, to come over and serve me," he responded to her settling back on the sofa with his arms stretched on each side of the back.

"Yeah, I cooked dinner."

"Yeah you cooking..."

"What did you come over here for Tony?"

"To get some of that sweet sex you always been dangling in front my face, but never gave me none. I want some of that tonight, right now," he said to her bluntly.

All she did is look at Tony and his words seem to hypnotize her. She has on the Baby Dolls that tie at the shoulder. She just reached up, pulled the strings on both sides and the black garment fell to the floor. Her deep chocolate mocha skin glistened in the low light like glass as he looked at her. She looks like glistening glass. Although

Tony doesn't get with all that romance crap it didn't stop him from imagining he is licking her all over right now.

It's all he could do to maintain his composure cause Phaedra didn't have anything on underneath but a thong. Her body's slamming just like he remembered, what little he saw of it that night at the hotel. Everything's bouncing and he swears she's twerking while she walked around trying to show him her body.

He got up off the sofa and went over to her. He stood behind her and grabbed her waist with both hands, pulling down her thong. She leaned back into his embrace and he unzipped his pants. He let his pants fall on floor and his underwear followed as Phaedra felt his excitement behind her.

She grabbed him and pulled him to the sofa behind her. All that's heard next is the sound of a condom wrapper being ripped opened.

****

A few hours later Phaedra laid atop Tony on her bed. It had gone down just as he planned and really, he could just bolt now, but decided to stay. After all, he wanted to be able to get down with her again. She's everything he has been waiting for. But damn it shouldn't have taken this long, it's been years.

"That was worth the wait wasn't it Tony?" she said moving off him as if she is reading his mind.

"Damn right. I got to get some more before I dart up out."

"That's all you came here for isn't it?"

"Naw it's really good to see you," he said automatically. "I came over here for some of that dinner you said you cooked that was unexpected."

"I cooked but that wasn't what you wanted to eat. I can warm it up for you."

"No you stay right here with me and tell me how you manage to open up a business, a hair salon right?"

"You know once I left the bank I was in between jobs. I was at the right place at the right time. I met this guy who owns properties and one of them was the salon. So I put up some money for the place he was selling. He has a business partner and they loan me money too. I still owe him some money but I pay that with the profits from the shop. My shop is doing really good but I could use a loan to get the debt paid quicker."

"What difference does that make, either way you be in debt with a loan?" Tony asked her like he is talking to someone clueless.

"Yeah, asshole but I'd be establishing a business loan and business credit, remember? I'm just paying those guys I'm not getting anything back to help me like a business loan would do."

"Oh yeah you right. Have you found a bank?"

"That's the problem I don't think a bank will give me a loan without a lot of red tape. My credit is good, but you know how tight the banks are today. It would take forever to convince them to loan me money and by that time I could really fall prey to those guys if they decide to do something shady," she said as she rubbed her leg over his.

He started to stir.

"How did you get two guys to get a loan from a bank for you?

"I smashed both of them," Phaedra said laughing. "That's what you want to hear right? Men."

Tony stared at her, thinking she probably did. She ain't no saint he knows that and she knows he ain't one either.

"It's your sweet thing," he said moving his hand between her legs. "I ain't judging you."

"Hey Tony you can get me a loan at your bank."

"What? Get you a loan. I ain't doing that. What you trying to work me? You let me go up in you and then you try and trick me out?" he yelled at her. "I ain't those dudes."

"I just asked Tony damn. You don't have to do it and for the record if I were trickin' I'd smash the head of your department, instead of bothering with you," she said glaring at him.

"Yeah it's a female, now what?" he joked.

She just kept glaring at him.

"Too funny," he said laughing at her shaking his head. "Yeah I'll help you get the damn loan. Now get back up here and remind me why I been hunting down this sexy body for years."

"By the way don't try me like that…I ain't no thot."

****

"Thank you Yolanda for your company this evening. I owe you a bit of thanks, because I almost had dinner alone."

"And I thank you Mr. Powers for the great dinner. I don't know when I had a chance to actually get out and enjoy myself."

It's true.

It has been almost two long years since Yolanda Prescott allowed herself to be close to another man. Not since the love of her life Bryan, had passed on. No, he was taken from her, murdered. Bryan's gone and she misses him so much. But she said to herself that this year she would change; try to move on and maybe find a companion. He would have wanted her to be happy and move on. She loves him so much but she has to do it. She at least she can go out and have dinner. Steve Powers has been a longtime friend of the family and she feels comfortable with him. Although he's much older, he's just right for her personality to date; a gentleman.

It may come to a time when he may want to become more than just a friend. She knows he would like to do that. Yolanda thought about it more. How could it be that she's now thinking about another man? She felt as though she's betraying Bryan's memory. She has mixed feelings.

The thought of it made her feel ashamed.

"I know this is a throwback thing to say but a penny for your thoughts," he said to her.

"I was thinking how much I had a good time tonight."

"It's only the company that I'm keeping."

Steve didn't feel as if he is laying it on too thick. He thought this is just what a woman needs to hear; at least this one. He's going to let her know it. He always had feelings for Yolanda, but thought against it because she was married to Bryan. He knew that she would never betray her vows. He was married too but not anymore.

Now that Bryan's out of the way there's nothing stopping him now. After all the two of them are alive, what can Bryan do for her now? She's a vibrant woman and she needs to be loved and made love to. So leave it up to old Steve to be the one to help her along the way.

He'll take care of his buddy's woman.

The only one drawback is the kid. It's not like he didn't like kids, it's just that he has a son already. He's two years in college and he has a daughter from a previous thing out on her own. He's not trying to be a father to anymore young children. He just started living at thirty-nine. So, scratch the relationship but he can still have some fun with the mama and accomplish what he set out to do at first.

"So what were you telling me, Steve, about your new businesses? You remodel homes, isn't that what you said?"

Perfect he thought right on cue.

"Yes, that's a portion of the business that my partner and I been in for the last five years now. It was tough getting it going but we have been moving these last few years in the right direction. I finally get to see a profit, small, but it's picking up. I'm still waiting on you to let me buy that old townhouse of yours so I can flip it."

"No. I can't do that," Yolanda said slowly as if this is the first time she is giving this suggestion.

She couldn't possibly part with that memory. That is the place where she and Bryan fell in love and lived together. That was his townhouse that he brought brand-new when he was single.

She also knows that he died there too, which is why she considered getting rid of it one day as well.

It's just too soon though to, want to make that kind of change. Too soon to, seriously give up something that's a connection to him.

They barely got a chance to be together in the new house, Bryan, Bryan Jr and her. This current house has become a tomb to some degree. She got trapped in her depression more than anyone really knows. She tries very hard to keep it from Bryan Jr. because he needs his mother to be full on point.

It's so hard.

One of Yolanda's older sisters moved into the home with her. She fell on some hard times she said and needed the help. Yolanda knew that wasn't true. The family was just concerned about her being in the new house by herself.

One of these days, she will probably sell this house to downsize to something more befitting a single woman and her son. Bryan left her with a few insurance policies that made going back to work not a necessity right now, not ever.

However, she will probably never sell the townhouse and she will never go there to live either.

That would be emotional suicide.

"I'm just not ready to part with it yet, but if I do, I will consider your offer Mr. Powers."

"Okay Mrs. Prescott, that's a fair promise. I'll be around anyway, so it won't make much difference."

She noticed what he said almost cementing the fact that they will be developing something. She has to be careful. She's moving into a territory that very few have experience in or success.

****

Later on after Steve, left Yolanda went to her bedroom, grabbed the phone and laid across her bed. Bryan Jr is spending the night at her mother's house so she has the rest of the evening to herself. She dialed a number and then pushed the talk button on the phone.

"What's up girl," Valerie said on the other end when she answered the phone.

"Hey Val, I'm just returning your call from earlier. How are you doing?"

"The real question is how are you doing? I haven't had a chance to really talk to you in a few weeks; we've been playing phone tag. What have you been doing; everything's all right?"

"It's been great. Bryan Jr over at his grandmother's and I'm just laying here relaxing."

"Girl what are you not trying to tell me but want me to know?"

"I'm just relaxing you know. It's been a while since I've had time to myself," Yolanda said thinking she'd better change the subject before she says something about her date with Steve. Too early to let the girls in on this. "How are things with Tony and you? Did you move out like you said you were going to do?"

"You have been out of loop for a bit. Yes, I did move and I actually broke up with him…"

"Aww baby, I'm sorry. You wanna talk about it?"

"Well I didn't finish. We did break up for three weeks but Tony called me last Monday morning bright and early begging me to come back."

"Who?"

"Girl don't play, yes Tony called. He's changed I guess. He asked me to marry him."

"Tony?"

"Uh Yolanda, girl what are you trying to say?"

"Okay, okay I'm just joking. That's good for you right?"

"Well once I gave him the cold shoulder for a few weeks he came back acting all pitiful. He must have felt that I was about to leave for good."

"I guess."

"You don't seem too happy with my decision."

"Well to be honest I don't know what to think about Tony in that regard, Val. He's like a brother to me and that's all I know I can vouch for. I don't know about him in a relationship so I definitely can't really speak on that. I do think that personally that he's not really ready for a commitment."

When she said it, she wished she hadn't. Most of the time being too honest with close girlfriends about their men can be sisterhood suicide.

How is she going to back out of this?

"Well…," Val started to say.

"Oh yeah don't forget Dawn's cookout is a week from Saturday," Yolanda quickly said cutting her off, trying to change the subject.

"I remember Yolanda," she said and then paused. "Don't worry about me girl, this is Tony Parker's last chance. Believe me Nathan Collins is waiting behind the scenes if he can't live up to what he says. But something tells me that he's learned his lesson."

"Who's Nathan Collins?"

****

When Tony got back home, it was midnight. He saw a car in his driveway. It's Sharnia, damn. He didn't feel like being bothered with her after that workout he gave Phaedra or better yet she gave him. She's everything that he thought that booty would be. She's beast. Sharnia ain't got nothing on this one.

He continued to look at her car and felt pissed. So this is what she's gonna do every night; pull this new girlfriend crap. He did this with Valerie. Thot's gotta go.

As he pulled into his driveway, he opened his garage door with the remote and parked inside. She got out of her car as he got out of his truck.

"I don't feel like no company tonight, Sharnia," he said to her from inside the garage.

He pushed the button to close the garage door before she got to it. He then turned around and began walking into the door to the mudroom.

The garage door stopped midway down and Tony hearing it, turned to see it going back up. Sharnia stop it from going down. Once it opened up fully he couldn't believe his eyes. There in the front of his garage Sharnia stood buck-naked, her dress on the ground. This is some next level shit right here. Sharnia's going for hers he thought as it peaked his interest. That damn Home Owner's Association is gonna be writing him a letter about this.

She stepped in and stopped behind the truck.

She ran her hands down her body seductively and then stepped inside the garage. Out of courtesy for the neighbors he knows is watching this; cause he knows he's got some nosey ass neighbors, he pushed the button for the garage door to go down again. He went to the back of his truck, while she stood there seductively watching him.

He opened up the back of his truck hatch. He grabbed Sharnia's arm and pulled her to him and he kissed her. She rubbed her body against his. He motioned to her pointing to the inside of the truck and she climbed up into the rear of the truck.

These thottie ass women that he deals with keeps his blood going stiff and strong, hot damn!!

****

Across PG, county Phaedra is on the phone talking to someone. She is laying in her bed still naked from her sex fest with Tony.

"I told you I'd get it…it don't matter how much and besides I don't want to get too greedy because I need to get that loan mainly to get the account. Once I get that then we can do what we planned…stop questioning me got damn it, I got this shit wrapped up. That's right I did it."

CHAPTER 4

A week later on Saturday the planned cookout is in full force at Deron's house. Tony sat looking around and drinking at the outdoor bar that Deron had installed on his patio. But he don't drink alcohol no more and no alcohol's being served at this cookout; according to the girls. This is the first outdoor event that Deron and Dawn has had at their home since the installation of the new deck, patio and pool. Tony couldn't help but feel proud of him. Deron took the modest house he got built and turned it into a real investment if he ever wants to sell it. Practically the entire yard has been, turned into a backyard oasis to include a fire pit, a small pool and lavishes extended patio. Like Tony always says to the guys there's nothing that his brothers can't do when they put their minds to it, just like him.

When Deron saved all that money in spite of Cheresse, nearly running through it spending it like it was hers. He was able to take some of it to accomplish a lot of things. Even though he had his head way up her cooch he still kept his business sense. He was still moving on what Tony taught him about finance. Before he was even thirty, he had this. That's what you do, pay the piper now while you're young and make those ends meet. Once you get that straight then you play.

Now they can play and play it hard Tony thought. But D, don't want to do like he did before; like what he's doing now is better than that. Lately it's been hard for him to catch up with Deron. He's been acting strange lately and Tony wants to know what's going on.

He won't go nowhere with Tony cause he claims he's always busy. When he talks to him, it's always about the Lord. It like D done zoned out. He even has some new friends, church going friends. It's cool though their still brothers. They still tight, he thinks.

Tony just kept watching all the many family members and friends running around backyard. Valerie, Yolanda and Dawn are sitting in the enclosed area with the children as they played in the kiddie pool.

Deron's cousin Paulette and her man Rick is here with their baby boy, his brother Frankie, his wife and his kids, his sister Matice and her husband and their kids, Dawn's three sisters and brother and their families, just endless people, parents, aunts and uncles. All these people came to party with Dawn and Deron and all Deron's doing is moping behind that damn grill.

Tony continued to keep his eye on him. It don't make sense, several times Frankie said he would take over on the grill. He's the one that always does the grill when they get together. Deron ain't trying to celebrate with the family.

"Daydreaming can get you done up Tony," a guy said to him as he walked up on his side.

"Yeah but when you make your move you better be ready, cause you know I always is. What's up Aijon," Tony said smoothly with a hint of humor and clasping hands with him.

"My man," Aijon responded. "Tony this my girl Tiasha, you know from Baltimore."

"Damn Aijon ain't nobody gonna slip up and mention no other bitch's name so he don't need to know all that where I'm from. I ain't hovering; do you. Hi you doing Tony?"

"I'm good Tiasha good to meet you," Tony said smirking at Aijon. "Aijon's tripping huh?"

"I told him he don't have to trip cause he used to be this big time football player. I don't need a sponsor. I got my own bank."

"Why don't you go fix me a plate so, I can talk to my man."

"Only because I'm hungry too nigga cause you ain't ordering me to do it. Where's the food Tony?"

Tony looked at her, smiled and pointed over to the outdoor kitchen where Deron is grilling food. He wanted to laugh at this chick. She's a true rat and with some bite. But she's a tiny little pretty, dark-skinned, beauty that can't be no more than twenty-five. She's wearing these tight shorts that puts that booty right out there with a low cut top. She got that. No wonder ole boy Aijon seems like he's charmed. Tony sees that she don't take no stuff. He could see himself laying up with her at least for the night. She's reminds him of Valerie but ain't got all that she's got, but she rides up close with that body. That's why he likes variety, nothing matters but the horizontal position in the end for Big T.

As long as he's known him he noticed Aijon likes them young as he can get 'em and still be legal. He thinks it's easy to handle them and get into their heads. Tony knows that's a lie. They ain't nothing but trouble and they never loyal; always posting on Facebook.

Aijon can't help himself though he's got a young mind. You'd think the nigga could pull the ladies and control them with his status. He's thirty-three, a former six foot three football player from Seattle with some cash flow; at least enough to be big in the DMV. He's a teenager in a man's body for real. Them early twenty's broads be trying to get on and he falls for it. The former football part isn't a career plan or a choice. He had a promising career at first making some real deep money. He was doing too much partying; in his short football career and got, sloppy on the field; along with some outside brushes with the law, minor stuff.

He moved to DC with hopes he would be picked up by the Redskins playing, second string at least but Tony don't believe they are interested. He still be hanging at the camp trying to be relevant. Hell he knows ain't no team gonna pick up that loose cannon. He's done.

They've been hanging partners for a year and a half now since he's moved his money into an account at Washington Federal Tony works at. They know a couple of the same women, another one of those Cheresse deals and that's how they bonded. All over cases of beer, Yak, Cîroc, Grey Goose, Henny, Jack, some shit he can't even remember. Of course, all types weed and yes did he mention some badass women? Some women Aijon imported to DC just for the weekend occasionally.

He has plenty of that action going on and Tony has the time. It's how he, Deron and Bryan used to get down even though his boys ain't never smoke no weed. He got to say he's having a good time hanging with ole Aijon. But still there's something about him that don't always set right with Tony. Like his mind ain't all there.

"Tony man that bitch's gonna make me jump outside myself one day with that fast ass mouth of hers, but that booty is good. We were arguing before we go here that's why she did all that. She goes all in and so do I," Aijon said boldly to him. "She knows she's up on my loot."

That right there. That's the big downfall of hanging with this dude Tony thought. All that bragging about what he got and what he can get. Who does that shit? He can't even handle his own women. Yeah everybody does it to some degree even himself but this dude thinks he's Russell Wilson or RGIII. Tony has his own shit jumping right now and he don't need no has-been football player trying to be one up on him. Sometimes he wanna say to him 'nigga just shut the fuck up' when they hangout.

This is what makes him miss his boys. If he could get his boys back to where they were before that would be living. But Bryan's dead and D is fucked up in the head, confused with religion.

"So this trip to Aruba's still on with those broads we scoped out two weeks ago?" Aijon said breaking his thoughts.

"I don't know cause I just got back with Valerie," Tony answered motioning Aijon attention to her. "I got to lay low until she gets comfortable again. She's been on my ass about other women and commitment. I think I'm gonna take her, instead."

"Yeah alright, it's cool. I'm still going though, with my boys so I guess I'll see you down there," he said simply. "So you gonna introduce Tiasha and me to your peeps?"

"Come on."

The two of them walked across the front of the deck towards the kitchen grill area. The way that Deron has the yard constructed is the bar area is the first place you get to when you enter through the gate of the fenced in the yard. Too bad D built that badass bar and ain't never gonna use it. Next to the bar at the back of the house is a large half-circled deck. On the left of the deck is the large walk-in kitchen grill area with a bar countertop for whoever wanted to eat there. The pool area is further in the back of the yard behind a semi-privacy screen across the patio that covered most of the backyard. There is seating around the small main pool and the kiddie pool.

Deron really went all out, Tony thought as he approached him. It is money well spent.

"Hey Deron man, I want to introduce you to my man Aijon Gant."

"Hey man, welcome."

"Appreciate that man," Aijon said real brief.

Tony and Aijon looked over to the corner of the bar area of the kitchen grill and Tiasha sat there eating.

"Tiasha, why didn't you wait for me?" Aijon asked her.

"Nigga I said I was hungry. You must not be over there flapping. Why you always complaining, I got your plate right here covered up? Deron's food is off the chain."

"Oh you already met?" Aijon asked with suspicion eying Deron and her back and forth.

"Yeah, you just don't walk up in somebody house and not speak to the homeowners or who's throwing the damn thing and eat their food. I got manners nigga. You know what you tripping I'm going over there with them girls cause you blowing me," she said as she looked over at Dawn and the other women sitting near the pool. "Deron which one is your wife?"

"Dawn has the blue on," Deron said simply.

Tiasha walked off tossing her empty plate in the trashcan that sat out along the way.

Tony started laughing because he couldn't contain it no longer. Deron smiled and looked on. He wasn't feeling Tony's friends.

"See what I mean about that chick. She about to be done. Deron, where is your cooler and ice at my man, I need a drink?"

"The coolers are over there near the screen, help yourself."

Tony and Deron watched as Aijon walked off.

"D, I hope you don't mind that I invited Aijon and his girl, we going to Crucial Lounge later on tonight when we leave; for some stripper action. You wanta come?"

"It's cool T and no I don't want go there, you know I'm trying to keep it right," Deron responded not really with any emotion.

"Man you need to get out. Ever since you got promoted again you been acting funny. That job's too much for you?"

"The job is fine. I'm good about staying in man. There's nothing out there for me, I got my woman."

"Naw D it's more than that. Something's on your mind and you ain't trying to talk about it."

"I'm good Tony. My thoughts, my problems, nobody can help me on this."

"On what D, what's going on?"

Before Deron could answer, Aijon walked up behind Tony with a sixteen-ounce plastic cup in his hand.

"Tony man, y'all got to try this Patron mixed with Red Bull. It's the beast," he said extended the cup out to Tony.

Tony looked at Deron for a minute before he responded to Aijon. He forgot to tell Aijon that this is supposed to be an alcohol free cookout. Just one more thing for Deron to stare him down on.

Dawn and Deron want to stop from serving alcohol around the children when they all get together. Some new rules he ain't down with either. Still what's he going to do but go with it because even though Valerie drinks with him; she don't care either way?

She could go months without a drink.

So of course, when Dawn and Yolanda said they weren't going to drink in front of their children anymore not even a glass of wine; she was down with her BFFs.

Tony was the odd man out in this group on that.

To him lately he's been outside the circle for a long time, that's why he gets it in with Sharnia when he wants and hangs with Aijon. They keep it real on all the fronts.

That's how he likes to get down. Sharnia for wild sex and Aijon to wreck up the city with.

"Hey Aijon let me yell at you for minute," Tony said to him as they began to walk away. "Deron you better get from behind that grill and get around seeing your family man," he said to him walking off.

Deron just nodded but he didn't move.

Once Tony and Aijon got off to themselves Aijon broke the silence.

"Yeah what's up Tony?"

"It's on me my man I forgot to tell you that Deron and Dawn don't want no alcohol at their cookouts."

"What? Who the fuck has a cookout at their house and bands liquor from the premises. That's fucked up."

"Well you know they go to church and all moving in that direction…"

"Church people Tony? You got me at a cookout with some damn church people. You want me to drink holy water on it too?"

"Hey man watch that. Those are my peeps. Deron is like a brother to me so you need to ease up."

"Yeah, yeah, yeah, I get it. Next time man let me know what's happening."

"Aijon I'm ready to exit," Tiasha said walking up on them. "You know they ain't got no drinks here?"

"Tiasha go easy with that. These are Tony's peoples, church peoples. Just take this drink and keep it light all right. We gonna leave in a minute."

"Church people, okay I got it. What the fuck you think I'm a damn demon? My peoples are church people. Nigga you be trippin'," she said rolling her eyes at Aijon. "But Tony your man Deron, I seen him some place before. I can't put my finger on it."

"So?" Tony responded nonchalantly.

"Well you don't think it was at church do you? I wanna say at some strip joint cause I be going to see the girls with my men just to go, I'm down with that," she said looking at Aijon.

Aijon just looked at her expressionless. He's boiling inside. This *bitch*, he thought is going to stand here and tell his buddy that she fucks with other dudes right in front of him. He should punch her slam in her damn face but he knows that's what she wants. She wants a payoff but she ain't gonna get his dollars. He's gonna get rid of her first.

"You see Deron at a strip club recently?" Tony asked her thinking this chick be trying to push that envelope.

"I remember something like that. Next time I see him I'mma text you with a pic, cause it be quite often."

"Yeah you do that. It's important that you do just that, alright," Tony said glancing over to Deron.

"Yeah I got you."

****

Deron saw Tiasha staring at him a lot. At first, he thought she was trying to catch his attention but it's something else.

Maybe she knows the truth.

Maybe Tony said something to her.

Whatever it is, it's not anything he's going to worry about. He's got too much on his mind already. Tony always picking up strays to be his friends on the side. He likes the ones that are always one hundred and revved up. Why can't he slow his life down? But Deron knows the answer already, it's a spiritual battle. This world has a lot of wild, risky, things that on the surface will make you think you're a god; but in the end they turn out to be fake.

Those things will destroy you eventually.

The Lord has been good to him, he thought, keeping him from that crazy nightlife he used to lead. He could only survive all that by God's mercy for sure.

Unfortunately, he can't seem to shake his past in his mind.

It's with him.

He's not letting his past die and except the promise wholly. He's still holding on to all.

His lust for one woman especially still stirs more in his memory than he would like to admit.

He still thinks about Cheresse and all that sex they used to have. He knows it's wrong but she just keeps coming back to him in his thoughts over and over again. She had his mind once and took every bit advantage of it. It was nothing that he wouldn't do for her. He was so hooked on her sex and starving for it daily.

They used to have sex every day.

He remembered the hot sex he would have with her in alleyways, loading docks behind buildings, between parked cars, apartment stairways, tennis courts and parks; anywhere they could dodge the police in DC and have wild sex. Then Dawn came and quieted him. She got in a place

Cheresse couldn't go, but Cheresse wouldn't let him be. After Cheresse broke Dawn and him up, he had that block of months he just went buck-crazy having sex with every woman that was available to him to purge the hunger.

She had unleashed his control again. He would take most of those women behind Cheresse's apartment building in the back near that damn dumpster and have sex with them. It was in the dark, in the backseat of his BMW and it was exciting. He had to trade that Beemer in because of the memories; once he settled back down with Dawn.

He wanted to be near her always and when he was having sex with those women, he was imagining he was having sex with Cheresse. Each one of those women got, used so he could play out his crazy sex games with her.

Finally, in the end, that wasn't enough.

The hunger still wouldn't die.

He had to get back with her to be with her sex again, to lay with her again.

He did get her back too.

All it took was a phone call and a few well-placed words and they were back in the bed again smashing the sheets.

Several nights they were together then.

But, it wasn't right and he started to realize that it wasn't right. He was living dirty and foul; and Dawn's love was calling to him. That's when the Lord started moving in his life unexpectedly. Things finally fell to the ground though.

Cheresse, Cheresse, Cheresse…

Thank you so much Jesus he thought.

Thank you for getting me out of that fire.

He was so far gone that he would have taken all his friends down to hell with him just to lay with her every night.

He's truly thankful but why don't he feel healed?

He should be happy now that he's married to the only woman that he could love, but he's not.

He's hurt.

All of this is his fault.

He feels he ruined everybody's life lusting after Cheresse and she didn't care one bit.

"Deron look who's here?" Dawn said to him pointing at the entrance to the gate.

He looked out towards the gate and saw his two friends Trevell Davis and Aries James with their wives coming his way. They are folks Dawn and he befriended from church. Lately they've been getting together the six of them going places for dinner, boat riding, bowling, trips everything Dawn told Deron that save folks do. He's able to hang out and have fun without all the risk that the wild side of the night brings.

He found it is no real difference then what he used to do except for a few things. The things like, drinking, unmarried sex and all that other turned up stuff his boys and he used to do in the wee hours of the night.

It's refreshing to be able to hangout and not hate yourself in the morning; or not have your woman lose faith in you. It's good to be able to honor the Lord while doing it. This is where he belongs not to slight Tony or even Bryan to be honest. Bryan's the one who showed him the way. Did he have to die in order for Deron to see the truth? It worked. He will never let him down again, he promised.

But what's missing now?

"What's up family? Glad you could make it," Deron said to them trying to perk up.

"Almost didn't because we couldn't get Brandy and LeBreya out of those shoe stores over at the Boulevard. You're on the grill again huh?"

"Yeah I got that duty but I'm about to get off it. My brother will take over."

"Dawn is that your son over there?" Brandy said. "We didn't bring the kids because they're out with their cousins."

"That's him. Come on let me introduced you all to my family."

Dawn and Deron walked off from the grill area stopping over by Matice, Paulette and Rick to talk to them.

This is the only thing that Dawn knows of that she can do to keep Deron upbeat. He's been going further and further into what anyone would think is depression. Having him intermixed with family and friends should do the trick. These past months have been something with his mood changing, declining into some zone each day.

But he won't talk to her.

At least he won't tell her the truth. She knows that there's something going on with him that she can't detect. He hasn't lost his job and she knows he isn't having an affair. She contacted his doctor and knows that there's no serious health problems. She had to beg the doctor to ease her mind about that. This week she's going to find out what's going on with her husband.

Tony who stood a way away at the pool area with Valerie, Yolanda, Aijon and Tiasha looked on. He just stared at Deron when he noticed Trevell, Aries and their wives had come through the gate. He wanted to see how Deron acted around these people.

He saw it too.

He saw how Dawn and him treated them like they used to treat Valerie and him. So that's what's been going on, he thought. Deron doesn't want him around now that he's gone all church going. These guys Aries and Trevell, Deron thinks they're better than ole Tony?

Oh okay, he thought angrily.

"Tony what's wrong with you," Valerie asked him quietly keeping her voice low.

"What do you mean?" he said jarring from his thoughts.

"You look like somebody stole something from you."

"Nothing's wrong," he said sharply.

Valerie didn't say another word she just went back to talking to Yolanda, so not to make it obvious that Tony seems bothered about something. It's something to do with Deron because that's who Tony's glaring towards. To her there's something going on between those two. Lately they haven't been that close and she can see it. Even Dawn been acting funny towards Tony. Something's going on she's sure of it. She has never brought it up to Dawn because she isn't sure yet.

****

The cookout went on for hours and Tony continued to watch Deron. Most of the time Deron just seemed to watch Deron Jr and Bryan Jr playing. He also noticed how Deron's mood would change from upbeat to low throughout the day, when he was off to himself.

This ain't surprising since his new buddies ain't here no more. They left with their wives a few hours ago. Fake asses ate some food and rolled the hell out. These are the kind of people Deron's now calling his new friends. They can't even stay for the whole damn cookout and was late as hell, what the fuck?

Now Deron's back to moping around like his best friend isn't here. Several times, he would go back and forth into the house just getting trash bags and other useless items that are already outside. Nobody seemed to notice but Tony. Even Dawn's not paying any attention to it. Deron seems like he's on drugs, maybe coming off X or something worse. Cause those fools who do more than weed and do X come off that stuff and be like a zombie. *Let me find out that when ole' hoe girl Cheresse spiked his drink that Christmas it hooked him on Ecstasy*, Tony thought.

When Deron went into the house this time and didn't come back out, Tony decided to go in to see what's going on.

It's time they hash this thing out.

****

As he sat there in the theatre, room in the basement it started to hit him fast. The memories of what has been bothering him these pass months. He guessed that having Bryan Jr over with Deron Jr. reminded him of the closeness that Tony, Bryan and he shared over the years. It's gone and he's the blame. The thoughts of it all pounded down harder on him than he has ever let it in the past.

I can't deal with this anymore, he thought as he sat down in the lead reclining chair.

Years have passed and he can't get the sounds from his mind; the voice.

He just can't stop thinking about that night and what he said to him, his last words.

He was too short with him.

He didn't treat him as a brother.

He heard something wrong and he was too short, too hasty with him.

He let him die.

How could he do that?

It's eating him alive the guilt.

He needs a drink that will ease his mind.

He needs to forget.

No!

Deron shouted in his mind as pounded his fist on the arm of the recliner. It's resistant to his punishment and he just kept pounding.

How could he let him die?

How could he let Bryan die?

How? How? How?

I should die, he thought.

He cried soundlessly in the silent theatre room and is glad that no one could hear him over the loud party music that's happening outside.

"D. What are you doing down here in the basement?" he heard Tony say, shocking him.

He was startled but he never raised his head to look Tony in the face.

"I should have died then too."

"What did you say?"

"I should have died then. Bryan shouldn't have died for me."

"D. What are you saying? You weren't even there. Nobody knew that was gonna happen. You know that right. There is no way any of us could have known that he was walking into that situation."

"He begged me to go with him, Tony. Bryan knew. He knew that there was trouble. He said it. He said he didn't feel comfortable with the alarm system. That something was not right at the townhouse. He begged me to go and I let him died on that cold floor. He called me for help. Why didn't he call 911?"

"D, you gonna have to calm down. The medical examiner said that Bryan must have gone into shock quickly. He wasn't reasoning. He just called the last number he dialed on his phone. Where's this coming from? Is this what's been going on with you?"

"Every day since I heard those messages, I've been listening to them over and over trying to figure out what made me turn off my ringer. Damn it," he pounded his fist again.

"You, been listening to Bryan's messages all this time, what the hell? D, that's…you need…"

"Damn it Tony before, I told you before how this is going to do me. It's messing with me deep. I told you I couldn't handle it. I killed my brother, it's my fault, and I can't even look Yolanda in the eye. I killed her husband."

Deron started pounding his fist on the arm of the chair again. He couldn't find the peace anywhere. He insisted repeatedly to Tony that it's his fault and that he could never forgive himself for what he's done.

He tried hating Cheresse for what she did by changing him and making him turn on his friends. He wanted to punish her but he couldn't because it was his own choice to set his friends aside for sex.

He wants God to, forgive him but can he forgive himself? Mostly will Bryan ever forgive him for taking his life?

Tony put his hand on Deron's shoulder. He didn't want to see him like this. It is terrible what happened, yes and it's been rough for all of them especially Yolanda. He remembers that when Bryan was murdered, he, himself blamed Deron for it; but it wasn't about Deron. The pain was talking. Deron didn't do nothing wrong.

It was about that selfish son of bitch, Carl that wanted to rule over a neighborhood. Bryan got too, close to what was happening with Carl and he took the opportunity to get rid of him when he could. He was always looking to gun down Bryan.

As he looked at Deron completely losing it sitting in the theatre chairs, he felt really bad for what's going on with his friend. Nobody should have to deal with this kind of guilt.

As he pulled on Deron's shoulder to ease up another small tiny hand patted Deron on his bowed head.

"Bryan, boy where's your mother? What you doing down here?" Tony asked politely.

"I want to hang out with the boys. Uncle De-on, Uncle De-on? Don't be sad, it alright. Daddy said; don't let the bad man steal your spirit. Daddy said he see you later."

Deron picked up his head.

"What did you say?"

He saw Bryan Jr. standing there but he didn't believe what he's hearing.

Is Bryan speaking to him, through little Bryan?

He has to be.

How can a three-year old boy think to say something like that?

He hugged Bryan Jr like a father hugging his son.

"Don't let bad man steal your spirit, dad-dy say that," he smiled at Deron. "Come I show you."

Deron and Tony followed Bryan Jr. upstairs to the first level. They went into the library where Yolanda put all the toys she brought for Bryan Jr. to play with today. He went over to his toys and picked up a teddy bear lying in the pile.

"You have to come down here," he said to Deron.

Deron stooped down and looked at the bear. It has a Teddy Bear's Workshop tag on it. He recognized it because he gave one to his son.

"Listen," Bryan Jr said as he pressed the hand of the bear.

'Remember Bryan Jr. don't let the bad man steal your spirit. God will always love you and watch out for you. I will always love you son,' the voice said resonating from the bear. 'I'll see you later on.'

Tony and Deron realized the voice is Bryan's voice.

"See daddy say that," little Bryan said happily.

"He sure did," Deron, said trying to be steady in front of the boy.

"D, that's the Bryan you need to remember man. Those other voicemails got to go man. You ain't gonna get no peace until you let it go."

"Yeah you're right, thanks Tony," Deron said agreeing with him. "And thank you too little buddy," he said to Bryan Jr.

Bryan Jr just flashed a smile like the one the little boy in Deron's dream years ago did.

He realized that God is really with him.

CHAPTER 5

The next day on Sunday, Audrey rode in silence in Cheresse's car on her way to the airport. She can't believe how driven she is to want to take care of business.

"By the time you get back Audrey, I'll have a custody hearing all set up," Cheresse said.

Audrey decided that she's going to return to LA to see if she could take more time off from work. She wants to make this sacrifice for her friend who she now knows is gravely ill.

Cheresse just left the doctors a few days ago and told her that it's confirmed that she has some type of terminal disease. Cheresse wouldn't go into details about what's affecting her body but she says she'll be beginning some sort of treatments real soon. Audrey cried with her the whole night wishing she could do more to help her. She's too young to be dealing with this and the thing with her parents is insane. They must don't know about the diagnosis because if they did they would be right here by her side. Cheresse's folks have always did anything to make Cheresse feel like she's special. So why not now?

They've always had her back maybe a bit too much at times. Maybe that's the reason why she can't take no for an answer. So, at this time you would think that they would be front and center.

She asked Cheresse why they weren't talking to her right now but she didn't give her a reason. At first, she thought Cheresse was lying as usual but this is obviously an indication that there's something going on between her parents and her.

Maybe Renita knows something. She's closer to Cheresse than Audrey. Between her busy schedule with working and the twins plus with Audrey living in LA; they've fell off from each other. It's been almost a year since she last heard from her and that was brief. It's just as much Audrey's fault as she wants to believe it's Renita. Because she hasn't tried to reach out to her either.

"Have you heard from Renita," she asked Cheresse.

"No I was going to ask you the same thing. It's been awhile."

"I'm going to call her while I'm waiting for my plane."

"It won't do you any good because her cell phone is disconnected."

"What? Why didn't you tell me? Something must be going on with her. This isn't like her. What about her home phone?"

"You know Renita had to get rid of that phone too because of the bills."

"No I didn't," she said as she started to worry.

"Yes girl I think she's lost her job or something."

"I'm going to fly up to Philly instead of going back to LA, to check on her."

"Girl you don't have to do that," Cheresse said quickly. "I'll drive up there myself."

"No you will not. I can't have you driving long distance."

"Audrey, don't start treating me like some sickly handicap, I feel fine. It's just my appetite, I'm fine. I'll just go up there spend a couple of days and come right back. I'll check on Renita to see if she's alright. Please don't treat me like that, I can't take that."

Audrey nodded and turned her head from her friend. The tears were rolling down her face faster than she could control them or wipe them away.

"Okay Cheresse."

Cheresse simply smiled.

****

The cellphone rang loudly with the latest hardcore Drake rap Valerie noticed. Tony and she sat together on the sectional sofa located in the family room at Tony's house watching a movie.

It rang a third and fourth time with the same ringtone.

"So you're not going to bother looking at the phone to see who it is?"

"I don't need to because I'm with you right now," Tony said nonchalantly.

"It could be one of your boys."

"Could be."

"Somebody wants to catch up with you bad."

"No matter to me," Tony said trying to be nonchalant about it because he knows what Valerie is doing.

"You know you want to answer that damn phone, so do it."

"If I look at that phone it's gonna be one of the guys or Erica, something that will take my focus off of what's going on right now. I have Erica investigating this unknown company that's been buying up all the property in this area. You know I'm trying to get this realtor thing going. But I'm enjoying spending time with you. After we finish watching this movie we can go upstairs and do a love scene just you and me. So let the phone ride baby."

"Humph," Valerie huffed as the phone stopped ringing.

She got up from the sofa, went directly to the phone, and picked it up. The phone rang again. She hit the button on the IPhone 6 plus and nothing.

The screen remained dark.

She turned around and threw the phone at him.

"Balls in your court, baby."

Tony picked up the phone while it rang and answered it.

"Yeah?" he said reluctantly into the phone.

"Why haven't you been answering your phone Tony?" Shania asked on the other end of the phone.

"I've been busy," he looked at Valerie. "What have you got on your plate?"

"Why are you talking like that...is somebody there?"

"Yes."

"Tony, see this is the reason why I left in the first place," Valerie said to him from across the room. "I'm done." She started to walk off.

"Look here stop calling me. I already told you that I'm back with my girl," Tony yelled into the phone trying to sound as convincing as he could to Valerie.

"You told me she left. I thought she left."

"She's back, so stop calling, out."

"Give me that damn phone Tony," Valerie said aggressively walking up on him. She tore the phone from him before he could react. "Look whore, stop calling my man. I'm only going to tell you once and he's knows I'm not going to tell him anymore. Don't come around here just stop tricking thot."

"Valerie, Tony don't want you. That's why he won't marry your uppity ass. You think you're better than everyone else."

"Chick I don't even know you and I know you don't know me. Whoever you are and wherever you are you don't get the news do you. October 17th, this year 1 o'clock. It should be a nice fall day for a wedding. I would invite you but I don't think I'm allowing anymore guest, bye, bye, thot."

She cut off the call and stood there staring at Tony.

"Valerie," he said just shook his head innocently.

"Make sure all your bitches get the message."
****

"I'm so glad baby that you are doing this," Dawn said to Deron. They both just got back home from Church. "I wish I knew you were listening to that every day for the past two years. You know I'm here for you."

"Nobody knew," he said. "I guess that's how the devil tries to get to you by isolating you and getting you away from the people that love you."

"Are you feeling better, really?"

"Yes."

"I still think you should see the Pastor about this, to talk to someone you trust and respect."

"I don't know Dawn. I can do that here with you."

"Deron, really? Yes, I guess you can but you need to see the Pastor, okay?"

"I don't want too many people to know about this."

"Deron no one will judge you either way. It's so that you can get it off your spirit and turn it over to the Lord."

He looked at her a minute before trying to protest again. Then he noticed what he's always known about the woman he loves. He's on every word she breathes.

"You know I'm in love with you right," he said kissing her deeply. "I'll give the pastor a call."

"First things, first baby you need to erase those messages from Bryan," she said to him. "You have to free yourself."

"I know I'm doing it right now," he said as he worked the screen of his smartphone.

****

"We all have things in life that we wished we could have done differently," the Pastor said to Deron as they sat in his office later that evening. When Deron called the Pastor, he picked up right away and insisted on seeing him immediately. "Jesus knows this Deron and he knows each one of us personally. He knows what we're going to do. He's not just going to sit back and allow you to suffer in your pain he will help; but he wants you to make that choice to come to him for help. Some choices we make and other are, made for us. There's a plan and it happens whether we move the way we're supposed to or not. The end result is that Jesus is the salvation; the healer that we go to that will solve those tough trails. You lost your friend because you think you made an unwise choice. What if I told you that Bryan wasn't thinking either? He chose to go to that house without calling the police to go with him;

therefore, making a selfish choice. It was in the dead of night. Sometimes we value things over our own very lives, things, people too, because we don't really know how tricky the enemy can be. I'm not saying that he was asking for what happened to him. I'm saying he wasn't thinking with the instinct for survival that God places in each one of us. Think back on a time, any time you think, man I just made it out of there with my life because something bad happened right after you left. That's God telling you that you need to go, you need to get up, you need to leave, you need to stop seeing her, don't go, don't leave, don't call, call. Sometimes all we have to do is listen to what the Savior has to say, but the flesh is strong it can get in the way. I myself feel sorry that Bryan had gone there that night too. However, it seems as if he was, obsessed with going there the way you tell it. And if you had gone with him who knows what would have happened to you. You may not have been here either. As you say, you were in a different place with your soul then. You weren't prepared for salvation so you would have been lost. Your steps were, ordered in this direction. Something secretly told you that it was too cold and dreary to be out that night. That was the Lord God, thank you Jesus. You said that you told Bryan that you would go with him in the morning, but he wouldn't listen. It was out of your hands. What he heard was his path and no one knows but the Lord what that is. But I can tell you I believe he's gone on to be with the Lord. I'll give you an example. You have to listen to God the way Job did. He listened to his faith and waited on God. Even when he lost everything, he continued to wait on God. He wouldn't even curse God when his wife and friends told him to do that and he surely did feel sorry for his lost. However, he simply waited on the Lord. When we become anxious about a thing or someone, we begin to make mistakes. We begin to block our blessings. In the days to come Deron, you are going to have to learn how to forgive yourself. Not for Bryan's death but for what you're really punishing yourself for. You have let it go Deron or it will torment you. In second **Corinthians 5:17** it says *'Therefore if any man be in Christ, he is a new creature: old things are passed away; behold, all things are become new.'*

The past, the old sins must die and be forgotten.

Don't let the devil fool you. He knows when you are seeking the Lord Jesus. He tried to dump all the pressures of the past back on you. Using your friends that aren't good in your life, even bringing back acquaintances that you have discarded from your life. He's very clever because he doesn't want you to reach glory. You have to let go of your past, the past that's still punishing you…"

Deron sat there not able to speak. His thoughts are totally on what the Pastor's saying. He heard the Pastor; he really heard what the Pastor told him. God's been trying to get him this level for a long time but he just didn't seem to want that. He feels like he didn't deserve God's salvation and he self-punished himself. He feels that he deserves what happened to him with Cheresse.

"Your past is always going to be there, but it doesn't have to rule over you. Reading the word and praying to the Lord will take those things from you and in time. Everything you need is in the Bible. Remember the Bible is **B**asic **I**nstruction **B**efore **L**eaving **E**arth. Sister Brenda H gave that insight to the congregation the other day and it's true. What you need to ensure, is that you're less and less exposed to your old life, even some people as you move on to your salvation. Sometimes people are there just for a season or two. A new life is just that, a new life…"

****

Later on that night around 11 o'clock, Tony's truck is, parked outside of gas station on route 301 south. It's sitting amongst some other cars that are parked on the property for mechanical service. The gas station is closed. Tony's truck is rocking even though the truck's engine is not running.

This is another one of his dangerous hookups.

"Ooh baby," the female voice inside of the truck screamed. "That's it, that's it right there."

"It's what you want, right? You've been calling for it… here it is now ride it like you tryin' to make a baby," Tony said aggressively and tauntingly to Sharnia.

All evening long after that run in with Valerie over the phone, Sharnia aggressively texted Tony's phone. He was able to divert the text from appearing in the messages area sending it to email. He later slipped away to his home office located his first floor library and access the email on his computer. After a few well-placed emails later and he has Sharnia riding his love stick like she's getting it for the first time. He loves when she gets desperate to keep him. She does it so that he will keep on being with her he knows how she thinks. She will do anything to be with him and meeting her down here on the side of the road makes this smash fest hotter than ever.

It would've been good to be up in his bed so he could really get at her but Valerie is there working on some papers from work. He almost didn't get out of the house telling her that he had to go see Aijon about some money he wanted to invest. Just his luck Aijon called him and Tony told him he was on the way. Since they been hanging, they've been covering each other like this. It used to be Deron that covered for him when he needed him but that's out the window. He should've taken her to a motel but he ain't trying to catch no crabs in no sleazy motel bed.

"Damn girl," Tony said after his release.

"You like that baby," Sharnia squealed. "I was creamy wasn't I, just like your vanilla right? I've been backed-up waiting on you; except that other night when I had to go to my drawer and go it alone. But baby that not you. I love you Tony," she said excitedly hugging him.

"Forgot that love shit Sharnia. You know you love this stick. You my whore right?"

She didn't say anything she just looked at him through the dark dimness of the street lights. He looked like Satan grinning; sitting in this dim light. She just started to, noticed the traffic she heard as it flew by more steadily than she expected at this time of night. It's back to reality.

"Right?" Tony insisted.

"I'm…that bitch Valerie is your whore. I'm your woman," she said angrily.

"You know you ain't my woman."

"Then what the hell am I Tony, your prize white girl?"

"I thought we were smashing buddy. Now you catching feelings."

"Tony," she said trying to talk quietly so not to betray her anger. "I've done everything you've asked me to do. I love you and we're good together, we're compatible. Don't nobody make me feel it like you, do."

"Come on Sharnia we're friends you know like friends with benefits. We make each other get it."

"Why the hell are you marrying her?" Sharnia exploded.

"I'm not."

"She said you are."

"She said that to piss you off," Tony said plainly.

"So you don't have a date set in the fall?"

"I don't have nothing…Valerie set that date."

"TONY, DO YOU HAVE THE DAMN DATE OR WHAT?" she exploded again.

"Hey cut that shit out. I ain't attached to nobody and I ain't marrying nobody either, that's what's up."

"Take me home. Take me home now. Take me home!" she screamed pounding on the dashboard in front of her.

"Okay I'll take your crazy ass home."

"Yes take me home!"

"You always tripping and you want me to commit to you, you're crazy."

"I'm not crazy you can't leave that uppity bitch alone."

"Whatever. When I get to your place just hop your ass out even if the truck's still moving, I ain't stopping," he said pulling out of the station onto 301.

The two of them rode together in silence.

Sharnia's so mad she wants to kick the windows out of Tony's truck. For Tony he enjoys how he has her mind so messed up that he can tell her whatever and she will do it. She so hooked on this caramel chocolate bar that it should be a crime.

CHAPTER 6

On Friday, Tony and Deron are at Pentagon City Mall. Tony called Deron to help him pick out an engagement ring. They've been at the mall for about an hour going to the different jewelry stores there until they finally found the ring Tony thought Valerie would want. Really, it is because Tony thought that the customer rep behind the counter is fine as shit and is trying to get with her. Of course she is flirting with him to get a sale, asking him stuff like *'are you sure you're ready'* and *'you might want to see what's out there'*. Deron decided to rescue the young woman because he knows she doesn't know what she is getting into.

She couldn't be no more than twenty-one.

She isn't no way prepared for Tony's antics.

He'd ruin her for the next man.

Once the ring was paid for, the guys went down to the lower level to the food court to grab a bite to eat.

"Hey Tony have you been talking to Sharnia lately."

"Naw, D. You know I don't get with her anymore. Why would you ask that?"

"I'm just asking. I know she's seeing some guy because she's been a bit preoccupied lately."

He really wanted to say she's been a real 'b' at the job lately but he's not trying to curse too much anymore. Besides, it's none of his business so he didn't press him, but Deron knows the truth. Still Sharnia all week long has been snappy and downright difficult to work with. He had to counsel her on Wednesday because she cussed out a driver that lost a gas card. Seriously a gas card. He's known her for over eight years and he knows how she is when she's upset.

Usually she shuts down and takes off days here and there. But she's very quiet and secretive about what's going on this time. Hell, if it wasn't for Frank Molten saying anything he would never have known about the sexual harassment charge until someone else was hired in Wendell Savoy's vacated position. Getting that position helped him reach Regional Manager quickly, no thanks for Sharnia on this.

"I got to say D cause it's on my mind. You sure hover over Sharnia a lot," Tony said slyly. "You sure you ain't been hitting that? You know before you and Dawn got in too deep."

"I know you're kidding right? I know you aren't serious."

"Yeah I'm serious," Tony said boldly.

"Don't worry my man Sharnia's been all yours," Deron said knowingly.

"I told you I don't do her no more," he said trying to sound convincing. "I haven't been messing with her for over a year and half. You know she's not on my level."

For some reason Tony wanted to keep his thing with Sharnia undercover Deron thought. Maybe he's beginning to feel something for her and if that's the case what about Val?

"So you and Val are making this move. I can't believe it. I'm happy for you man," he said trying to switch gears of the conversation.

"Yeah it's time. My baby wants to get married and my baby Valerie gets what she wants."

Man, Tony's rubbing this thing in deep, Deron thought and he didn't know why. This is how it's been these days' tip toeing around every conversation like they don't know each other's dirt. Like Deron doesn't know that Tony's lying about wanting to get married. Lately T hasn't been so careless with Deron's personal business and even when he did, it was to Bryan; so that don't count.

Why would Tony think that he would betray him to Val?

"Well you know Dawn and I will be there."

"Shit D you the best man like I was at yo' wedding. I'm sure Dawn is Valerie's bridesmaid."

"That's cool."

"What you ain't trying to stand up for me?"

"Come on T, stop tripping. You know I'd be happy to do that."

"You drifting D."

"Don't know what you mean man," he said and then before Tony could say anything else on that. "What's up with that dude Aijon? Is he trying to get back into football or is he slumming?"

"What you mean by slumming D? That's kinda street for you lately."

"I didn't mean anything by it. It's just an expression and I'm just making conversation."

"I don't know what Aijon's doing man," Tony said eyeing Deron with scrutiny. "You know how it is when you got a lot of money to burn and a lot of women and alcohol to spend it on. He's made some good business deals and got some good property. I'm just glad I got him to invest at least a mill in something that's been able to turn a profit. He only had that 2.5 million left to do that. My buddy he'll get it together, you did."

"I guess," damn was that a dig, Deron thought?

When did this conversation get like this? Before, they've been able to talk about anything. Now Tony's on guard or is it him, Deron thought. Maybe he's not really interested in Tony's wild friends stupid spending habits with his cash, been there done all that, with Cheresse.

"Naw seriously D, he and his girl Tiasha plan on getting married soon too. I'm the best man at his wedding too."

"Well they're going in the right direction if they do. But from what I saw at the cookout they don't even know each other like that."

"There you go judging. Next thing you gonna say is that me and Valerie got no right to get married cause we ain't ready."

"Don't put words in my mouth. Man I'm not saying all that. I'm not saying anything about you and Val. I'm just saying."

But really he does think that Val and T aren't ready to get married. They're like night and day and T's never serious about one woman. Things haven't changed all this time. So no it's not that they shouldn't get married he knows they're not going to do it. The last thing that Tony's going to do is make another commitment that even matches his time with Monica. That marriage did something to him that he hasn't dealt with yet.

But Val is nothing like Monica.

"So what are you saying?"

"I'm just saying that ole girl was looking at me and I thought she was trying to hit on me."

"Oh no D that ain't it. She said she seen you somewhere before but couldn't remember where; that's what she told me."

"Oh yeah she didn't know where?" Deron asked nonchalantly.

"Well…"

Tony got cut off by a loud voice booming above them over the food court. At first, it sounded like it came from over the speaker system in the mall, like some kind of emergency announcement.

"Deron! Hi Deron. De----ron!"

Everyone on the food court started looking around to see where the loud screaming voice is coming from. The female voice sounded so loud that it caused a lot of the people to be alarmed.

These days you can never be too sure.

Even Deron couldn't tell where his name is being called from and he slightly recognized the voice. Tony being a little quicker he looked up towards the upper levels.

"What the hell is that?" he said pointing up to the upper level. "Deron isn't that…isn't that, that crazy chick, Crystal?"

Deron looked up to the direction that Tony pointed.

It *is* Crystal.

All this time he's been silently ducking her, avoiding going over to Paulette's new place just so he wouldn't run into her. He misses his cousin but he doesn't miss all that drama that Crystal's has caused him over the years. Plus, she practically stays over Paulette's new place.

He doesn't know how Paulette can take it.

Paulette moved into this bad new townhouse in Bowie, Md. otherwise known as Bougie, Md.

You can't tell her nothing now after she won that half million playing Lotto tickets late last year. Boy, she has a lucky star in her pocket. Two tickets in two different Lotto's totaling up to the amount. She brought the place for cash even though Deron tried to tell her to let Tony flip her money first. Rick stepped in to convince her because he didn't want to pay a mortgage. Tony was still there to get her a good deal on that townhouse though.

Rick's been right there enjoying that money like everybody knew he would.

He hasn't been working steady since he quit his job at FEDEX Field and the money came. A perfectly good job working as a mechanical engineer there and he quits. Said he was going to start his own business but that was a year ago. Deron just thinks he got tired of fitting those barely-legal girls he messes with into his lunch hour. He knows he's not going to find no other woman to put up with that nonsense but Paulette. She doesn't seem to mind that he's just floating into one job after the next.

She still doesn't get it.

She had that chance to get him out of her life but she didn't want to let him go. Especially after the baby came but they haven't got married yet.

"That's her? Damn, Deron, you sure get desperate during your booty drought," Tony joked sounding like he really wanted to stress the point to embarrass Deron.

"Deron wait right there I'm coming down. It's so good to see you, yessss! Don't move baby. I still love you," Crystal yelled down to him.

People are still trying to figure out who Crystal is yelling to. He tried to get up as fast as he could from the table not even looking up again to acknowledge her. He just wanted to get out of her sight as quick as possible.

"Deron don't leave I'm coming down. Ooh I can't believe it, baby it's you. I love you," she continued to scream.

Now people realized for sure who she's screaming at.

Some of the people were laughing because Crystal did look like a great big something jumping around on the upper floor hanging over the rails. It is just plain ignorant. It's clear to Deron from the quick glance he got of her that she appears to have gain at least fifty pounds. She's already tall and awkward looking now she looked monstrous.

"D, Crystal looks like a big ass great ape with a baboon booty. She blew up like a balloon. I thought the chick was gonna jumped down on this level. I was waiting for her to swing down onto tables to the food court like a recon mission," Tony joked. "Please man if you ever get single again try to get yourself some on a regular basis."

After that, Deron just ignored her and bolted faster as the screams from her increase with each step.

"Deron, Deron, De---ron…!"
****

When they drove off in Tony's truck, they cracked up joining on Crystal and talking about how close Deron got to facing her.

"Man I know she knows you married," Tony said cracking up. "I know Paulette told her. That chick's crazy as hell."

"I don't know what's up. What's the likelihood she'd be here at the mall? This is Paulette's fault and I'm going over her house later to say something to her."

"Naw D let's go now. I wanna see you get into Paulette's ass about Crystal. I need something funny to take with me on my trip to Aruba."

"Aw dam…excuse me, man I forgot you were going out of town with Valerie."

"Yeah in three days…," Tony's voice kind of trail off. He caught that. It's some bullshit that D feels like he got to hold back who he really is for religion, Tony thought angrily. He don't have to pretend to be a goody two shoes, they're grown ass men. No offense to Dawn but she done watered D down to some kind of wimp. He can't even express himself like he used to. Tony decided to himself that when he gets back from Aruba he's going to help his brother get back to himself.

Set him back on track.

Damn even Bryan wasn't this damn crazy with his religion.

****

Tony came home from Aruba seven days later. He told Deron that he and Val got into it several times and almost got arrested on the beach. He's still on vacation so Deron took off from work early to hang with him. He decided to go over to Tony's because he started to notice the things he'd say on the sly especially the last time they were together. He don't want T thinking he's not trying to be down with him anymore. So he wanted to do something they used to do when either one of them goes out of town. As soon as they get back, they give each other the rundown on their vacation. These days their vacations are different than they used to be. Sometimes other people would go on vacations with them instead of going together like they did before. Tony would do a guy's trip with Aijon and some other dudes. Deron would do couple of trips with some of his new friends from church. He don't know why he and Val don't go with them sometimes, but sometimes Tony seems uncomfortable around Deron's friends. Maybe because Val and him are having issues.

As intelligent, as Tony and Val are he thought, they can't seem to have a steady relationship. Deron knows that Tony's pretty much the cause; because that's his MO. He can't figure out where Val fits into all this. She can't possibly like the difficulties that they keep going through.

What's her motivation?

Now that she knows how T really is, he may finally have met his match. Maybe she's just like him. This is someone who takes him as serious as he takes her, or not, he thought.

Unlike Tony who had once predicted that the girls' friendships wouldn't last because it wasn't real; he couldn't be more wrong. Dawn, Yolanda and Valerie have stuck very close by each other. He almost envied them because he realizes that Tony and he have shifted slightly since he doesn't hit the streets anymore.

He noticed that brotherly bond that Bryan, Tony and he used to share isn't really there anymore. Is Bryan's death to blame? Their party lifestyle was notorious years ago.

He has to admit that those were some good times.

Now Tony's about to turn the big thirty-two and their friendship seems miles away. They weren't partying like they used too and who knew that was a big part of their bond; partying. But he wasn't really happy with where his future was heading then; at least he thinks. Having the fun yeah but not that Cheresse crap. A lot of crazy things happened the last few years too crazy and it changed his life forever. He guessed it was time to take a mature step to life. He's always been a little more serious than the average guy his age anyway.

It's time to settle down and get serious about life.

He's, definitely meant to be with Dawn.

"Now can you get with this or what D?" Tony said boasting of the sexy semi-nude, beauty on the TV.

Listening to him as he showed him the sights of his vacation on his thumb-drive, Deron tried not to get involved. He's still very new in his walk and with Tony; it's a constant battle not to revert to his old ways. They've had a lot of bad fun and Deron has to admit it to himself that it's hard not to wish he was still in it. Sometimes he wished he could return to his former life just a little but he knows that life was leading him to destruction. The way he was going.

If he went back it will send him over the deep end.

"Tony I'll be alright but will Val? Does she know about these women you've filmed?"

"Naw, why would Valerie be interested in this? It's my vacation flick. She don't concern herself with things she knows she can't control."

"Then why are you editing it?" Deron interjected with a hint of sarcasm. "Why don't you show her all the sights?"

"See D, I can't expect a humble guy like yourself to actually understand the frankness of our relationship. You being all churchy and all new. So I'm not gon' go there with you."

"Yeah, thanks you answered my question perfectly."

"See this girl here, I was about to bring her back here to be my maid before I found out that she makes more money than me. Most of those hoes were down there either by themselves or with a girlfriend. Man there was so much pussy on the beach that I thought I was on a Victoria Secret photo shoot. No wonder a man can't find a good woman, they're all down on the islands vacationing. I'm telling you man we need to go someplace together real hot, real soon.

My boy Aijon, I know he'll go," he paused, the video and turned back to look at Deron. "And before that halo on yo' head form a complete circle."

"And what happens if we do pull this off and our women decide they want to go away together by themselves, frankly I'm not feeling that."

"You gotta point."

Tony pressed the play button and the scene continued. The next scene that came up showed a nude beach. Wall-to-wall island women are there with nothing on but the umbrellas in their drinks.

There weren't too many men in booty heaven.

All the women are tight, like they were filming a Sports Illustrated magazine, a porn movie or something.

"Well this is my cue to check out that new PlayStation 4 game you got T," Deron said quickly as he bolted out of the room.

Tony watched Deron as he walked out of the room heading for his game room and shook his head. He got to hand it to him he thought, he's staying true to growing with his family and God. Even when Tony plays devil's advocate, he can resist the temptation and he does try to play devil's advocate. Because he's too young to be cooped up in love and trying to be a nice guy.

He's got to break Deron.

****

A little while later Deron came back into the room. Tony's still watching his vacation video.

Eventually Deron thought, that the two of them would outgrow the small things that bond them together. Partying, yeah that was something that they all had in common.

So what now?

What will they do?

Will they go on living their lives checking in on each other from time to time or will they just stop hanging altogether. They've been friends, brothers for a long time.

He supposes it'll all work itself out.

"I guess the scenery started to get to you huh," Tony smirked at Deron. "Check out the one in the blue striped, earrings, I got that two hours before liftoff."

"Man, you need help."

"What?"

"Maybe you're a sex addict you ever think of that? That could be the reason why you have issues settling down."

Whoosh Deron thought.

He didn't mean to say it like that.

"You mean I need to settle down like you? No thanks. I like what I'm doing's just fine. You get more freedom my way and variety. I don't get bored. You might wanna stop stressing yourself out trying to be all in love, Mr. Nice Guy and get yourself some evolving booty."

"Evolving? You mean revolving, don't you?" Deron said shaking his head.

"No I mean evolving. Whenever the one you with can't make the program, evolve to the next hoe."

"That's funny, you and your logic T. You know me I'm going to keep on trying that one on one approach and stay married."

"That's on you," he said pointing to the TV screen as he paused it to show Deron the latest semi-nude female on it. "Just like that ass was on me three days into my vacation."

"Man you need to cool down. Val's the right one and you might mess that up."

"Yeah I follow you and D, Dawn's is the right one to be with. Don't you, mess that up."

Retaliation and always the hardcore approach. His brother's going too far left that Deron don't think that he'll be able to get to him.

"Don't worry God's got me."

"All I want to know is you gonna hang with me on my birthday cause I got an all-nighter planned?" Tony said ignoring Deron's last statement.

"I don't know Tony. What are we doing?"

"No I'm not telling you. I haven't hung out with you in a month of Sundays and you ain't gonna cop out on my birthday like you did last year."

"You know how it is man."

"Man church folks party. Don't get me to exposing that myth. Some of those church folks you be at bible study with be the same ones gettin' it in at the club. I know I seen Aries at 9.9 one night."

"Man, that's on him, but I don't believe it."

"Those guys that were at your cookout are some fake ass Christians, D. I know I saw your boy downing some drinks at 9.9."

"Tony what's your point?"

"Your dudes get it in like I do. Ain't nothing changed, just different nigga just trying to hide in the church. They still got party in them."

"What's the point?"

"You know what; it ain't about that my nigga. The point is you can't hang with me cause you think your crew is better to be out in public with than me. Cause you trying to be churchlike and all, the image. What I think is that you just too uptight."

"We back at that? Just monitoring my walk man that's all."

"You taking this shit too seriously," Tony's voice rose.

"It is serious. Jesus is serious," Deron responded agitated as well.

"Too serious for you to hang out with your brother, right?"

"You can hang out with me by going to church. Then you can understand what I'm talking about. You used to go when Bryan was here."

"And the Lord didn't help my brother when he was laying on that cold floor dying either."

He looked at Tony for a second.

"What up with that?" Deron said hearing something in his tone.

"Nothing forget it. You gonna hang with me or what?"

"Are *you* going to hang or what? Do it to honor Bryan's memory."

"D, you ain't got to use Bryan over me like that. You not gonna convert me."

"Well you act like you don't care about your salvation. Somebody got to help. He shared that with us for a reason, but I'm not holding him over you like that. All I said is that you can hang with me too sometimes at my spots."

Tony thought about it.

The only way he's going to get Deron back to his old self is to play it his way. He's fucked up in his head still about Bryan, feeling guilty and shit thinking he got to hide in the church.

He needs a way out and Tony's gonna give him one.

"Okay man you win. I'll go to church with you," Tony said quietly.

"What did you say?"

"Damn it D I said, I'll go to church with you."

Deron just shook his head. Tony just don't seem to get where he's coming from. His life is now for the Lord and he has no intention in slowing down. He can't tell Tony how good the Lord's been to him because it's beyond words. He got him over his guilt about Bryan now that he's dealt with it the right way; with the help of the Pastor. He feels better spiritually than he has in months since Bryan's death, like he had a black hood over his head all this time. It's already a real battle but he's going to win it.

Don't Tony know that he still gets that feeling for his old life? It's always there.

But the promise is that God's going to be with him, through it and work it out so he won't fall back to that fast life.

"This Sunday."

"Okay man but you going out with me on my birthday, the whole night next week."

"Alright man we're hanging out but don't let it get too deep alright?"

"You know ole' Tony's got to get it turnt up, man."

CHAPTER 7

"You know Tony; I don't know why I let you talk me into coming here," Deron said as the two of them walked through the doors at Club P. This place should've been a no go on his list to be at tonight. He don't know why they just didn't go shoot pool like he suggested on their way here.

Club P is the latest strip club that survived the revamp of DC. It's true that Washington, D.C. is fast becoming like some sleepy city with these small pubs here and there; sort of like San Francisco.

Hardly any of the raunchy stuff is left and Tony don't like that. He like to turn it up all the way to one hunnit and Deron knows that's why they're here. He likes running the streets late at night doing risky shit; that keeps him on edge.

Now there's streetcars, condos and too many damn neighborhoods that call the police when you get too loud. If it wasn't for this club downtown on Georgia Avenue, northwest he wouldn't come into the city.

"Because it's my b-day and besides if I'm going to be going to church with you sometimes, not to join the place, I'm just saying, just so you know that, just rolling with you; than you can come here with me."

"Man, really? That's not even close. You can't compare the two."

"Uh whatever D, forget that shit. Let's get this party started. They got this bad ass broad that they just unleashed on us last weekend. She is bad," Tony said as he sat down at one of the tables.

"Tony," Deron said as he sat down reluctantly. He is uncomfortable. "I can't be here, really. Let's go somewhere play some pool and grab a bite."

"Damn D. you uptight again. Let's have one drink, one drink and watch two strippers and we out, all right? Besides

I got something else planned but it's not due for another hour or so."

"I'm not staying in here that long, seriously man."

"Look man you're blowing my birthday and I know you ain't trying to do that on purpose. Just relax and be about our brotherly shit and have some fun."

"I can't believe you man. I...," Deron said shaking his head.

"D. yeah-yeah-yeah, fuck that, look what's coming over here," Tony said looking past Deron.

Deron turned around to see a fine woman coming his way. Obviously, she is coming to take their drink order. Her body is phenomenal and he had to shake his head to get the thoughts out that are creeping in.

He hadn't been looking at her face at first; but then he started to, notice. The more she walked up on them, the more she started to look familiar.

"I'll be damn D, that's your girl Nelicia," Tony said.

Deron looked at her and couldn't believe it. It is Nelicia James. Nelicia in this place? She works for the Washingtonian Magazine. She has a job as a freelance photography or at least she's did when he met her a few years ago. At any rate what in the hell is she doing here and dress like that; and what did she do to her body because she is slamming with some new boobs.

"Deron Stone, what are you doing in here? Hi," she said bending to him to hug him and then sitting down at their table.

"Following behind this guy," he said thumb pointing to Tony.

"Hey Tony, baby. Where you been?"

"Just like you, around baby."

"Oh I see. Y'all are going to play with me like that. It never fails with you men. Once you give a man some they play you," she laughed.

Same ole Tony, he never changes. Sleeps with everything walking, Deron thought.

"Well you just fell off the GPS didn't you? I tried to shout at you but you changed your cell on me," Tony said.

Deron just sat there trying to not to get in the conversation. He didn't need for Tony to know he's been with her but something tells Deron that he already knows. Nelicia can't hold water. He didn't need all of this temptation from his past. If he didn't know any better he'd think that Tony is setting him up. Strippers and now Nelicia, with new boobs, this is some bull. What's the likely hood of this happening at the same time?

Boy Tony is really a trip. What's next?

"Nelicia, give us about ten minutes. Come back and have a drink with us on me."

Nelicia nodded to Deron and got up from the table.

When she left, Deron addressed Tony.

"You want to tell me what's happening or do you want to pull out some more women from my past?"

"Man I just thought you seemed kind of miserable and needed to get out of that boring church life. I'm trying to turn you up again; at least for my birthday. Stop tripping about the past and enjoy the here and now."

"Look T., there's nothing boring about God. It's my soul, not just some fad."

"I'm cool with it really D, but you seemed like you were missing stuff, so I wanted to get you back out in your element."

"The Lord is my element now. But it's my stuff, I'm not saying you need to change, that's on you, but I can't be in here; mainly because I don't want to hurt Dawn."

"Being in here ain't gonna hurt Dawn. You just having fun, not making a porn movie."

"It's the temptations Tony. Things like this strip club, these things are my triggers. I just don't want to get out of control."

"Sounds like you crazy to me. Just relax, we just out on guys night. It's my birthday and this is how I get it in. Now you don't have to be 100 like me but you gots to have some fun D, damn."

"I ain't crazy Tony, I'm saved."

"I got it D, but damn it's..."

Rather than listen to Tony try to convince him why he should chuck God to the side to sin; he cut him off.

"Tony order your drinks or whatever, I'm here, we're chilling, let's get it popping; but make it quick. I'm not going all night."

Tony heard the words coming out of his mouth but he knew his buddy isn't down with this no more. D, really has changed and for good; but it's still a long night ahead. It ain't over yet. He just wants the old Deron back and it'll happen. He has more treats for the rest of the night. Something's gonna catch Deron's attention.

"Oh yeah, and I know Nelicia is no coincidence either. I'm not cheating on my woman and I'm not coming here no more."

"I gotta try buddy...," Tony smiled as he felt his cellphone vibrate.

He looked down at the phone after taking it from his hip and saw that it was a text from Sharnia. He deleted it without reading the message. She ain't gonna ruin his night tonight, time to turn up.

****

When Nelicia returned to the table, she sat down with them. This is part of the strip club's rules. The server could sit at the table with the patrons as long as they brought several drinks. All the girl has to do is to keep getting up to get the drinks.

This didn't happen too much at one time with other table competing for the attention because it cost payroll to have this kind of action. This is right up Tony's alley because he likes to get on like that.

"So Tony, you seen Phaedra lately?" Nelicia asked.

"Nah we don't hang like we used to, not since that night, you know. Remember when we used to be everywhere together?"

Even though he nodded his head, Deron thought in his mind no, because he didn't know them like that. They were just objects back when he was turnt up.

"She's a trip huh," Tony, asked just to respond. Tony thought it was a good idea to lie to Nelicia about not seeing Phaedra lately. It ain't her business anyway. Too many questions would come up.

"I know right she was a hell of a trip that *night* wasn't she? I wanted to bust her slam in her face. It's just as well, she's a bitch anyway."

"Whoa, you two use to be criminals together what happened?"

"You know how it is when money gets in somebody's eyes; they flip on you. She's been hanging with some guys that helped her put the money down on her salon and gave me the finger. You know I couldn't even get her to give me a free weave. That's a bitch for you."

Tony and Deron sat looking and listening to Nelicia go on and on about Phaedra. Especially Tony, who was all ears to knowing the other side of the Phaedra that he didn't know.

He'd been dealing with her for a few months now. He can't put his finger on it but Phaedra's up to some shit that he'd better watch out for.

He can feel it.

Trying not to seem too obvious Deron sat in his chair silently, just smiling. Every now and then, he would look at the stripper that's performing. He's surprise how comfortable he feels sitting in Club P. He's even more surprised that he sat there listening to Nelicia rag on Phaedra and the memories of sleeping with both of them came to his mind. By now, Tony probably already knows that he's been with Nelicia. No need to let anybody know that he's been with Phaedra too. He shouldn't even have brought it up in his mind. These are the kinds of things that make him just want to forget that he was that out of control.

He keeps telling himself in his mind that it was a long time ago and he's changed. He's happy now with the way everything turned out and being here didn't make him wish that he should be doing anything else.

At least he wants that to be true.

When the next performer came up on the stage, she immediately started to pump it up more. The music she used and the way she started to gyrate her body very fast. She began whipping her body around and around real fast. You can tell she's trying to make the men rush the stage, which a few of them did at first. Then more of them surrounded it like mad male dogs after a bitch in heat.

It was enough to get both Tony and Deron's attention, which annoyed Nelicia. Only because their attention instantly left from her to the one on the stage.

"Who is that, Nelicia!?" Deron asked, not really thinking that he sounded kind of lustful.

"Oh that's some trouble making freak, Shinique; her show is so tired. She does that same ole thrust pumping body every time she performs. I don't like it cause all she doing is whining her body up and going faster and faster. It ain't all that and I can't believe the men always rush the stage like they do."

Tony kept staring at her and Deron noticed him doing it, but the look on his face kept changing from amazement to something else.

"What's up with you T, you act like you know her or something?"

"I do and so do you. Look a little closer man."

Turning his attention back to the stage Deron stared a little harder at Shinique.

"Nope," he said shaking his head. "Don't know her."

"Yeah I know cause it looks like she lightened her skin or something, but that's that damn Mocha."

"Mocha who?"

"The stripper that helped Felicia setup Bryan. You know setup by Bry's fake ass buddy, Steve Powers. That's that hoe I know it."

"From the bachelor's party?" Deron asked.

"Yeah that's her. I should go up there."

"What for?"

"I got to say something to her."

"For what, now who's tripping over the past? Man let that go. They didn't stop nothing, Bryan and Yolanda got married anyway."

"Naw it's the principle behind it. These strippers live by a code these days. What goes on behind closed doors stays behind closed doors. She violated that and I wanna know what went down; to see if Steve told her to do it."

"Man what code? Tony that crap's petty. You worry about meaningless things. It won't change nothing. Drink your drink because I'm going home, in a few."

"D. I'm trying to be easy right now, but you blowing my high. I was only joking. I ain't gonna mess with that hoe. I was joking. Hell," he said looking down on his watch. "I'm good too, let's cut. It's time to catch the bus. Nelicia," Tony said nodding to her and getting up out of his seat.

****

Outside in the parking lot Tony and Deron stood there. Tony looked at his watch instead of pulling out his keys to his truck. Deron silently chastised himself for not driving his own car. He already knew that Tony intended to be out until daybreaks and why would he think that would change. Now they're standing outside of the club and for what?

"Tony, man what's happening? You ready to roll?"

"Chill D, I got everything under control."

Then out of the club came Nelicia and six more women. Each one of these women were stacked up high. Video vixens and some more shit Tony thought. They must've been imported from South Beach or the west coast. They must think they're going to a video shoot. All of them wearing tight dresses barely covering their ass.

Just like Tony likes it.

They walked over to where Tony and Deron stood.

"Tony, Andre said this is all he could do and all you need," Nelicia said pointing to the other women.

"Yeah, well that ain't what I paid for," he said bluntly. "And you can tell that bitch right there she can turn around and head back in the club. I don't want no home wrecking snitches on my bus."

"Who?" Nelicia asked turning to look.

"Shinique, Mocha whatever her damn name is right there and get me some more girls," he said pointing to Shinique.

Shinique looked at Tony and then turned her head.

"Alright but now *I* got to be the one to replace her and bring some more girls?"

"Hell yeah, I didn't give Dre power of attorney over my shit. You call him and tell him I'mma need some of my money back or some more women, sumethin'," he said looking back out to the entrance of the parking lot and then at his watch. "But you know what we'll get to that later, they can meet us. Our ride should be coming right about now…," Tony said with a sly smile pointing to the entrance of parking lot.

Everybody looked in the direction of the entrance of the parking lot. A Party Bus pulled in the parking lot. By the looks of it this bus seat over thirty people. This is right up Tony's alley. The more room the more party.

The bus pulled up right in front of Tony and everybody else. The door opened and music, alcohol and a faint smell of weed hit them all in the face.

"What is this Tony?" Deron asked as if he's pissed off.

"D. you know how I like to take it to the next level baby and do it big. I got a party bus for my birthday and we guys and these thots are heading out of town for a few hours, destination unknown. Welcome to Tony's world the whole other life…"

"Aw hell no…I mean no man I can't do that."

"Come on Deron it'll be fun," Nelicia said stopping as she passed by the two of them on her way to board the bus. "We can catch up on old times."

"Nelicia get yo' ass on the bus and get them girls right I got this," Tony said disgustingly.

Nelicia stepped up on the first step and turned halfway around to face Tony.

"Look here nigga, you don't own this," she said patting her ass. "Don't get to ordering me around because you're paying. I got class. Fuck with me and I'll shut this shit down."

"I'mma need you to get yo' ass on that bus, chick," Tony said to her again ignoring what she said. "D this is phase two of my night my man. The party's just getting started, you gots ta ride."

"Man…"

"Come on D, don't let me down."

In those split seconds that it sometimes takes to make a decision, Deron thought about all the time that's passed. How the bond between the two of them has been shaky? They haven't been much like the brothers they say they are.

Years ago this wouldn't even have been an issue.

Deron would've been down with whatever Tony was down with and that would be it. They were a singular mind then but sometimes thing change. They're getting older and taste in things became the difference. He's not thinking he's better than Tony, he's thinking different now that's all.

He's glad his life is settled now. All that chaos that was in his life before, he didn't like that. The women that he began to encounter later were beginning to be a hindrance to him until he met Dawn.

Cheresse was the biggest problem and who probably turned him off to the fast life. She came in and changed it all with her games. Just plain poison. If he hadn't pursued her he would've been all right but would he have been motivated to seek God?

God does everything for a reason.

He needed to go through that hell.

She was the hell in his life.

A dirty *habit* he couldn't stop lying to people and himself to be with; because he was addicted to her.

Well really, it's Tony's fault, he thought. He should've told Deron about it in the beginning instead of having that damn Parker pride that sometimes gets him in trouble. He would've left her alone or at least watched himself with her. Instead, he went in blind.

Now his boy looks at him like a stranger and truthfully, to Deron, Tony's a stranger to him. A year or so of catching up with him here and there; is why they're conversations are a struggle.

So with all that he decided to board the Party Bus.

He's made up his mind.

Tony just smiled.

Good, he thought his boy Deron's back. Once he sees what Tony has in store for the guys tonight he gonna get turnt up for sure.

****

Before he opened the door to the rest of bus, Tony and Deron stopped at the driver. Tony wanted to make sure he knew where to go. Once that was clear, he opened the door. The sound of the music blasted off the walls. The first thing besides the bus being, packed with about fifteen dudes there are three poles, mounted along the center of the bus. Each pole a stripper is dancing around or riding on it. Nelicia and other women were far in the back with some dudes. They were doing something with them huddled up in the corner that Deron and Tony couldn't see.

"Tony, Happy Birthday man," Aijon yelled to Tony.

"What's up my dudes, turn up time?" Tony yelled back.

Aijon looked at Deron and nodded to him. He wasn't expecting Tony to bring him after all ain't he supposed to be in the church? What's he doing on this bus cause it's about to blow. He must be trying to be uncover with his shit which is cool but don't run it like you better than the next nigga. Tiasha was dead on it he thought when she said she saw him at some strip club. This nigga is fake.

"Aye Deron what's up boss man," one of the guys said stepping up to him.

"Mark hey man what's up," Deron responded clasping hand with the guy he also knows as Tony's buddy, Cert.

In his mind, Deron isn't sure he's going to be ready for all these blasts from the past. Also, Tony's boy Aijon is looking at him as if he tried to pull up on his woman or something. Hope this guy don't get out of hand when he gets drunk; because he don't want to take it there. He's trying to stay leveled out and not get in no trouble. Then there's Nelicia and now one of Tony's running partners that used to sleep with Cheresse. The one who told him how she really gets down and Deron continued to be with her.

"I ain't know you was gonna be on tonight," Cert said to Deron.

"Yeah it was a last minute thing," he said looking back at Tony. "But I'm in the place now man. My boy T is bringing in his birthday right," he said trying not to seem like he didn't want to be there, which is true he rather be home with Dawn.

Cert turned his attention to the guy next to him and said, "Man this nigga right here gave me my shot when I used to work at UPS. My man right here is boss nigga."

Deron didn't bother to correct Cert either he's drunk already or he don't remember that he used to work for

AUPA not UPS. This is going to be a long night, he thought.

****

An hour went by on the Party Bus. Tony is in full swing circulating through the bus clinking glass with the other guys edging them onto the strippers that rode the three poles nonstop. Sometimes a dancer if she's requested will trade places with Nelicia or the other ones doing lap dances and other stuff. Deron did his best to keep himself even nursing some ginger ale the bus provided in its refrigerator. Every time Nelicia came over to him, he just waved her off or gave her some cash to keep it moving.

He must look mighty gumpish to some of the other guys on the bus; him trying not to interact with none of the strippers; but nobody said a thing. They probably noticed how glad Tony is that he got on the bus mainly because T kept saying it, toasting a drink every five minutes to their friendship.

"Deron man what you got in that cup?" Cert said.

"Ginger ale," he responded.

"Aw no man we gotta fix that shit. You gotta drink with me man. My nigga," Cert said getting up from his seat and going to the small liquor bar.

Once there he grabbed a red cup, bottle of clear liquor and a bottle of cranberry juice, he quickly came back.

"Man we gonna drink some classic shit, vodka and cranberry juice. I'ma add some Red Bull, you?"

"No man, I'm good I ain't drinking no more tonight, I got to get up early in morning."

"D. you know you lying," Tony said interrupting them. "You can have another drink damn. Come on Cert pour that shit stop holding on to it like you trying to fuck it."

"Nigga hold on…"

Cert handed Deron the red cup. Of course only to save face and hold down Tony's mouth, he took it. When he did that Cert immediately followed behind it with the vodka bottle, pouring and after that poured cranberry juice. He did the same for his cup but added the Red Bull and then handed the bottle to Tony. Tony poured the vodka but added some grapefruit juice on the other side of him. He also had a Red Bull and poured that in as well.

"D. you gotta try this shit with Red Bull. It'll get you there I ain't lying," Tony said shoving the Red Bull at him.

"Uh, uh not where I'm heading T."

"Man add this shit," Tony said to Deron like they were teenager and he's peer pressuring him.

Once the Red Bull was, added to Deron cup, Tony raised his cup. Cert followed and Deron reluctantly raised his. Then down the line Aijon, the other guys, Nelicia and strippers stopped moving, then the ones that had cups raised theirs. The music is still loud but everybody could still communicate with each other.

"Too my boys especially my boy Deron for coming out to celebrate with me, that's what up. Nelicia get yo' girls shaking that ass," he ordered her and then he addressed the other dudes. "Turn up niggas it's gonna be a long night."

Everybody guzzled his or her drink and Tony watch Deron drink his, slowly but he finished it off.

Instantly, his mind started to churn into a haze.

****

About forty-five minutes later, Tony looked at Deron and he seemed buzzed. He was on a fourth drink, talking loudly to Cert.

He buddy's back, he thought.

The other dudes and strippers busied themselves with what they were doing sexually to each other.

Aijon who sat in the back of the bus on his phone came up to where Tony sat. He stood over Tony and motioned him to stand up so he could talk to him in private. They walked off from where the others were on the lengthy bus. Tony saw the cellphone in his hand and hit the roof.

"Nigga didn't I tell you no damn cellphones on this bus. I ain't ending up on Facebook, Twitter or Instagram so Valerie can be on my ass," he snapped to Aijon.

"I got the memo man, I ain't taking no video. I got to show you something," he said raising his phone to Tony. "Tiasha just text this link to me to remind…"

"Yeah I'll see it later."

"No, it's about your man…"

"Come on Aijon shit, I'm trying to get with this stripper. I'll see it later."

Tony brushed past him and went back to where he was sitting. Damn Aijon is a damn pest sometimes he thought.

Time to take this party to the next level, he grinned. Tony got Nelicia's eye and whipped his pointer finger fast in a circular motion. Immediately she blew a whistle that is around her neck. Next, she dropped what clothes she had onto the floor and the rest of the women did the same thing. Nelicia went straight for Deron. He saw her coming towards him and got caught up with the haze of the alcohol and her fine naked body.

She looks hotter than before when they slept together.

Tony sat on the right of him and the other woman came to him. Nelicia and the other stripper straddled Deron and Tony each at the same time.

Wrapping their legs around them.

"What's yo name, chick?" Tony asked with a smirk.

"Is that important?" she asked.

"I like it when we personal it makes the sex better," he answered.

"Malaysia."

"I like that, that's what's up," Tony said and then he pulled her down to him closer. "You can unzip it when you ready."

All Malaysia did is giggle and did what Tony told her. This is what she does, her job and she's damn good at it. It helps that the men are fine and in shape. This one right here got that thuggy about him and she likes that. It helps her get in the mood and really get turnt up. The one Nelicia's on is cute too and they got a football player up in here. She wants to get in with all of them cause that's steady cake once she hooks them. These other girls don't know what they doing cause their amateurs. That's the ticket, to get with these high-end guys that want to slide out on their women for some new experienced booty. A woman that knows what they like. That kind of money's a free for all up in here and she's gonna get it. But she knows from experience that if she pops her ass on Tony tonight he'll be coming back week after week for this; more dollars.

"Your turn Deron," Nelicia said looking at Tony and Malaysia. "I knew one day we'd get back to this, baby. Tony told me how you been playing devoted husband and how she ain't giving it to you like you want it. He says she's changed you. I'm gonna change you back."

Once again, Deron thought Tony is running off with his mouth. So much is going through his mind. How the hell did Nelicia get here to doing this? She's a freelance photographer. Dawn didn't change him, she helped him become something better.

She helped him didn't she?

Damn Nelicia's sexy like shit right now.

He's pretty drunk.

It must be the Red Bull addition to his liquor. He never mixed that stuff in when he used to drink. As much as he wants to get up from this seat, he enjoys her sprawl all over him bouncing slightly.

Damn he miss doing this shit.

He should try to get out of here before he can't resist her any longer. Because right now all he can think about is, Nelicia's fine body on top of his and the way she's moving.

Almost as if she's reading his mind she reached down, grabbed his penis through his pants and rubbed it until she got its attention. Then she moved towards his zipper and started to pull on it. With her, other hand she reached behind him on the ledge of the tinted window. She picked up one of the many condoms that lined the ledge. She tore at the package with her teeth and it snagged open. As she held Deron in her hand, she brought the condom down to put it on.

"Nelicia," Tony yelled to her getting her attention.

Once he got her attention, he shook his head.

She shrugged her shoulder, then leaned in and started kissing Deron passionately as he passed out.

CHAPTER 8

The next day at noon, Yolanda, Dawn and Valerie are having lunch at Olive Garden in Bowie Town Center. Today is the day that Yolanda has decided that she is going to tell her best girlfriends that she's seeing Steve. She knows that she will receive from them that first initial shock but they will get pass it. They should be happy for her because it's been a long time since she's been out of the house with a man.

It's not like he's about to be her lover or something.

Right now, he's just a very special friend.

She doesn't know where his head's at right now but she's sort of sure that he wants to take it slow too. After all, he just got out of a messy divorce from his wife, Serena. He says she's been trying to bleed him dry but most men say that after a divorce. It makes the new women in their lives more sympathetic to them. Come to, think of it Serena did seem somewhat hostile towards her at times. She acted as if she never liked Yolanda. Even when she last saw Serena at that New Year's Eve party at Tony's house, just before Steve and she separated.

Even so that's not all that was going on with those two.

Bryan and she may have been trying to live a Christian life but she certainly isn't naïve to the ways of the world. Of course, she's carrying that on with herself and her son. She won't let any man think she's going to be an easy lay.

He'll be sure to know he won't succeed.

"So what time did you say Tony and Bryan got in last night, Valerie," Yolanda asked.

"You mean this morning, the sun was out," Valerie responded plainly.

"That's when she called me, to let me know Deron was alright. I kind of thought he would end up following Tony around all-night," Dawn said evenly. "With those two together we never know what they're going to be up to," she added as she shook her head.

"Right," Yolanda agreed.

"Well don't you think it's time they got back on track; they haven't been male bonding lately?" Valerie asked the two of them.

"Well I hope they weren't doing too much drinking," Yolanda said looking at Dawn and watching her squirm a bit.

She knows that Dawn doesn't like what went on with Deron last night. But if she has learned anything about being with the Lord she knows that the flesh is weak. That being said as time goes on the desire for those things drift away but it won't happen overnight. Deron has been good in his walk and honoring his agreement with God, but that doesn't mean there won't be slips.

"They were drunk as skunks, especially Deron," Valerie said watching Dawn's reaction. "I don't know how Tony got him into the house?" she laughed.

There became this awkward silence at the table. Dawn tried not to think that Valerie seems too amused that Deron got drunk, hanging with Tony. She knows he stopped drinking about a little over two years ago. Not that he was an alcoholic before but because he felt that, it was part of his issues back then. This could be a concern but she won't make a big deal about it because with what's been bothering Deron lately. She's just thankful he didn't start back drinking earlier trying to ease his pain. It could've easily gone that way too.

"Val, there's no need in looking at me. Deron is not a saint and for that matter neither am I. Just not a thing else I can say about it," she said simply.

Yolanda just turned her head to the side.

She noticed here lately that there seems to be a little tension between Valerie and Dawn. Yolanda wasn't sure if it is because of the guys. Yes, there has been a slight change in Tony and Deron's friendship. It may be due to Deron's newfound faith but that's how things go and especially since Bryan's not here anymore to buffer between the two. She knows Val didn't expect Deron to keep running the streets with Tony just to maintain their friendship; does she think that Dawn does?

When Bryan found his faith, he told Yolanda that he would probably lose his two best friends. Only because at the time Tony and even Deron were fully out there running the streets; like all three of them did at one time. It bothered him but it bothered him more not, fully pursuing his walk until the boys just adjusted to it. Bryan even headed Deron in that direction before he was, killed. Valerie must feel awkward because everyone knows how off the hook Tony is about everything.

He can't even be faithful for five minutes, but nobody can tell Val that.

"What's going on with Deron anyway?" Valerie asked. "He seems a bit uptight lately."

"Ghost from the past I guess," Dawn said reluctantly.

She's not going to let Valerie bait her into saying something that she shouldn't. She didn't want to tell the girls anything about the recordings, mostly Yolanda. Tony must not have said anything to Val about it either. He's probably thinking the same thing about Yolanda too. Sometimes Tony does surprise her. It's best to let everyone stay on the path of healing. It won't be easy on Deron because of his guilt but he'll get through it. Yolanda well, the lost will always be there, but she'll move on too as well, Dawn thought. It's easier for her because she had just met Bryan but she felt the lost all the same.

"Cheresse is back again?" Valerie blurted out. "He's been talking back with Cheresse?"

Dawn blinked rapidly.

Val's on the attack and she has a feeling it is because of their last conversation. But just not that, lately it's been like a tug-a-war dealing with Val and she didn't know why.

"No girl, we've been saved from that demon. Deron had a little stuff on his mind but now he's fine. He saw the pastor and he helped him."

"It must've been serious? What was it?"

"So girls I have something to tell you and I want, well I just want you to know that's all," Yolanda said interrupting Valerie.

It's obvious to her that Dawn didn't want to tell the two of them about whatever it was that's bothering Deron. Val's not really being herself lately. She seems on edge. She was actually trying to corner Dawn about this and make her tell them.

"So what's this news," Dawn asked smiling.

"I'm seeing Steve Powers."

****

He could barely rise up because his head pounded like someone is hammering a nail through his brain. Deron could tell that he's hung-over. He hasn't felt like this in a long time. This a familiar feeling from his earlier drinking days when he didn't know he had to hydrate himself before drinking. Damn Tony, he thought. This is what he was scared of that he would go back to his old life and that's not what he wants to do. Some people would say it's 'all right' it's just that 'one time' 'you can handle it just keep it in moderation' but that's how habits and addictions find their way back in peoples' lives. It's just a slow walk back to the afflictions, that's not going to happen to him, he thought. With Tony, it's turnt up all the time, with no stopping at the red lights.

It was Tony's night and so he celebrated with him, it is what it is. Now the only problem with all of this is that the last thing he remembers is Nelicia sprawled on top of him feeling on his penis. After that, he don't know what happened until he got in T's truck to come here. Either Red Bull is a dangerous legal drug that should be banned or he's been out the loop too long. No night of drinking should've knocked him off his feet like this.

He could see its noon by the clock beside the bed. He's at Tony's house in his usually overnight room, though he hasn't been over here like this in a long while. All that stuff that was going on with his guilt about Bryan kept him off the radar for a minute. The pastor helped him, he really did. So again he's not going to let this one slight night out with the fellas knock him off his path.

Reluctantly he got up out of the bed he was in and looked around. Looking down at himself, he could see all his clothes are still on. He was extra drunk last night because he usually strips down before bed, even after he's been out drinking. He decided to make his way out of the room to check with Tony to see what happened after he passed out.

He'll probably lie but Deron knows when he's lying.

Please God, please don't let me find out that I slept with Nelicia last night, he thought.

That will hurt Dawn so much.

"Tony," Deron yelled out urgently as soon as he walked out of his room.

"D, I'm down in the sunroom," Tony yelled back.

Of course he's up bright and early, this is his routine. This is right up Tony's alley to be out with his boys all night drinking and smashing women then get up with no effects like usual.

"Foods' in there," Tony said pointing to kitchen as Deron entered the sunroom. "Valerie fixed it before she left to meet Yolanda and Dawn for lunch."

"Shit, Dawn, I mean…"

"Don't worry about it buddy," Tony said. "Just like before our women know the deal. Dawn knows you're alive and well."

"Thanks," Deron said as he relaxed. "I want to know what went down last night T. the truth."

"What D.?"

"Come on Tony don't play. You know what I want to know. Straight talk, did I sleep with Nelicia?"

"D. I ain't gonna play with you. You had a good damn time finally and it was off the hook. It's about damn time. Everybody got turnt up on that bus. I had a good damn time too," he said reminiscing in his excitement.

"Tony!" Deron yelled at him.

"But naw man I got your back. I wouldn't let you down like that after you set your belief aside to party with me. Nelicia wanted that stick bad, but I had your back. Shit a few years ago big brother Tony would've let you smash the hell out of her and think about it later. It must be your church thing rubbing off on me, "he said shuddering. "But I tore Malaysia's ass up y'all hear me."

Deron just shook his head.

This man is off the hook.

He really thinks that last night was a good thing. It may have been for Tony because that's where he is in his life. It wasn't to Deron however, he went against everything that he set out not to do, mainly drinking. He is definitely relieved that nothing happened with Nelicia. He wouldn't be able to explain it away to Dawn, not that. With Dawn, a man can only be drunk and unaware one time if that and he's used up that little trick one too many times before they were married.

He's bless that she came back to him.

"Aw man I'm not ever doing that again."

"That shit was fun, that's all I'm saying, damn fun. We got down Tony Parker style. Welcome back D," he said extending his fist for a pound.

Deron looked at the fist and then back to Tony.

"Where's the food?" Deron asked ignoring the fist-pound.

Tony shrugged his shoulders and pointed to the kitchen. He then grabbed the remote to his smart TV and went to sit down.

"Y'all take your time you hear," he said to Deron mockingly as he felt his cellphone vibrating.

Deron excited the room shaking his head again.

Picking it up Tony sees, that Sharnia's calling again and it's getting on his damn nerves.

Ever since that day he dropped her off at her house and told her he'll call her when he needs some she's been acting crazy. He should've ran her ass over. She's been texting him left and right; damn she's real desperate. It don't make no difference he's does what he wants and he's not gonna let this crazy thot run him down.

Tony brought up the internet on the screen and then fiddled with his phone. He scrolled down to his messages and found the text Aijon was stressing him about last night.

That nigga was hard-pressed for him to see this.

It's a website and he entered it into the search engine.

Once he completed that, Tony pressed 'OK' and a website popped up. Just as he thought, it's some bullshit Aijon wanted to show him; a damn porn site. Why in the hell would a grown ass man want to show him a porn site on a Party Bus full of live strippers, fine strippers at that? Hella fine, especially that bad ass Malaysia. He gonna see that again if that's the last thing he does.

Aijon, that fool's crazy, he thought.

It's one of those amateur sites that, Tony has heard about that's circulating around internet, especially this one that's local, here in DC. He read more of the introduction message left by the administrator, the gist of the site and some bullshit. On this site everyday jokers and tricks that want to be porn stars can upload their home sex videos on this site and get paid. It works by the number of hits each video by the owner gets. What the hell, it's like a thousand of vids, Tony thought.

What the hell am I supposed to see?

He likes porn like the next dude but he's not gonna watch it when he can get the real thing at any time. He got three main bitches and more's on the way. The harvests have been ripe this year as it's been since he was fourteen; so Aijon can keep this shit. He'll get it in when he gets with Sharnia again or Phaedra, definitely Valerie…Malaysia, hell Nelicia too.

"Let me read this text again," he said to himself aloud.

After he re-read the text, he saw what he missed, the title. He went back to the screen using his remote.

"'SeXmas Lovers', he said to watch 'SeXmas Lovers'."

Tony put in the website's search engine the name 'SeXmas Lovers'. The video popped up and started playing. When the video came on the first thing that showed on the screen is a woman's nude booty, a redbone. She's twerking it right in front of the camera, close up. That instantly caught Tony's attention walking off screen. The next thing he saw is a naked man lying on his back on a bed and the woman walked back into the scene. She started crawling seductively up the bed to get to him. Once she got up to him, she kept right on going until she straddled his face with her thighs on both side of his face. Tony kept right on looking thinking this is all right. This went on for a bit and then the woman moved back her until they pressed real tight together. After that position the man moved, flipped her backwards to mount her and she laid her head back. That's when Tony saw both their faces. It took him back for a second that he knocked his glass over onto the floor; that sat on the table beside him and it broke.

"D, Deron," he yelled like he's getting jump on the street. "Get the hell in here, now, quick, quick; you got to see this shit. You won't believe this shit."

****

"Okay you two can stop looking at me like I have two heads," Yolanda said.

"I'm just shocked Yolanda, that's all," Dawn said.

"I know I'm shocked," Valerie added turning her head.

"Why?"

"I guess we're just not used to you dating, let alone Steve Powers. Isn't he married?"

"He's divorced Valerie."

"Oh," she said. "I just didn't see this coming."

Again, at the table there's an awkward silence. Yolanda knew she was going to get this reaction. Steve is not very well, like by Deron or Tony. Bryan would always tell her. He didn't know why they didn't like him. When she first met him, she didn't detect anything that would cause someone not to like him; so she couldn't explain it. Bryan simply said the guys were always cold to him, especially Tony.

"I know I didn't either," Yolanda agreed. "But he's a friend and things are moving at the slowest pace possible. I mean we're not getting married or anything."

"But don't you feel sort of…," Valerie started to say.

"Strange? Yes, I did at first but he's a friend and I'm comfortable with him. It isn't like I have been looking at him the whole time I've known him. You know I would never do that."

"Yeah girl, no one's saying that," Valerie said.

"No baby, no one's saying that, we know better," Dawn added.

"It's really a coincidence," Yolanda continued. "He came to me wanting to buy the townhouse and at first I was like I would consider it. He began to draw up papers…"

"Hold on, he drew up papers even though you told him you would only consider it?" Dawn asked suspiciously.

"Well no…ah yes you can say that."

"So this guy is trying to buy your townhouse and now he wants to date you? Uh, uh that sounds like trouble," Valerie chimed in.

"Well he knows that it's not for sale, not now and not ever."

"So you think he's into you?" Valerie interrogated.

"Val, why do I feel like you have something to say?"

Like always is what Yolanda wanted to say.

"Yolanda, this guy was a friend of your husband that nobody liked. Now he's trying to move in on the still grieving widow and trying to take her property from her. What do I have to say?"

"Okay Val, that's enough," Dawn said. "I think that there is a cloud of mistrust here but it shouldn't be directed at Yolanda."

"This isn't about me and Tony, Dawn," Valerie said sounding a bit irritated. "This is about a no good man that is devious to the core and shouldn't be trusted. Tony and Deron both don't trust him. They think he's the one that tried to break you and Bryan up Yolanda by bringing that stripper to that bachelor party. You can't ignore that."

"That's why I'm telling you that I'm taking it slow, well other reasons."

"Which also is not any of our business," Dawn added.

"I understand that we should mind our business, but if it was me, I would like someone to tell me what's going on."

"Humph," Dawn said.

Valerie stared at Dawn for a minute thinking how did they get to this point where the two of them are always disagreeing lately. Dawn doesn't see what she sees because her life is so mapped out perfectly. She had that one blip with Deron but she's not dealing with shit every week. She should try walking a mile in her shoes and maybe some of that faith really will be, really tested.

"You know I know who I'm dating. But I'm not blind to it. That's why I'm also taking it slow too and I also have a backup."

"Oh boy, Nathan," Dawn sighed.

"Really, Dawn, nothing makes you happy?" Valerie said defensively. "I'm sorry if my life can't be as perfect as yours but I'm only dealing with the cards that are dealt to me right now."

"My life is not perfect, point one. I keep trying to tell you that. Point two you choose to be with Tony even though you know he may not be right for you. So whose fault is that?"

"I take the blame. But like you said it's my business and you should mine yours."

"Okay girls it's getting too Tony and Deron right now," Yolanda said jokingly. "Need the two of you to go into your corners and remember that each one of us at this table is concern about the other. That's why we're such good friends. Our sisterhood is tight, right?"

"Well yeah nobody said anything's wrong, I'm just venting," Valerie said.

"Yes that's right," Dawn agreed. "But I do think Val that you should end one thing before you start another. That way you will know this is what you really want."

"I ask you before about this guy but you never got around to telling me. Who is this Nathan anyway," Yolanda asked?

"I used to date him in college. Dawn met him the first night I met her at Friday's with Deron. Nathan Collins and I were on a dinner date during the first time I saw Tony's true colors. I should have kept on with Nathan, but at that time, he was trying to move to Atlanta and I didn't want to move there. So we just kept in touch here and there. He was engaged to be married last year and that's over now. He just moved here from Alabama and decided that Maryland is where he wants to settle down. And he wants to settle down with me," she smiled. "But no Dawn, I'm not jumping on it. I wish I had your drama free life."

"Really, Val?" Dawn said annoyed that Valerie keeps on making the same comments about her relationship. "Be careful what you wish for, you just might get it."

She is being careful but Tony isn't trying to make any of her wishes come true. They've been off and on arguing too many times during their relationship from day one and there's no getting to Tony. She's not going to let her life pass her by trying to maintain something that not there. She wants a husband and some children. It just may be possible that Tony's not interested in her anymore and that's a fact she may have to face.

She's going to need to exercise other options.

Does she want to remain with Tony, yes? But she definitely not going to wait for him too long to make up his mind.

****

"Let's back this up for a minute D," Tony said pushing the start button again. "That's you and that hoe Cheresse. How in the hell did you let her film that?"

Deron stared at the screen in shock. He just shook his head in disbelief. Not only did he not have knowledge of her filming this, he has no memory of having sex with her like this. It's a complete blank. There's no way this could've happened but it's right on the screen.

"Tony man give me a minute to take this in," Deron said beginning to panic. "What is this on?"

"This site it's an amateur porn site. It's real popular on the east coast. Some west coast porn star created it cause he got tired of being short changed on money every time he did a video shoot. It works like this, you and yo' girl make a sex tape and upload it here. The more hits you get the better chance of you getting some big bucks. It's almost like YouTube but you really get paid. A one-time deal if yo' video is hot and they got a flick they can stream anywhere and anytime they want, overseas, local, states, big shit."

"I get it," Deron said annoyingly.

"Over a two million views gets you about fifteen grand if the rumors are true."

"Who gets the money?"

"In your case yo' hoe girl Cheresse gets all the tokens. I mean you didn't know anything about this so she had to upload it. That chick is off da chain. What you gonna do about it D?"

"I have no clue," Deron said without thinking. "Damn it, Dawn is going to kill me."

Tony laughed shaking his head and Deron looked at him.

****

"This is supposed to be some kind of joke?" Deron yelled at Cheresse through the phone. His head's still pounding from the night out and the alcohol. An hour later, he was able to remember her cellphone number something that was shocking to him that he did. But he has to face the facts that she was more to him at one time than he wants to admit. He is still over Tony's house and Tony just sat in the background of the sunroom watching Deron talk to Cheresse.

"Who the hell is this?" Cheresse said on the other end, tauntingly.

"You know...ugh...," he yelled then calmed down some. "You know who this is Cheresse. Why'd you do that?"

"Deron Stone, hi. It's been a minute. I'm flattered that you still have my number. Does your wife know you have my number cause I don't want her calling me with no bullshit. I have moved on with my life."

"Humph, I can't tell," Deron said angrily. "This upload to the porn site was done recently. I don't see why'd you did that?"

"Deron Stone are you about to cry? That's so sweet that you would cry for me. You'll do a whole lot more crying when I'm done with you."

"Look I'm trying to be as patience as I can with you but you don't seem to want to show me any respect. I want to know from you when did you film this crap and why would you upload it to the internet? I want to know from you personally before my lawyer asks you. You need my authorization to do something like that."

"Don't threaten me with that shit Deron," she said condescendingly to him. "I just wanted everyone to see how we used to get down. People will ask you why in the hell would you married that boring ass nun and not stay with me as hot as I am."

"Nobody's going to ask that dumb question. They know a psycho when they see one and that's all the reason right there."

"I'm psycho alright but I got paid," she said to him tauntingly.

"Not for long Cheresse. Again, I didn't give my authorization for that release. You and I both know that as soon as I get my lawyer on that company's ass they're gonna pull your petite scene from the net and it'll be done that shit and you," he shouted as his anger exploded.

He tried to keep his cool and not let her take him there. Things like that were important to him that he keeps under control. He knows he can't be perfect and it's been slowly seeping out. Cheresse knows how to take him there fast.

"Yeah that's the Deron I like to hear. I feel it down between my legs, ooh. You know you can't pray for a body like mine."

Even though he heard the crude way, Cheresse mocked his salvation he continued to listen to her. Her voice always has a way of cutting through his strong sense of right and hook him. He has put a stop to this.

He has to stop trying to hang onto Cheresse.

Is he doing that?

He's been doing good in his walk with Christ, with Dawn and even putting to rest that thing about Bryan recently.

But he hasn't hung up the phone yet.

Is that all his salvation was used for to get him through Bryan's death? Is this what he really wants is to do live a holy life right now in the prime of his life. There are restrictions that hasn't been easy for him to follow lately and as much as he wants to blame Tony and Cheresse, it's his responsibility.

God has never turned his back on him and he knows that, but…

"Look I got to go," his voice now betraying his thoughts.

This woman is an adversary to the woman he loves. There's no reason to consider her as nothing but that. At every turn, this woman has been hell for him and now she's back at it again.

"I love it when you sound like this baby. That means you still got me on your mind. The video made you remember that didn't it? You need to get back on this body and show me how much you miss me. You need to leave that slut…"

"Hold up, don't bring Dawn into this. What needs to happen is that video gets off that site. That will end that."

"Yes it will but what about all the sub-sites that have probably pick our fuck fest up? You forget, you just found out about this but it's been pumping for at least six months now."

"I'm not going to let you send me backwards with your crap. Don't worry about it, I got it. You won't be hearing from me again," he said ending the call without hearing what else Cheresse has to say.

CHAPTER 9

Monday, morning around 10 o'clock sharp a woman walked into the large office suite hurriedly.

"Tony Parker please," she said to the receptionist urgently.

"Oh I apologize; Mr. Parker is in a meeting. Do you have a later appointment?"

"No, I'm his fiancée, Sharnia Burkefield and this is an emergency."

"Okay, I will try to reach him," she looked at Sharnia curiously because Tony doesn't act like he's engaged.

Sharnia nervously tapped her foot as she waited by the reception desk. All this time Tony has been ignoring her calls and her texts. She drove by his house from time to time and nobody answered the door. She even went as far as to walk around the back of the house but nothing. He is avoiding her. He promised her that he isn't going to marry Valerie. Now it looks like they've been trying to patch things up and she knows, they're playing house again. He told her she's the one. Well at least he said that they aren't going to stop their thing.

It's taking too long for the receptionist to contact him and it's pissing Sharnia off. He's avoiding her and she knows he's doing it on purpose.

This is the last straw.

"To hell with this," Sharnia screamed aloud. "Tony where are you up in this bitch. You think you can do this to me and then hide from me uh, uh not me. Where are you," she screamed as she began to walk steadily around the suite then down the hall.

The receptionist ran after her as she started to open office doors and screamed Tony's name while walking with a fast pace down the corridors. They both got to a hallway that led either left or right. The receptionist turned right and

Sharnia headed left. She banged on the doors that were, locked and most of the staff started coming out of their offices as she brushed aggressively by some of them in a huff. The receptionist by now found Tony and he went up the office corridor to find Sharnia.

At the same time, two-security officer came up running pass Tony and he quickly followed them. No doubt, one of the staff called security and told them where Sharnia is exactly located. What the hell's wrong with her coming downtown to his office and causing this shit? That's why he don't fuck with her no more. Security should take out their batons and beat her ass down, cause if he gets a hold of her it ain't gonna be good.

"Miss you need to come with us."

Tony heard one of the security officers say down the hall.

"I'm not leaving until I speak to Tony Parker. He works here and I need to talk to him NOW!" she screamed.

Right on, that cue Tony appeared as in a blink and Sharnia charged at him. She jumped at him and started pounded on his chest.

"I hate you. I hate you. You said you aren't going to marry her. I hate you."

Security grabbed Sharnia's arm and set her down in a chair forcefully with one throw.

"Miss, you need to stop this and either you leave quietly or we're going to have to you arrested," the security officer said.

Sharnia thought about it for a while. This is not what she planned to do when she came here. She was only going to suggest that they talk in his office. She was going to tell him how she really feels and what she really wants. What happen, how did she get to this point? She guesses it was when the receptionist told her he was in a meeting and she remembered all those time he would lie to Valerie the same way. Sharnia would come down here after four and he would screw her in his office for hours. When Valerie would call, he would tell her that he was in a meeting and laugh about it to Sharnia. The shoe definitely wasn't cool on the other foot and she thought he was lying to her now.

"I'm leaving," she said as she got up her anger mounting again. "Tony Parker, I'll see you later," she said to him pointing her finger on his chin.

She walked off in a huff and security followed right behind her closely. She turned over a few computers and the set of financial books that were sitting on top of a small credenza as she exited out of the suite. She just couldn't calm down. She hated him so much.

How could he keep on treating her this way?

Tony followed but made sure he stayed a way back. All of the employees that worked in his suite piled out in the lobby area and now gawking at him. He is on blast right now and not how; he wants to be. He didn't know she was going to go off like this, but maybe he should of since the last time they talked. She almost broke the window out of his passenger door to his truck when she slammed it hard getting out. This bitch is wild he thought. When did she get like this? This is some embarrassing shit right here and he knows this don't look good to management.

His supervisor stood right there beside him almost like Hillary Clinton.

"Tony, you know you're going to pay for those computers right," his supervisor said, then she leaned in closer to him. "Also when you finish picking up everything I think you may need to take some time off to handle your private business. I won't press charges against your girlfriend. You do damn good work around here but you're suspended one month maybe more."

There's nothing that Tony could say. Sharnia came right up, in here and jacked things up for him royally. She did it in ten minutes. He knows that his boss is not going to suspend him for no month but he knows better than to argue with her now. Hell, he could've been fired.

That stupid ass chick.

****

Later on in the day after Tony left work in disgrace, he ended up over Aijon's house. Aijon is going on about that stupid ass chick, Tiasha he's got racking his brain and Tony's regretting he came here. Don't nobody want to, keep listening to that shit all the time. He should keep a better leash on her. He was gonna call Deron but he thought against that. Too much stuff's been going down and he didn't want to scare D off. Next thing you know he'd be right back on church watch again and that's something Tony don't want. It took him this long to get him to be comfortable enough hanging with him again. No disrespect for the church but that's for old people that don't have nothing to do, he thought. Unless in those cases like Bryan whose woman got him hook he had no choice. Soon D is gonna be back in the fold full strength and then Tony won't be hanging out with this wildin' out psycho Aijon.

He pissed Tony off when he first got over here. The first thing he brought up is that sex video Deron did. He was clowning on him and making jokes, calling D a fake ass Christian. He don't know nothing about that man and what he went through. He thought he was gonna hit Aijon in his mouth. Even though for himself he don't choose that life he ain't gonna sit around blocking another man if that's what he chooses. He saw that when they went out for his birthday. For some reason Aijon, don't like Deron. Even before, he met him; even before he knew anything about. Tony can tell. He never showed no interest in getting to know him when Tony kept mentioning they should all hangout. In fact, he don't seem to like Cert either. The more, Tony hangs with Aijon the more of a whack job he gets. He's always talking shit about people like he's better than the next one. He can't even control his woman and he can't stop talking about it either.

"Tony I'mma kick Tiasha ass to the curb. I ain't gonna be sweating no chick, not with all this cake I got. Shit right now she should be running my bath water instead of running with her hoe girlfriends," he said doing the quote sign with both hands.

"Oh yeah, speaking of that. That's something I been meaning to talk to you about. I need to get with one of them girlfriends Tiasha got. I saw them at 9.9 recently and I'm really shock I haven't bang not nay one of them yet."

"That's because you said you don't like them young like that."

"Well I might've been too quick on that. As long as they over twenty I can get with it, hook a bruh up."

"Alright," Aijon said before changing the subject. "What the hell is up with your vanilla spice?"

"Who Sharnia? Who, the hell knows. That bitch's cut. Ain't no chick gonna come up on my job and get me suspended."

"Should've smacked her ass around some, she'd get the message then."

"Yeah like you doing Tiasha," Tony said just letting that comment marinate in Aijon's head.

Visibly Tony could see that he got the message. How you gonna tell me about handling my woman? Not two minutes go by that you been complaining about yours, Tony thought, dumb ass. That's why brothers need to mind they own business when it comes to another nigga's woman.

"Man I'm blown with this shit," Tony said deciding to keep the conversation moving. "From now on I'm only hooking up with class, professionals. You know the ones that let you fuck with them cause they ain't got time for no relationships, unattached," he said as he laughed. "You know they can be some freaks."

"That's the only way to get down. Pour another drink man."

"Naw, I'm heading out right now. I think I'm gonna give a friend a call and see what she's up to."

"Yeah, I'mma find out where Tiasha is. I swear I'm gonna smack that hoe."

Yeah-right Tony thought.

****

About an hour later, Tony is at his house. This unexpected vacation is gonna be cool with him but he wished he'd planned a getaway. He hasn't told Valerie that he's gonna be off for about a month yet, he wants to see how he could use the time off to his advantage. It's time he enjoys himself but he sure hopes that he didn't lose his rep at the bank. Overseas and upscale clients aren't gonna want to deal with him at the bank or on the side if they get wind of this; or at least he's gonna have to work double time trying to gain their trust back. He's already facing clients thinking he don't know shit cause he's a brutha but he can make nine out of ten of them tons of money.

Damn if he's gonna let Sharnia screw his stuff up.

He thought about it and figured the best way to get over something like this is to lay up on something nice and tight. He knows just what it takes to make it feel good and who can do it. He picked up his phone and tapped the screen. Phaedra's number popped up and he tapped the screen again.

"I was just about to call you," she said giggling.

"Oh yeah, what's up?"

"I need you to help me invest some of my profits. I need money fast and I can't pay your fee."

"Shit Phaedra, I already got you the account now you want some free investment advice too. My pockets' bleeding over here," Tony yelled into the phone. "I'm trying to run a business not give away handouts."

"You didn't say that when you were laying between my legs. I just need some help getting my start. In my account I have some profit I'd like to flip; you gonna help me or what nig-ga?"

"We still on tonight," he asked slyly. "I mean if you gonna work me, I got to be working yo' ass too. I gotta get sumethin'."

"Hah, hah," she giggled. "You so nasty, I hate you."

"I hate you back and I know you working me."

"Tony, somebody's always doing something to you. I'm just asking a smash buddy to help me with my cash flow. You don't hesitate to ask me for some. When I start rolling in dough you can get that commission you're always going on about."

"I'm just being real. You know it ain't love right?"

He wanted to be sure that she understood that because of the recent crap with Sharnia. He doesn't need another side chick flipping the script on him and falling for him like an addict.

"Believe me nigga there's no love here, I can't stand you."

"Oh I'm so hurt," he toyed with her. "I'll be over there at nine. I hope you don't have to go to work tomorrow."

"I have a twelve thirty at the salon, why?"

"I'mma knock that bottom out all night. So you might be lucky if you wake up at one," he said to her trying to let her know on the sly what he wants to do when he gets there. He don't want to be bullshittin' around because he knows how these broads like to talk you to death; especially when they know you want the business.

"You better bring your paperwork if you coming here."

"I told you, you working me."

****

"Hey Tony," Erica Fontanne said to him over the phone. It's the next day in the afternoon. Tony just got home from Phaedra's house after their all-nighter. Once again, Phaedra went at him like she had something to prove. She definitely got something up her sleeve and he's gonna be watching her like a pit-bull. Still that ain't gonna stop him from enjoying a taste from that body every opportunity he gets, he thought. Of course Valerie wanted to know where the hell he was all night and of course he used Aijon and getting too drunk at his house to drive as an excuse.

Erica called him as soon as he walked in the door and he had to pick up the phone before he catches some zzzs. He's about to be out and about tonight and he needs his energy. She has the real estate information he's been expecting.

"I got more info about those shadow investors buying up all that property in DC. It looks like they are going to be a problem for us in the city, there's not much prime property left. Their money seems to be coming from everywhere. The one thing I did notice that stuck out a little further than the other stuff is your buddy's neighborhood here in Maryland."

"Deron's neighborhood, what's happening with that? Are they the developers or the builders?"

"No not Deron, the other one, Bryan. The same company has brought about forty-two out of about eighty townhouses over the last four years. It's been hard on them because the people don't want to move. They're spending a lot of money to get that community. They use different names but it's the same company once you trace the companies down to the parent one. They have businesses as well as funding them too like a couple of lounges, convenience stores, hair salons, car wash…"

"Hair salons? Look for PM Hair Designs."

She paused some before she answered him.

"Yep, that one's on the list. Somebody you know?"

"Yeah actually. No big deal though. They loaned her some money and she's paying it off soon."

"Soon? Her business' that good cause she owes them some loot. She just opened that saloon recently."

"So it at ain't that much."

"Ain't much? She owes approximately one hundred fifty thousand to them. That's current."

"What! She said she only had 'bout forty to go. So she borrowed less than she owed from my bank."

"Maybe she just wanted a little business funds so she would have some spending, you know renovations."

"She also invested her profits. You'd think she'd pay that loan to them down. I don't get."

"Nothing strange there Tony, she's trying to flip her profits with you so she can eventually pay those guys off right?"

"Naw it's some bullshit local company she invested in. She wouldn't take my tip. Some company that has about three strip clubs. I think Club P is one of them.

"Hell she could have invested in something safe like Google or Apple something; that's moving. A strip club here in the city is not a guaranteed investment."

"Yeah, but she claimed that was the only thing she felt comfortable with. The company has some other businesses as well, like restaurants. I'll email the info to you and you can trace them as well. Now that I think about it I better check this shit out."

"Maybe she thinks she'll get a quick buck. Like I said for renovations and spending."

"Naw she said she wants to get out of debut. That was the first thing," Tony said assuredly while he thought about it. "You know I'm gonna ask her about this."

"I know you are."

****

"So let me get this straight," Phaedra said to Tony over the phone later that day. "You're concern about where I put my money?"

She wasn't gonna do it but she stepped away from a client to talk this nut. Ever since she's been back seeing and messing with him he thinks he owns her. How far is she willing to go to let these no good ass men disrespect her to get her business going? Once she gets it going she's done with these petty broke men who think cause they make six figures they can treat her anyway they want. Her next stop is a millionaire. That's the kind of money she likes. She'll get him to open up a chain of PM Hair Designs salons. Tony's sex is good but she ain't no dumb chick.

She knows how to make that dollar count.

"You know it ain't like that, I don't give a damn about that trivial shit, the fact is you lied," he said flatly. "I don't want you to think I'm all up in your business but I most definitely don't like to be played. Been there done that and ain't doing it no more."

"So how am I playing you? I asked you to help me get a loan that I got to pay back to a bank you don't own. It's not your money. I asked you to help me with some stock investment and you've done that. Now what? What's the problem Tony, because I'm not licking your balls when I asked you for shit?"

"Oh you got jokes," he laughed. "I just want to know why you lied about the amount. If you needed more then you should've said so cause I won't be able to get you another one, not with your collateral."

"And I didn't ask you either. I got this. You're not the only one who knows how to work a dollar. I know what I'm doing. I've already doubled that loan and I'm gonna be paying it back soon."

"These guys that you have as investors they some heavy hitters. They been aggressively buying up a lot of property throughout D.C. and Maryland. They working overtime. Who are they?"

"What do you mean?"

"No stuttering on my end *who are they*?"

"Jerrell Lewis that's my contact and what? It looks like you've been doing some checking boo."

"Yeah every time I put my name on something in black and white I got to check it regardless of how good the poo-poo is."

"That's all you think of and I like that about you," she said trying to soften the conversation to switch it around and paused. She has said more than she should. "You coming my way later?" she finally added.

"Why, you need some?"

"That's not what I asked."

"I'm asking."

"Yeah."

"Thirty minutes."

"No I'm at the salon."

"So?"

"I got clients, later."

"I got this."

"Come around back and call me."

"I want it to smell like strawberries."

****

The next day at work in his office Deron decided today would be the day that he talks to Sharnia about Tony. Neither, one of them want to admit that they're seeing each other but they are. Really, it doesn't have anything to do with him except for the fact that he's Sharnia's supervisor. It's really affecting her work and he wants to know what the problem is. He thought that day in his office a few years back was the last time, but was not. Her work is definitely on the decline and Deron thinks it something wrong in her personal life. Her whole personality has changed and for the worst and that's where it's becomes his problem. The staff are starting to complain and he can't cover for her anymore. Just this morning she slammed a file cabinet so hard that it knocked over the glass vase that was on top of it; while one of the drivers was in her office talking to her.

It's uncomfortable that he can't talk to her like they normally would do because she's changed the game. She won't talk. When he promoted her to the position of his assistant, he thought he was getting someone that's as hungry as he is to become the top at their company. However, lately she hasn't been with it. Heck Vera Stanton, the former assistant he fire wouldn't have been this bad.

It's just becoming ridiculous because he warned her about Tony and she ignored it. Right after that fight then, they talked for hours after work. He thought he made it clear to her. Now everyone has to pay the price for her bad decisions because she's pissed off. That's something that he's going to have to put an end to, real quick.

He got up from his desk and went out of his office down the hall. As he took the strolled towards her office, he felt a weight on him. He again blames Tony. Once again, he's the one that causing Deron these unnecessary headaches; just like the party. Now it's reflecting on him badly.

Everyone's looking at him to fix this thing with Sharnia. If word got around, which it shouldn't, but if word got around that it's because of his best friend, he'll be blamed. They're already trying to secretly sabotage his position as new Regional Manager. A brother always got to work hard.

No one expected him to move this fast in his career but he is now in that position. The most dedicated employee that the company has employed in over ten years, their words not his. He happily took the position. Of course, others thought of their favorites but that doesn't always make the best choice. Besides, for the last few years he's been getting it in with finishing up his degree. He plans to stay on top.

So of course, he's not going to risk this liaison with Sharnia to interfere with his career growth. One day he might make it on the Board of Trustees, token or not he's going to make it and he's going to deserve that spot because he's a bad brother.

So Tony and Sharnia be damn.

Entering into her office, Deron heard the phone on her desk ring just as he walked up to her desk and she answered it. She turned her head away from him in her usual fashion when she didn't want anyone to hear her conversation.

While he stood there, he glanced at her monitor screen. By the position of her desk, it made it easy to do that. She didn't seem to realize him looking at her screen. On the screen, it is something relating to residential sprinkler systems. It explains the operation, function and how to, disable them. Now if she had a man that cares about her, she wouldn't have to look this information up herself. He would be doing it because she's his woman.

Tony's only concern is for Tony's address that much is true. He could care less what Sharnia's needs. Why can't she see that? The document from what Deron could tell is very detailed and thorough; she's going to need that.

Then he noticed Sharnia looking at him.

"Hold on a minute baby, "Sharnia said. "Deron is there something you wanted?"

"I wanted to talk to you but you're on the phone. I can wait. There's nothing critical going on," he said backing away from her.

She went back to her call as if he hadn't been there.

This was the second time she's made him feel uncomfortable and this has got to stop. It's only because he considers them as friends but now he's noticing that something is changing. Later he has to talk to her. No matter how hard it will be to get through this talk. He has to do it for the company.

****

Later that day Deron again walked in Sharnia's office and towards her desk. He's sure he has this dumb look on his face. How do you tell someone that's hell bent on being with somebody that you know is no good for her or him, not to? Heck he was just like her a few years ago. Tony's his buddy and all but he's not right for Sharnia. For some reason it works for Val because lately Deron has noticed that Val gives Tony a good run for his money. Maybe she's just used to it. Sharnia on the other hand is too sensitive and soft. She'll let Tony run all over her and who's going to have to listen to all that drama once he messes up her mind, Deron.

It's not that she told him that she's seeing him but Deron can tell. It's all in her aura. She's the same way she acted when they were sneaking around before ago. Except now since Tony's been pissing her off she's been pissed off with everyone she encounters.

"Hey what's up, you've been kind of quiet lately?"

"Everything's good Deron, I'm just quiet."

"You know it worries me when you get like this."

"Worries you? Why should it worry you that I'm quiet?"

"We're friends, I'm concern about you."

"Oh."

"What's bothering you?"

"Nothing."

"If there's anything that I…okay I'm just gonna say it…it seems like Tony's got your mind occupied and that may not be a good thing."

"Uh huh."

"You know that Tony's still with Val right?"

That she knows isn't true because she just talked to Tony over the phone earlier. Deron needs to step back and mind his own business she thought giving out wrong information. It's enough dealing with Tony. What if she tells Tony he's doing this then she would be wrong; but he's getting on her nerves?

"Do you give Valerie this much attention and advice or am I the special case?"

"You know it's not the same thing."

"I'm just getting tired of you treating me like I'm some kind of side slut. I'm a grown woman and you're in my business."

"You and I go back further than Valerie and me. I'm not taking sides but I've been in a ménage à trois before. I know how much trouble it can be. I almost lost my woman."

"All that really doesn't have anything to do with me Deron. I know you mean well and all believe me I really do appreciate it, but my life is not one of your projects. I'm alright really."

"Okay that was straight forward. I didn't say anything about your life, just Tony."

Sharnia simply stared at him. She's bothered by the way; Deron keeps interfering in her situation with Tony. If he didn't know Tony, he wouldn't bother her with it.

"Just back off," she said frustrated.

"Okay Sharnia dang, I'm just concern."

"Don't involve yourself is as plain as I can say it."

"I just don't want to see you hurt, you and I are cool."

"Deron, I'm a big girl. If I think that I'm getting too far involved, I know what to do. I'm having a good time right now and frankly I don't need a father-boss on my job telling me what to do."

He's sure she didn't mean to sound as blunt as she did at that moment.

"Why don't you tell Tony to stop seeing me? Why is it my responsibility? Just leave me alone about it."

"I got it, your life; your deal."

"Is this going to affect my job?"

"What…?"

"Is this going to affect my job?"

He didn't say anything else.

He should tell her how her attitude on the jobs been and her work's been the pits; but he knows he'd be caught in a trick bag behind it.

He looked at her for a minute and then walked off to his office. Once there he walked in and slammed the door shut behind him. He's not going to take part in that anymore.

It's getting too much like employer and employee instead of the friends he thought they are. She wants to mess with Tony knowing how he is than she should do it. He's only trying to watch out for her because he already knows how Tony is do her. The sooner she becomes a liability he's going to boot her.

What Sharnia is looking for in him will never materialize. He thought she would understand his risk. He's Tony's best friend and frankly, he's betraying him by trying to assist her. He's not betraying Tony per say but he's betraying the code. Normally Deron wouldn't do that but Sharnia is peeps and this whole thing has him caught in the middle. This is one more thing that Tony has been reckless about over the years messing with somebody who works under Deron.

He didn't pay too much attention to it before because after the fight a few years ago he thought it had ended. Tony surprised him because normally when women don't take Tony's side he usually kicks that woman to the curb. Not only did Sharnia come to Deron's defense that day but also she embraced him in a manner that made Tony think they had some dealings before, the two of them.

Of course, that wasn't the case but T doesn't know that.

He's always dealing with things on adrenaline. Popping off when it's not necessary, but regardless that's his boy.

He hopes this thing with Sharnia won't get out of hand. They don't need to get into it over her like the way the thing with Phaedra kicked off.

CHAPTER 10

About a week later, Yolanda and Steve are out to dinner. To Yolanda they were having a good time and she's enjoying his closeness. Even though they keep it friendly, she could see herself falling for him if she gave herself the green light. It's just too early though and things are moving too fast. She hadn't really noticed it until her last talk with both Dawn and Valerie. First off, she didn't believe what Valerie said about Steve because she's never seen an inkling of deception from him. She wished Valerie had kept that to herself because she doesn't want to start questioning herself about him now. Things are going great. No one more than her expected to, never have to deal with her heart again. She thought she was going to remain single and honor her husband, but that isn't realistic; life goes on. However, she didn't think that she would be drawn to Steve so strongly. She thought that she would get a chance to test the waters not actually find someone that she really liked.

She looked at him in silence as he took bites of his food. It is different from when she was with Bryan. It didn't start off with Bryan like this and of course she's had boyfriends before him. There wasn't this air of suspense and intrigue that isn't like what she feels right now. She wants to feel comfortable and it seems as if there's a fight to remain calm. Is she trying to stop herself from feeling anything for him in order to, not offend the memory of Bryan or is she just simply scared.

Steve noticed the awkward silence that suddenly appeared at the table. They were engrossed at first in a deep conversation and then it fell off into this silence. Is he losing his advantage over this situation? He couldn't let happen when he is so close to being with her and possibly getting that property she has. He'd been looking at her even when Bryan was alive. He thought that at one time he could have gotten her to have an affair with him. He realized that wasn't going to happen once he found out she's in the church. He must've read her intentions wrong when she used to look at him with those pretty brown eyes. She never used to take her eyes off him and he used to move around to see if she was really looking at him. His ex-wife Serena used to accuse him of entertaining her advances or rather her suspicious looks at him. She is a crazy bitch anyway he thought, that's why he left her ass.

"It seems like I'm always asking you what's on your mind," he said to her sweetly.

"I know."

"Well," he reached over the table and grabbed her hand. "I want to know everything about you so don't hide from me."

He wants her to look at him as sincere and romantic. It's the only way he'll be able to get with her. Bryan didn't know what to do with her but he does. Bryan was too wimpy and she led him around like a puppy. Once they get together permanently and he gets control of that money he knows Bryan left her, his businesses will be off and running more than now. Of course, he'll do right by her and keep her as his prize because he earned her, but she will let him lead her. He knows what to do with a woman. Hell if Serena didn't drink so much he would have stayed with her but who wants an old drunk around. It was messing up her looks. She wasn't like that when he met her. She didn't show that ten-year difference that she has over him until she turned into an alcoholic.

To think the courts makes him pay her alimony for being a drunk but he had to. She should be paying him for staying with her all this time. His money was, tied up in hers and of course, he had to stay to get some of the land that her uncle left her. He died right after Bryan did which was perfect timing as if he had planned it himself. Unfortunately, the land got tied up in some ligation between Serena and her other siblings. Those damn nasty ass relatives can be a pain in the ass especially siblings.

So he had to move on with something else and he didn't want to wait any longer to sleep with Yolanda. Now she has him on hold waiting for her to get past being with her husband's friend. It wasn't like they were best friends Bryan had that stupid ass Tony and Deron for that. They just grew up together. Really it wasn't a friendship to him it was who could get to the finish line first. He has seen to it that he's going to be first. Besides Bryan was a boy compared to him, Yolanda needs a real man.

"I'm not hiding from you; I'm taking it slow."

"I told you before that you're safe with me."

"I know that. I'm taking it slow because I don't want to rush into something that I don't think I can handle right now."

"In my opinion all you have to do is let go. You do have to move on you know?"

"I know that but I'm just scared and I need to be cautious."

"Well take all the time you need because I'm not going anywhere, I think I'm in…," he cut off his words.

Yolanda lean in as if she wanted to hear what else he has to say. She felt herself do it and caught herself. Straightening up she thought she'd better change the conversation before it goes further into the area she didn't want it to go.

"Steve that reminds me, I need a service guy to do some work at the townhouse. I have something wrong with the air conditioner unit or at least that's what my handy man Easton said."

"Oh yeah what?"

"He doesn't do air conditioners that's why he said get an air guy or service guy."

"Heating and Air Conditioner repairman."

"Yes do you know one?"

"You know Yolanda; I can take that townhouse off your hands any day now. It can be too much trying to maintain two properties."

"I already told you that it's not for sell, Steve. And don't start trying to scare me with that story about that other developer that's trying to force people out in that neighborhood. Not everybody's moving."

"I'm just trying to help. I don't want you getting into a bad business deal. Better to sell when you can get the price you want and not what someone wants to give you."

"Well Yolanda Prescott can't be scared that easily."

"I know that's why I'm falling for her so quickly, because she's one of a kind."

"Flattery is not going to get you that townhouse."

"How about if I asked you to marry me, will that at least get your attention?"

"What?"

"Marry me Yolanda, I love you."

"Steve, no, I can't…"

"I know but I love you and I want to be with you. If you, marry me now I will spend the rest of my life trying to show you."

She didn't know what to do or say. It makes sense for her to move forward. Bryan has been gone for two years now and maybe it is time to move on. The thought of it made her heart ache. Steve's been so good to her these past few months. However, it would be risky to get marry so quickly.

****

Later the two of them were sitting in his car in front of Yolanda's house. Steve reached into the backseat and grabbed a large envelope from there.

"Well look I got these documents for you to look over, just to see the offer okay."

"I told you that I'm not going to sell."

"Yolanda you can at least see what my business is all about. What if we start dating seriously I want you in on the ground floor of this?"

"Your business will be yours, I won't be involved in that."

"Do it for me, just look over the documents please."

She thought about it and felt what harm it would do for her to look over the documents. At least she can get an idea on how things work in the real estate world.

"Okay Steve. I'll look them over."

"Good I'll walk you to the door."

****

On the next day, Cheresse walked into AUPS boldly.

"Deron Stone," Cheresse said to the receptionist with no pleasantries as if she was ordering the hired help.

This is what Cheresse has, been waiting for the day she could serve Deron with these papers and she didn't have time for this bitch, she thought.

"Deron, there's someone here to see you," the receptionist said into the phone as it connected. "He's coming out."

"I'll go meet him. I know the way around this small ass building. This is not some suite on 17th and Penn NW."

Cheresse walked off from the reception desk leaving the young woman who sat there offended by her abruptness. As Deron opens his door, Cheresse appeared right there. She walked pass him into his office without being asked to come inside. Deron just wave to the receptionist that it's alright and she nodded.

He thought, as he looked at her that this isn't the way he wanted to end his Friday and begin the weekend.

He noticed first off that she lost a lot of weight a whole lot of weight but she still looked good. She still had that sexy shape and he was surprised that he still looked at her like that. The clothes she's dressed in are high-end and she wore them like a high fashion runway supermodel. She must be in somebody else's pockets dressing like this.

Then again, it could be the money from porn site.

"Just couldn't stay away could you, Cheresse?" Deron said as he walked back to his desk to sit down. "Just couldn't do me that one small favor huh?"

"I know how much you love my attention."

"Putting me on a porn site wasn't enough attention?"

"Oh yeah you're still on that. I got that copy of the stay order from your lawyer to the owners of the porn site. I'm not giving any money back believe that," she said sitting down in one of the chairs that are placed in front of his desk. "Anyway just like clockwork every nine months, I like to drop in to see my lover in the flesh," she added laughing.

"Why do you keep coming back? There's nothing here for you. Did you think blasting me on the internet like that would bring me back?"

"Well as much as I know you think everything is about you Deron, I'm here on business."

"We have no business between us Cheresse."

"Not business with me not yet, business with my firm. I personally wanted the pleasure of delivering this to you. Even though you'll get this in the mail. I couldn't resist this," she said humorously as she reached into her large Louis Vuitton tote bag and pulled out an envelope. She laid it down on his desk and then looked at him. "You've been served," she said laughing as she went out the door to his office.

Deron watched her as she left and then diverted his attention back to the envelope that laid before him on his desk. There's always something unfolding with Cheresse. She knows he won't hurt Dawn and that's the reason why she gets away with some of the stuff she does. That's why he hasn't said nothing about the sex video yet, he doesn't want Dawn thinking anything negative about him.

Again, he has to resort to lying to her and keeping secrets to protect her. That he knows never gets him anywhere as he quickly found out before. But he has no choice, he hasn't evolved into that brave man that everyone thinks he is yet.

He reached down and picked up the envelope dreading the day he met that woman. Tearing into it he pulled out the documents and of course it's a court summons that Cheresse has charging him with something stupid. Probably suing him for defaming her in that video. She would try to get a civil suit just to tax his pockets so he couldn't move on with Dawn, but she's not going to get him.

He took the silence to read the document and the first thing he read is, 'Audrey Lorraine Butler vs Deron Alexander Stone'. The document went on to reveal that this is a child custody hearing and the first hearing date is set for three days from now. The letter is, dated ten days ago. He should've got this at his home. Why did Cheresse deliver it? Is it real? He read further down the letter. What is this? Audrey wants full custody of Deron Jr. She gave up her parental rights to him.

She said she didn't want to be a mother.

Why is she turning on him now?

Once he got his mind together, he went to his cellphone and searched for Audrey's number. He kept her number for no particular reason other than the fact that she's Deron Jr's Mother. Pushing the spot on his smartphone to connect the call, he increasingly became agitated.

The call connected and immediately went to voicemail. He waited for the greeting to end and he left a message.

"Audrey, this is Deron, what in the hell is this?" he said aggressively into the phone. It's hard now to contain his growing anger. "Why in the hell would you do this and send Cheresse here? I need you to call me right now, right now. This shit is not gonna fly."

He hung up the call.

He sat down in the chair at his desk and looked at the picture of Dawn, Deron Jr and himself.

Why Lord is this happening?

****

Three days later around one o'clock on the day of the hearing Deron and Dawn made their way through the halls of the Upper Marlboro Court House. They had just come out of the courtroom. The hearing was, cut short because the custody judge had a prior hearing that ran into their time. They drove from there to Yolanda's house and Deron dropped Dawn off. She's hanging with the girls while Deron goes and picks up Jr from his mother's house. He didn't notice as he drove off Steve exiting the house from the front door before Dawn closed the door.

Dawn walked into the morning room where Yolanda was sitting with Bryan Jr. in her lap. He restlessly leaning on her trying to fight his sleep. Valerie is there too. It felt odd passing Steve Powers in the doorway knowing that now he's trying to be with Yolanda as a boyfriend. Really to be honest although she doesn't dislike Steve she does however still share Deron and Tony's concern about him. Wow, she actually agrees with something that Tony thinks.

Dawn sat down across from Valerie in a small wicker-cushioned chair. She has a strange look on her face. Once she caught Dawn's eye she motioned to the end of the large wicker sofa that sat against the wall facing the windows and the small end table beside it.

There on the table sat a set of forms and Dawn looked back at Valerie for clarity. Valerie mouthed the name 'Steve' when Yolanda wasn't looking as she went on and on about Bryan Jr's latest adventures. Dawn simply shook her head wanting not to do this behind Yolanda back, right in front her face. Valerie is beginning to become pessimistic in their friendship. It's like she's pissed off inside and that if she's not happy no one should be happy even if they are. The two of them have been having their fair share of disagreements lately but Dawn knows it's not intentional.

"So Steve is really pouring it on Yolanda," Valerie said.

"Yes he is," Yolanda said wanting to continue talking about her son. "Dawn is Deron coming back to pick you up?"

"No Val's going to drop me off."

"Oh, I was going to let Bryan stay up longer so the boys could play together but I guess it just as well he hasn't taken a nap yet. You know how cranky he can get when he's fighting his sleep."

"Are Steve and you going out again tonight?" Valerie asked.

"Val, don't you see that Yolanda doesn't want to talk about Steve right now," Dawn said intercepting the question.

"I didn't know that subject was off the radar for today. I'm sorry Yolanda."

To Valerie she felt like Dawn enjoyed making her out to be inconsiderate. Nobody knew that Yolanda didn't want to talk about Steve because she's the one who let on that she's seeing him. Now since she's inquisitive about the details of their thing she being intrusive. But no one stop getting involved in Tony and her affairs. When they ride to Dawn's house, she's going to have a talk with her. Something's wrong with the two of them and they're getting out of hand. Mainly because she's not going to keep being check by another woman.

"No problem Val, I'm just distracted with Bryan right now. Besides there's nothing to say," Yolanda said. "You know I'm going to put him down for a nap."

She got up and left the room with Bryan Jr in her arms he had fallen asleep just that quick.

"I don't see what the problem is that I said anything about Steve."

"It's becoming an obsession with you and it's making Yolanda uncomfortable. She's not going to say it but you can tell she's uncomfortable."

"Well then that means that she shouldn't be with him."

"Valerie, let Yolanda handle her own affairs."

"I am but *I*," she said as she got up from the chair she was sitting in and walked over to the end table with the documents on it. "Want to know what these papers are that Steve is so insistent that she sign. I heard something about a good faith offer. Why does she have to sign a good faith offer?" she asked picking up the papers to read.

"Why are you into that?"

"I don't trust Steve and if you're not going to help be quiet so I can hear when Yolanda comes down the stairs."

"You can hear her on the baby monitor over there," Dawn said pointing to the baby monitor on the counter. "Don't you hear her she still in Bryan's room?"

"Good because I need to go to her office library to makes some copies," Valerie said walking off toward the office library.

"Valerie, no what are you doing?" Dawn tried to call to her in a lowered voice.

There was no use.

Valerie entered Yolanda's office and went straight to the copier machine that sat on a table by itself. She turned it on from the power save mode and dialed her selection of print on the touch screen. She fed the pages through the top feeder and waited as the prints came out quicker than the copier Tony has at his place. Then she re-fed the pages flipping them over once again into the top load and waited for the copies. Once she finished she grabbed the originals and the copies then hurried back out into the morning room. She half-expected Yolanda to be waiting there with her hands on her hips wondering why she's copying her personal documents. Instead, when she returned just a disapproving Dawn is sitting there with this disapproving look on her face as if she's Michelle Obama. Dawn stared at her intensely as she placed the original documents back on the table and then she placed the copies into her tote bag.

"You know I'm going to tell Yolanda," Dawn said to her.

"Please don't do that. I'm only trying to help. I'm going to let Erica Fontanne look these over and if they're legit than I will apologize to her myself but what if I'm right?"

"About what Val?"

"Steve is a sleaze and a liar."

"I think you're overdoing it don't you think? You're letting the problems of your relationship overtake you into thinking everybody's going through the same thing as you but that's not true."

"You know Dawn you keep saying that but you don't know what you're talking about. I'm looking out for a friend."

"I'm going to tell her."

"Don't tell her."

"No, I am."

"Don't tell her, I mean it."

"Don't tell me what?" Yolanda said appearing almost out of nowhere.

The elephant's now in the room and there suddenly became this awkward silence; as neither woman wanted to be the first to speak. Valerie simply looked at Dawn swearing the woman to secrecy silently with her expression; popping her eyes out.

"Valerie stole your outfit ideas girl," Dawn said as Valerie exhaled silently.

"What outfit?"

"You remember when you showed us that outfit online, the one you said you were going to wear to that play *Wrong Woman at the Wrong Time*? Val went out and brought it."

"I can't tell you nothing can I Val?"

"Well you know me," she said nervously. "I just had to have it."

Dawn shook her head openly. To Yolanda it is to chastise her for the outfit, but to Valerie she knows Dawn disapproves of what she did.

"Well one thing Val, it had better be right on point," Dawn, warned her. "Stealing an outfit could ruin a friendship," she added laughing, but Valerie knows she's serious; only trying to cover-up the meaning from Yolanda.

****

"So what do you think Erica," Tony asked her as she sat on his computer in his home office.

Tony, Valerie and Erica are in the office looking over the papers that Valerie made copies of when she was at Yolanda's the day before. This space is something that Tony's very proud of because of what he was able to do with it.

It's a renovated space on the first floor from the room that he used before as a storage room. A pretty good space for an office right off the family room. It's good to get some use out of all this office equipment he stocked in here preparing for his realtor slash financial advisor business.

"The document seems like a standard good faith deal between the buyer and the seller," Erica said to him not taking her eyes from the screen.

"But Yolanda said she isn't going to sell. Is that binding?"

"No it's just good faith that if they do business it basically won't be outside of what they discussed. But as long as she didn't sign anything or especially as long as she didn't get a third party to notarize the signed document she still good. Then there's always the thirty days to make up your mind clause. There's all sorts of ways to end a contract but time is of the essence."

"Then I did jump to conclusions?" Valerie said.

"I wouldn't say that," Erica said. "There still the question of why there's a beneficiary deed form mixed in here with the other documents and it's signed?"

Erica noticed that Valerie is being extra nice to her tonight. Usually she doesn't have too much to say to her, just a couple of cold words. That's probably because in the back of her mind, she thinks Tony's sleeping with her.

Been there done that and ain't doing it no more she thought. She doesn't ever have about that.

No matter how much she enjoys the friendliness even if it's temporary.

****

Two weeks later Yolanda met Dawn and Valerie for lunch at the Cheesecake Factory on Clarendon Blvd in Arlington, VA. It's crowded as usual but they manage to get a booth in the center of the restaurant away all by themselves.

"Well girls, today is the day," Yolanda said happily once they sat down. "I have some news to tell you."

"The world's waiting with bated breath," Valerie, said musing in her mind.

"Bated breath, Valerie?" Dawn asked.

"Nathan writes poetry and he knows what to do with it," she responded.

"Uh, uh, dangerous territory girl," Dawn said.

"I'm a wild card remember? Besides, it's refreshing; having a man wine and dine me for a change and not want to gouge me out every time we're together. Better yet, remind you every five minutes of what he does for you. I want a man to declare that I'm his woman and be about it. I'm just saying."

"I get it Nathan's the one. So if he's the one then why don't you leave Tony alone and invest your time in Nathan?"

"Not sure I can answer that question. I guess I want the best of both worlds, a wild card."

"Trouble."

"Well *Steve* is the one," Yolanda interrupted. "Remember *I* am the one who called this lunch date together just so I could break the news. We are official."

Dead silence hit the table.

Dawn simply looked at Yolanda as if she is disappearing right before her eyes.

Yolanda has confessed her love for Steve Powers.

This is unimaginable.

"Well don't the two of you talk over each other," she said amusingly.

"I…I don't know what to say," Valerie said.

"Say 'I'm happy for you, girl' and let's celebrate with a glass a wine. No children around."

****

Later that evening Deron and Dawn were at Olive Garden, in Bowie about to sit down for dinner. They were waiting for their table to be, called. It's been a rough week for them because Deron had to tell Dawn about the porn site and the video. It took him a few weeks to tell her because he wasn't sure how she would take it, plus after having to tell her about the custody hearing that suddenly came up. To Deron it didn't go well because she didn't say a word to him she just got up from him and walked off. Once again, Cheresse is causing another stir in his life.

Why is Audrey helping her wreck his life, he's never done anything to her? He knows why Cheresse is doing this because she can't get over the fact that he doesn't want her no more.

As much as he likes to think that he's that good in the sack it's pass all that. Her ego is just that big that she won't allow something that she had belong to someone else. If he were to go back to her, she would play the same games that forced him to leave her alone in the first place.

Dawn's being so perfect about this but how long is she going to stand by him through all this.

"Your table is ready Sir," the hostess said to Deron.

The hostess led them to their booth and they followed her around the corner towards the back of the restaurant. She then gave them a menu once they were, seated.

"Deron, I'm going to the restroom, I'll be right back," Dawn said as she got up and walked off around the corner.

He watched as she disappeared around the corner and thought to himself that he has ruined everything messing with Cheresse. She's still affecting his relationship. But he didn't know he was going to meet someone like Dawn, he didn't get that lucky, blessed before. He felt that he deserved a love like hers but he didn't know he was going to get one. The devil works this way when he tries to destroy you from the inside out, he sends someone like Cheresse.

****

Dawn adjusted her clothes while she stood in the stall. It's incredible what the two of them are suddenly going through. She's not going to let Audrey take her child away from her. No matter what the court decides. She gave up her rights and she stepped up to be Jr's mother when Audrey abandoned him. And it's no big surprise that Cheresse is back again involved with this.

What kind of woman is she posting sex videos on the internet of her ex? Dawn doesn't even want to think about that right now. She didn't want to think about any of it now. The devil is busy once more.

She opened the door to exit the stall and she thought more about all of this. It'd be better if tonight the two of them not speak on any of their issues. She thought instead when she gets back to the table she'll tell Deron what Yolanda told Val and her today about Steve. It's best to get it out of the way so that there will be no surprises from meeting up with him accidently. Especially since Steve's going to be around for a while. She knows that it will be awkward at first.

As she walked towards the sink and mirror to wash her hands, she noticed the woman standing, leaning against the wall. It only took her a moment to recognize her.

Cheresse, she thought.

Of all the restaurants for her to be at why, is she here at this one, right now? Cheresse stood against the wall staring at her. She is dressed surprisingly in one of those new Armani suits; the jacket, skirt and all that Dawn saw when she was in Niemen Marcus, with Valerie recently.

This is a joke.

A jezebel trying to dress like a professional woman.

What Deron ever saw in this woman is still a mystery to her?

This is what she wants Deron for, to be her cash-cow to buy these things to make her feel like she's something she's really not. They were quite the opposite pair weren't they? Him with the cash he saved before he brought the house and her wanting him to spend the cash on her, pitiful.

There's no reason to talk to her Dawn thought. All she will do is try to provoke her to a confrontation and she's trying to have a pleasant evening with her husband. She still has to consider the custody hearing. She may have to go back to the table, get Deron and leave. No more public displays like what happened on M street.

"You know you're just a rebound chick for real?" Cheresse said as the other woman started to wash her hands ignoring her. "Deron don't really want to be with you but since you and your uppity whorish friends' been poisoning his mind he can't think. Really bitch he wants me deep down inside."

Dawn still didn't say anything to her she just watched her own reflection in the mirror as she washed her hands.

This woman is getting on her last nerve.

Everywhere she turns Cheresse Bennett shows up and tries to ruin her life. All she wants to do is cause problems between Deron and her. But all Dawn has to do is stick to what she knows, Christ and not entertain her silly behavior.

But it's so hard.

"So bitch did you like our little porn movie we made together. I gave him the present he really wanted. That dick was all up in this pussy that Christmas day. It was many more days after you two broke up and well you know how he do," Cheresse taunted her by patting her vagina.

Ugh, Dawn screamed in her head.

She is so vulgar.

A hood rat in fancy clothing she thought.

No, she hasn't seen the video yet but Deron did tell her about it. She doesn't want to see it. She just wants it to go away like everything that Cheresse does.

This woman…

"I thought you might let me borrow him tonight," Cheresse cut off her thoughts. "Because I know you can't be satisfying him. You can't even give him a baby. I hope you know that Audrey's baby is never going to be yours. You're just a fake ass baby stealing momma, barren as dirt," she said.

"I'm the only mother he knows," Dawn forced herself to, only say. Who told her that she's barren, there's nothing wrong with her. This woman doesn't know anything about her. "Well, okay bye, bye," Dawn, added as she started to exit the restroom.

Cheresse took a swing at her as Dawn tried to exit the restroom. Instead of connecting her swing, she ended up falling into the sink. She turned around to swing at Dawn again and this time Dawn forcefully pushed her back. Cheresse was stunned as she fell back into the wall. Shocked, Cheresse didn't move, she just held the side of her shoulder from the pain of hitting the wall. It was harder than Dawn intended it to be. She prepared for another attack from her. Cheresse just straightened her clothes and herself up.

"Oh you got some balls huh bitch. Okay you want to see me, it's on," she said moving towards Dawn.

Just then, two female servers came rushing in, stepping in between them and pushing Cheresse back.

"I told you, Priss I heard some shit in here," the tall female said. "Y'all got to go or we're gonna call the police."

"I'm leaving bitch, don't touch me again," Cheresse said angrily to the server.

"Well stop running your mouth and go."

She pushed pass them and hurried out of the restroom. Dawn stood there not moving and the two watched her, waiting.

"You too," Priss said.

CHAPTER 11

"I just want to know where we're going that's all," Deron said from the passenger side of Tony truck as they rode together Friday, mid-morning. "The last time I went somewhere with you sight unseen I got drunk. I'm not doing that again. Ain't doing that no more."

"D. give that shit a rest. We're going to Howard County."

"What's up there?"

"Jessup Prison."

"What are we going there for, to see somebody?"

"Yep and if I hear, what I think I'm gonna, hear, they gonna be putting me up in there too."

"Man don't go up there starting anything. What's going on? Who's up here?"

"D just sit back and enjoy the ride, visiting hours isn't until one. I got this I'll let you know what's happening as soon as we get settled in. Meanwhile why don't you finish telling me about what went down with Dawn and Cheresse while y'all were at dinner?"

"It was funny as all get out," Deron, said laughing. "Cheresse followed Dawn into the restroom. She tried to swing on Dawn and got shoved into the wall. I think, no I know for sure Dawn enjoyed that. She's secretly wanted to do that for a long time now or worst. Man we got kicked out of Olive Garden. Dawn was pissed. I've never seen her that mad except that night when Cheresse ran up on us at Friday's. I guess she's doing that again. She looked like she wanted to fight her then. I'm not advocating for any kind of violence but Cheresse makes you forget about turning the other cheek," Deron said seriously.

"Huh man."

"Anyway man forget about that. What do you think about Yolanda and Steve Powers getting together?"

"Man you know I can't stand that son-of-a-bitch. He's really my point for going to Jessup. You know Valerie copied some forms Steve left for Yolanda to sign. Some docs to sell her townhouse to him; don't ask just listen. So in with the papers was a beneficiary deed and that paper was signed by Yolanda. But the rest of the document was blank. That means anybody can fill it out with whatever property they, want. I want to know what the reason for that paper is."

"Are you serious?"

"Yeah."

"So what's the trip to Jessup for?"

"It's just a hunch but Steve is too hyped up about buying Yolanda's property. I heard Valerie talking to Dawn about it before but didn't really start to connect some stuff until later."

"What stuff?"

"That's what I want Carl Daniels to tell us, why Carl Booker's name is on over five of the properties that Erica had on the list she compiled for me and is Steve his partner."

"I remember that other name. That's what Bryan knew Carl as. What's up with the alias?"

"He was a working crook but working for who is what I want to know?"

"Damn T since you been off from work you've been doing some heavy detective work. Can't tell whether you work for PG Police or PG Housing Authority."

"I told you D, I wasn't gonna be suspended for some thirty days, I been working from home, tele-work. I called my supervisor two weeks ago and told her if it's gonna flow like that then I'm out."

"And your supervisor took that?"

"Yep."

****

Once they got to Jessup Prison, Tony and Deron went in. They went through the normal checkpoints and sat patiently waiting on Carl to arrive in the visiting room to talk to him. At least Deron sat patiently.

"This is some bullshit man having to wait around for this nigga to get here. We ain't waiting for the President."

"They have to get him here Tony. It's not like visiting your son. You get more courteously out of these guards then you do Katrina when you go to get TJ."

"D. you got me there."

The two of them laugh and then they saw Carl walking out with one of the prison guard. As he approached them, walking through the rows of other families and friends visiting his fellow inmates; he didn't recognize Tony and Deron. Deron looked at him and couldn't change his stare from the man. Here comes the man that changed all of their lives. Now they're face to face. The last time he saw Carl was court over two years ago. During that time, he just wanted him convicted; now his thoughts are something worse. He wasn't expecting to feel this way but this is it. For Tony it's business as usually. Although he felt something to him, Carl's right where his murderous ass supposed to be. Showing any kind of emotion is not going to bring Bryan back. There's just not anything he could do about that but get information to make sure his buddy's wife is safe.

That was his silent promise to Bryan is that he's gonna protect Yolanda and make sure his son is okay. Between him and Deron their going to be all right.

"Y'all wanted to see me?" Carl asked.

"Yeah?" Tony said.

"Why did Jerrell send you here or something? I don't know you."

Jerrell?

Phaedra's Jerrell, Tony thought.

What does he have to do with this? Keep cool Big T, he thought to himself. You gonna get your answers and some.

"We came to ask you some questions. I'm Tony and this is Deron, we're friends of the man you killed."

Carl's first instinct is to look the two of them up and down for a sneak attack but realized they couldn't hit him in the visiting room without going down themselves. He kicked himself mentally for talking before he knew what's happening. But it didn't matter to him anymore this is where he's going to be for the next thirty something years and the devil ain't gonna ride him through it.

"What do y'all want with me, revenge, because I made my peace with God?"

"Naw Carl we want to know who sent you to that townhouse that night to kill Bryan. We know somebody did. We heard what you said in the courtroom, which was really nothing. We know the only reason you got caught is because Bryan ID you and DNA evidence. But we want to know who sent you there?"

There was a long pause as Carl contemplated how he's gonna answer. When he got to the jail after his sentence, he said he's going to take that night to his grave and not relive it. He knows his life is messed up but he's alive even if he's in jail. Once he started talking to the Christian brothers that he bonded with in here, he started to realize that he had to get that monkey off his back or it was going to be a rough stay here at Jessup. So he started talking to the pastor that visits the jail and confessed his sins.

"I used to work for this guy name Jerrell. He set me up in a townhouse a few rows down from Bryan. They paid my rent and all I had to do was wreck up the place and smoke weed. I got some money on the side and it was supposed to be my gig until the whole community sold."

"Why was you using the name Carl Booker?"

"I wasn't using that name, it's Daniels."

"Okay so you saying you were set up to be the neighborhood thug?"

"Yep."

"This was a plan?"

"A plan to make everybody move out of that neighborhood but Bryan started to be a problem. He started to get the people feeling safe again by promising to get more police in the community and he did. So I was told that I needed to rough him up a bit when the gambling, smoking and drinking behind his backyard didn't get him out of there."

"But he did move. He was out of that townhouse before you killed him," Deron said. "Why did you kill him?" he asked trying to hide his anger.

He had to say it.

To just get it out.

"I was told to rough him up a little because he still wouldn't sell his property," Carl responded to Deron. "The other part was my fault I'm gonna be honest with you. If I could take it back...well you know."

"You still didn't answer my question," Deron said a little too abruptly.

"Yeah I know. I was expecting him to be there because I was told he was gonna be there. Before I went I had smoke some weed and been drinking. I went over there and broke into the back door that was easy. The alarm was supposed to go off and if it didn't then I had to go in and wait for him. It wasn't long before he came through the front door. He must've sense something cause he headed right straight to the back of the house and found the door broken into. He came back up front, I hit him from behind, and he fell to the floor. I started to leave out running past him. All I had to do was rough him up. He grabbed my foot and I hit the floor myself. Next thing I know he whipped out this Taser and I couldn't let him use it on me. I just did it. I pulled out the gun I always carried and I did it."

Deron and Tony just sat there in shock, with Tony just shaking his head repeatedly.

There's nothing to say.

They relived a night that for everyone on some level found it hard to get over.

This is what happened to Bryan.

Tony wanted to steal Carl in his face forsaken his thoughts of being calm. He knew if he did though the prison guards would be on his ass before he was satisfied.

"Who told you to go over Bryan's," Tony asked trying to rise above his feelings.

"Jerrell called and told me to go over there, bust a window and leave, but when I was about to walk down to the house I got a text on my cell."

"A text."

"Yeah, it said to go inside if the alarm system was off and rough Bryan up because he was coming to the house."

"Who did the text come from?"

"Don't know, I thought it was Jerrell but who knows where it came from. It wasn't the same phone he called me from. But I was gettin' paid so you know…"

"Jerrell got a last name?"

"Lewis."

Yep, that's the dude Phaedra knows he thought.

"Jerrell Lewis got a business partner," Tony said bracing for the name he figures he will hear is Steve Powers.

"Naw, I don't know no other partner. I deal with J."

"Alright," Tony said not really, telling Carl whether he is finished asking him questions or not. He just got up out of his seat and started to walk off.

Deron nodded and followed suit.

Carl just sat there and the prison guard came to retrieve him.

"Hey Tony," Carl called to him. Tony and Deron turned to face him. "I'm sorry I did that to your dude."

"Oh yeah, well tell it to the devil while you burn in hell, muthafucka," Tony responded to him harshly as he turned again and walked to the exit door.

****

Once the guys got back to Tony's truck he is able to cut loose with his temper. As much as he wants to get with the get down while he was that close to Carl he don't want to spend no time behind bars. Not when there's still somebody to find for this. That's why he always pays his child support. As soon as he got behind the steering wheel, Tony pounded his fist repeatedly on the steering wheel of the truck.

"Damn it D that nigga should be done up. Man I wanted to go on his ass. He killed Bryan in cold blood man for nothing. We got to find out who sent him to do this. Whoever it is they wanted Bryan dead. They had to know Carl would kill him. Anybody can see that crack head is unstable. Weed my ass. We got to find em D."

"Yeah, I know let's roll T," Deron simply said.

****

At home, Tony is still up late thinking about what Carl told him and Deron earlier today. It's all beginning to make sense. Deron told him that Bryan seemed almost obsessed about going to that townhouse like he knew something was wrong. What if instead of sensing it, somebody told him something was wrong. Tony's nodded to himself because that just makes common sense. His friends all think that all he does is get with women, drink and smoke weed and spend money but he ain't stupid.

Something ain't sitting right with all this.

Carl said that new buyers are trying to buy that community no matter what; hell Erica said the same thing. Like he said, he would cause all sorts of shit in the neighborhood and scare the people right out of there. He was supposed to be the neighborhood trash and he was. He had a free townhouse to live and wreck up in and everything to go with it. He remembers now how Bryan would complain about the parties Carl threw a lot. People hanging outside in the parking lot, taking up people parking spaces and the police really couldn't do anything. Because by the time PG came to the scene, everything was set back to order. They paid him to be there as the troublemaking nuisance and he was sent to Bryan's townhouse to rough Bryan up. But why that neighborhood?

So who knew Bryan was gonna be at that crib that night at that time he thought?

Deron knew.

Yolanda she knew.

But somebody else knew, Carl's accomplice.

Somebody that had to talk to Bryan before or after he talked to Deron. If he could get D to focus some more on that night rather than being messed up about it, he could get some more insight on this.

Then he thought about something.

Maybe Yolanda can help.

****

The next day Tony went over to Yolanda's house. When he rang the doorbell he half expected Steve Powers to open the door, which would be awkward. He is relieved as Yolanda opened the door holding Bryan Jr in her arms. She looked at him before she unlocked the heavy storm door, then pass him. It's shocking to see Tony coming over without Valerie in tow. Since Bryan died, he hasn't really paid a visit to just come see her. She knows that he isn't doing it out of anything other than the fact that he has gotten into the routine of only coming over for events. There was a stretch of time when she wasn't receiving visitors when they showed up to give her support because she was so depressed. During that time, she thinks a lot of her friendships were changed.

Death does a lot of things to people.

Sometimes you just can't get a hold on it because people don't always say what's on their minds. A lot of times they just act out. Too much speculation goes on and those who left out of the equation are sometimes hurt the most. She didn't treat Tony or Deron with much consideration initially. Deron especially because she wanted to blame him for Bryan's death. She wanted so much to aim her pain at a face because she knew he should have gone with her husband that night. But as the Pastor told her, Deron did exactly as he was ordered to do. His responsibility was to tell Bryan exactly what he did which was not to go, 'go in the morning'. Bryan chose to ignore the warning. It was a subtle warning but it was there. So she had to free Deron from that burden but she never did, silently all the time she still blamed him.

One day soon, she's going to have to sit down with him and let him know this. It's important to her as well to him, although she doesn't think that he picked up on anything because she's been cautious not to let him.

"Hey Tony, what brings you by?" she said once she opened the storm door.

"I wanna say I came by to see my little sis and my nephew," he said as he walked into the house and stroked the boy's head. "But I got an agenda," he added hugging her, then walking into the family room to sit down.

"Val and you aren't having any issue are you?"

"No," he answered curiously wondering why that would be the first thing on her mind. "Something else."

"Of course not I don't know why I asked you that," she answered realizing what she asked.

"Yolanda, I know things with Valerie and me are up and down a lot so you don't have to tiptoe around me. Besides I know how females like to get together and talk so I know me and Deron are first on the list."

"Sometimes, but that's just between you and me. I'm glad you guys are behaving yourselves."

"We're cool. I hear you have a new friend," he said deciding to put that out on the table and change the subject off him and Deron.

"I hear Deron and you are not going to be happy about it."

"We'll manage because we love you, ha-ha. You women do talk a lot."

"Uh huh."

"Well I better get to what I want before you kick me out. I want to know if I could get Bryan's cellphone, I mean you still have it right?"

Wow, that isn't supposed to hurt like that when she heard his name or when she is reminded of that night. She steadied herself as she prepared to answer.

"Yes I have everything from that night. Why do you want it?"

"Okay here's where the kicking out part comes in. I can't tell you."

"Can't or won't?"

"Both."

"Tony what's this all about?"

"Yolanda it'll take too much time to explain and basically stir up some stuff that may not need to be stirred up and I want us to be cool. Nothing's going on, I'm just trying to work a theory out. So I'm asking you to trust me."

"Oh boy when you guys say stuff like that it is best not to know."

"Okay so can I get the phone?"

"You have a week and I want my phone back alright."

She didn't mean to sound so bossy or territorial about getting the phone back but she has her reasons. She hasn't had opportunity or a desire to go through the phone to get all of Bryan's memories from it. It was, just put up and away once she was able to get it from the police. She guesses she always had it so it would always be there. Now Tony wants to take from the house and it becomes an issue.

But she has to trust this man who she considers to be her big brother, no matter how out of control he can be at times.

"No more than two days, promise."

"Am I going to find out about this, ever?"

"One of the first people to know if I'm right but if I'm not then no, I'll keep it to myself."

"Fair enough. So while you're here would you like me to cook you something? Besides you're going to have to charge the phone."

"Umm no I can charge the phone at home…," he started to say but he knows that he hasn't stopped by her house in a long while just by himself and changed his mind. "Yes, I would like, if you're gonna cook."

"I wasn't but it's not everyday family drops by," she said handing him little Bryan Jr. "You can babysit."

****

That was more than Tony expected as he drove away from Yolanda's house. It was a meal and what he set out to, do. He even got to play uncle for a few hours. As much as he pains him to admit something as weak as this is, he really does miss those times being over Bryan and Yolanda's and being with them.

Before he was with Valerie, he was over there all the time and it was always food, fun, a lot of talk and laughs. Half the time there wasn't even any drinking just good family fun.

Since his sister has been married for the last ten years and living in Richmond, Virginia, he spent a lot of his down time with his new family of friends, Deron, Bryan and Yolanda. He never goes to his parents.

Now with Bryan gone everything fell off the normal routine. He's like a wildcard trying to match with some other cards in the deck.

****

Once Tony got home, Valerie and he activated the phone that is fully charged. Yolanda had given him the passcode and he thought man Bryan was all about that woman. He couldn't imagine giving his passcode to Valerie because he knows she would be all up and down his phone asking him questions about his contact list. Bryan didn't have to worry about that because Yolanda was just that kind of woman that she didn't do the suspicious, sneaky chick thing. His attention went to the phone. He knew exactly what he wanted to see and hear, but not in that order. Bryan's phone is an IPhone and it's easy for Tony to access the messages; even the ones he deleted without completely deleting them from the phone.

Tony scrolled down the saved voicemails to the date and around the time when Bryan was murdered. He instantly saw Steve Powers name several times even on the date of Bryan's death.

Curious he went to the first one that was several months prior to Bryan's death after they'd moved out of their townhouse. Valerie just sat beside him patiently and quietly trying to figure out what Tony is doing.

'Hey Bryan, SP here. When are you going to let me buy that townhouse of yours and get it off your plate? I'll give you a fair market price and even kick in some incentives, let me know buddy.'

The next voicemail was a few days later.

'Hey buddy, I get it you're still honeymooning with your fine wife; you lucky dude. We don't have to talk about anything yet but I really would like to get that property off of you. Don't forget dinner at my house on Sunday. Call me.'

The one after that was the month of the murder, several weeks before the actual night.

'Bryan have you been getting any reports from your alarm company about glass breakages? You might want to keep an eye out for your place because some of the neighbors are saying that break-ins are starting up again around there. I been watching that townhouse I brought like a hawk. Catch up with you. I'm still interested in buying.'

Before Tony went to the next voicemail, he thought he should check for deleted voicemail that may be on the phone. There was one deleted voicemail from Steve

Powers. It was one day after the New Year's party Tony threw at his house a few years ago.

'Bry, you got to call me when you get this message buddy. Serena didn't mean what she said to you. I am not and have never been interested in Yolanda. I wouldn't do that to you man. We're like brothers. You know how drunk and suspicious she gets all the time.'

"Tony what is all that about?" Valerie said breaking her silence.

"I don't know," Tony, said stumped himself.

"Well did Bryan ever mention that Steve's wife thought he had a thing for Yolanda?"

"Naw, this is the first time I'm hearing about it. But I tell you what, it doesn't look like Serena was far off the mark, does it?"

He didn't say anything else as she shook her head, he just went back to the active voicemails.

The voicemail he is about to listen to was in the same week of the murder; Wednesday.

'I don't know if you heard but there was another break-in right near your townhouse. Maybe you should start coming by more often at night and checking the place out before you settle in, especially on the weekend. Things look like they're getting serious. I can come by and we can ride together sometime if you want.'

Tony pause before he played the last voice message. This was the night. The message was, left earlier at 9:36 PM. His thoughts were running around in his head and they weren't good thoughts.

Something ain't right about all this looking back on it.

The missing pieces are adding up.

He pushed the message.

'Hey man I'm calling to see if you put your alarm on at the townhouse. I got word that Carl's been in your backyard probably peeping in your windows. Just want to let you know. I tell you what I'll meet you over there. I'm leaving now.'

Bryan listened to, this message Tony thought. Instantly Tony went to the text messages because he remembered seeing something before he went to the voicemail.

10:05 PM can't make it man, somethin' up

"That muthafucka's dead. I'mma see to that shit," Tony yelled out as he sprung up from the sofa and started pacing the floor like a maniac.

It's like an explosion to Valerie as she heard Tony cursing and yelling aloud at the top of his lungs. As many times, as they have gotten into it she has never heard him sound this angry. She didn't know what happened. What is going on? They were listening to the voicemails and as soon as he saw the text, he went ballistic.

"Tony you need to calm down. What's going on? What did you see?"

"It's that son-of-a-bitch, Steve Powers. He set Bryan up to go to that damn townhouse that night to kill him. Aww man I'm gonna kill that dude I ain't lying."

"Please calm down I don't understand what's happening, how do you know that?" she said frantically, trying to make sense of what Tony's talking about.

"Valerie it was him. Carl said that he was supposed to break a window and roll out. Then somebody else texted him and told him to go into the townhouse and rough up Bryan. Steve, that's who, he knew that Carl would kill Bryan. He had to know. That nigga wanted Yolanda and that property."

"What are you saying? Why he would do something like that? I mean people do stuff like that but Steve, I can't believe it?"

"He's with Yolanda now isn't that enough proof? I'm going over his house right now."

Tony walked off from Valerie grabbing his keys from their usual spot on the foyer table that stood there. Then he headed to the kitchen, into the mudroom towards the garage door. Valerie followed close behind him.

"No Tony you can't do this. You're going to get yourself in trouble. You already know that Steve doesn't like you and this will give him a reason to get you locked up."

"I don't give a fuck that nigga's mine. Ain't nobody gonna fuck with my family like that."

"Tony no, what, this is crazy."

"Valerie take yo' ass back in the house now."

She stopped and stood transfixed as he opened the garage. Normally she would protest because he doesn't talk to her like that and not get some shit back. This time however, she obeyed silently, in fear that if she said anything else he would get even angrier than he is already. Once he passed through the entry door, he hit the panel for the outer garage door to go up. He jumped in his truck started the engine and tore out of the garage backing out to the street in one swift move. Then he sped out of the neighborhood.

Valerie closed the garage door crying uncontrollably. She has to do something. She ran to her cellphone and called the only person she knew that could get the help she needs. She pushed the call button.

"Dawn, I need Deron quick," she said hurriedly through the phone skipping the usual greetings.

"Val what's wrong you sound upset? I…," Dawn paused. "Deron, Val's on the phone come quick something's wrong," her voice could be heard away from the phone.

Seconds later Deron appeared on the phone.

"What's going on Val?"

"Tony is gone crazy," she said hysterically.

He could hear the panic in her voice. As much as he knows that Val has cried wolf before about Tony and her relationship, something is terribly wrong right now. He began to panic himself but he pushed those feeling back down to talk to her. Dawn looked on curiously as if she could read his expression. Deron pushed the speaker button so she could hear.

"…and it had something to do with the two of you going to Jessup to see Carl. He got Bryan's cellphone from Yolanda, heard some voice messages, read a text and went off. Deron I think he's gonna kill Steve if he gets to him."

"Where is he now?"

"On his way to Steve's house."

"Okay Val, I'm gonna call him to see if I can slow him down. Hold on…," he said as he passed the phone over to Dawn.

"Val I'm on my way over," Dawn said reassuringly.

Deron walked off hurriedly to his cellphone and retrieved it as he ran out the front door. His car is, parked in the driveway. He quickly got into it and drove off. Once he got on his way, he called Tony and the call connected to the Bluetooth in his car before Tony answered.

"What D," Tony said as he answered the call angrily.

"What's going on with you man?" he asked calmly.

"I know Valerie called you. I ain't got nothing to say. That nigga put a hit out on Bryan and I'm gonna hit his ass," he yelled as he ended the call.

"Tony man you…," Deron said to him as he noticed the call ended.

Tony must be blind mad because he don't usually just shut down like that unless he's ready to do what he sets out to do. He has to get through to him he thought.

He hit the call again and Tony answered.

"Tony what the hell are you doing, slow down man before the cops get to you," Deron yells through the cellphone. "The way cops be doing out here these days."

"D. stop calling me damn it, I'm gonna kill that dude. I never liked that son-of-a-bitch anyhow, now I know why."

"Come on T; let the police handle this, man pull over."

"Turn around man I know you coming this way don't you get involved in this."

"What's it going to solve. Let's get the police on this."

"I'm gonna feel better. I'ma avenge my dude."

"And what about Yolanda? She needs closure too. This is just going to take her to another level. What if you get locked up or worst? How do you think she's going to feel with all the men in her life leaving like that? She might self-destruct don't you care about that?"

"Damn it D you know I love Yolanda, that's my little sis. I promised Bryan at his grave that I'd look out for her and I ain't letting that slimy bastard get that man's wife."

"Then you got to lay low on that T. It has to be the right way. Let's talk this thing out. Don't let this be the last time I hear from you man. Let's handle this together."

"Man," Tony yelled as he lifted his foot off the gas pedal and eased off the road. "Yeah I'll meet you back at the spot."

CHAPTER 12

Later on that evening just before it got dark, Deron and Tony were back at Tony's house with Dawn and Valerie. Tony called Erica to come by so she could shed more light on what's going on or at least if he could tie Steve into all of this. Erica is in his home office surfing through the computer for information. Dawn, Deron and Valerie are talking amongst themselves. Tony paced his family room like he's waiting on the stock market results.

They all agreed that they wouldn't call Yolanda until everyone is on board to Tony's theories. That incensed him that they wouldn't take his word for it cause they take him as a hothead. He knows shit because he goes off his instincts. He never liked Steve Powers because always thought of him as a fake friend to Bryan. Bryan couldn't see it because he was always too loyal to a fault. But when a nigga you done known since you were a teenager start acting funny around you it's time to wake the fuck up. Steve wanted Yolanda and got Bryan out of the way, nah, maybe a little but what he wants the most is that townhouse. He already has a townhouse in that neighborhood and getting Bryan's ain't nothing to kill somebody over. There must be something else to gain.

Erica said that there's a company trying to buy up all the townhouses in that neighborhood. That's a big thing. Well okay his townhouse and Bryan's it might be worth something to whoever's trying to buy the whole neighborhood. So a builder is trying to get all that land. Probably to knock the townhouses down to build something else there. It's not that much land and the area isn't enough for commercial; so more houses have to go there. That neighborhood is older and the surrounding areas are as well. Not much is going on around there and that's why it was so easy for Carl to run it down.

"I got it Tony," Erica said emerging out of the office and appearing like lightning in the family room. "This is what's going on. A large land project's going into effect in the next year or so. It's been held up due to some financial problems but it seems to be moving steady now. A large amount of houses, townhomes and condominiums are to be, built on thousands of acres of land. This is big time. Bryan's old neighborhood is part of the land that's being brought by a large builder. There's a company and it's like the mother company of a bunch of subsidiary ones about five companies. These companies have been busy buying up a lot of the adjoining property to your buddy's neighborhood. But I don't see where they get all this money from."

"What do you mean?" Tony asked.

"You remember when I told you about that company that's buying up all those townhouses. Well this one is one of the masters. But their income is not like that to be going top buyer and yes I finally found your boy Steve Powers listed as one of the owners. It's all in the courthouse records if you dig deep enough. He used the name Steven L. Powwe, P-o-w-w-e. I thought the name was too close to be a coincidence so I ran his credit because *I* can and found out that he uses that name often," she said boldly.

"That's it y'all," Tony declared almost thrusting out his chest to pump it up. "There it is the reason why Steve Powers had Bryan killed. His goal is to get that whole neighborhood and wants Yolanda too. We gotta go tell her."

"He knew that Bryan wouldn't stop fighting for that neighborhood and time was running out," Deron agreed and added. "Just like Carl said he was only supposed to break a window. Steve was the one that texted him to go further. It's obvious. He knew they would get into a fight."

"Now you on it D. Let go we got to get to Yolanda and I swear if he's there that's it."

"That's a big stretch isn't it Tony," Erica asked.

"Well I'm adding in those good faith papers that Val found," he said. "That proves he wants that property. I know it's gonna take a little push to get Yolanda to see but she's gonna see it if we got to stay over there all night, let's go y'all."

Everyone got up and started out the room to the door.

"Tony, if you want I can stay and get this stuff printed," Erica said. "I'm sure you're going to need all this evidence laid out neatly."

"Okay E," he said, then pulled his keys out and separated a few from the ring. "I'm going to leave you these spare keys just in case you need to step out. If you leave before we get back, you can leave the keys on the foyer stand right here."

He dropped the spared keys on a desk in the foyer that stood evenly against the wall beneath the stairway and headed out the door. By now, Deron and Dawn were out the door but Valerie waited for Tony.

She stared at him and he noticed her.

"What?" he asked.

She just shook her head and walked out the door in front of him. How close is he actually with Erica? It was bad enough sitting there while the two of them played *Law & Order* detectives; with all the sexual tension to boot. Things like this really makes her glad that she set a date with Nathan. It's time that she explores other opportunities because Tony is just not serious. The engagement ring he gave her is just a formality to shut her up; she knows that now.

So what's keeping her with him she asked in her mind?

As she got into the front seat of his truck, she couldn't answer that question as hard as she tried.

****

The drive over to Yolanda's house didn't take but ten minutes. That's the beauty of how they all planned to live around each other when they moved into their homes. Well they moved around Tony. Deron isn't too far away as well. They would just keep on with their lives, watching their kids grow and in Tony's case have brothers he never had growing up. Didn't see Bryan's death coming damn it he thought. He misses the man that has become his brother more than he could ever let on and he'll be damn if he lets anything happened to his little sis. His own sister and he were never that close because his parents weren't close to each other. They didn't teach that. The four of them, his father, mother, sister and him learned how to be intelligent drones living in their middle class home, with nothing but ambition to live with. He made it too and he's a success. He's only scratched the surface of what he can do and these chumps better watch out. But his success ain't what it used to be because his boys aren't where they should be, by his side.

He felt his phone vibrate against him interrupting his thoughts. He waited for the phone to stop vibrating before he acknowledged the phone. He looked down at the new smart watch he just got. He saw the text and the missed call is from Sharnia. Here she is again bugging him and he's got shit to do. He'll call her later and set something up.

He feels like some rough action tonight.

They all got out of the vehicles that they were riding in and walked hesitantly to the front door of Yolanda house. Deron rang the doorbell and they all waited patiently for Yolanda to come to it. Deron noticed how Tony, Valerie and even Dawn slowed down as they approached the door so that he would be the first one to it. It's just how it is all the time; they always get him to be the responsible one. The one to always either fix what's going on or share the bad news. In this case it, may be both that he will be accomplishing this time. At least he won't have to calm Tony down because Steve's car is not here which means neither is he Deron thought.

As the door opened all of them were surprised to see one of Yolanda's sisters, Sherry. She's the one that stayed with Yolanda after Bryan was laid to rest. She held little Bryan in her arms as she stood behind the storm door.

The looked on her face worried Deron for some reason and he couldn't explain why. She opened the storm door.

"Hey Sherry how are you it's been a while?"

"Deron, how are you? Hey everybody," she said looking past Deron and to the rest of them. "If you're here to see Yolanda she's not here."

"Oh. Well can we wait for her because this is kind of important?"

"She's gone out of town and I don't know when she'll be back."

"What, where did she go? Is there something wrong?"

"You all come in," she said and led the way to the family room.

Everybody piled in as quickly as they could. They're wondering where Yolanda would go all of a sudden and not take Bryan. Dawn knows that she wouldn't have gone out of town without saying something to Val or her; so something's odd.

"Sherry what's going on? Where's Yolanda?" Deron asked her almost demanding an answer.

"Las Vegas," she said shaking her head in protest.

****

Yolanda and Steve settled back in their seats as they watched the rest of the people board the plane. Yolanda's happy but she's very nervous at the same time. It's not every day that a woman makes a heavy decision like this but this is how it should be this time around, spontaneous.

She's going to marry Steve Powers.

There is no sex involved. She had to see if he wanted her for love and not because she's a lonely widow. Not because he thinks that, she needs the touch of a man. This really looks like the real thing and of course, she will always love Bryan Prescott. But it's time to move on.

"You are more beautiful to me now that you've said yes to me than ever," Steve said breaking the silence gazing longingly into her eyes. "I won't be able to keep my hands off of you."

"Steve," is all that she could say.

What's wrong she thought?

It is his way to compliment her.

Why is she trying to make this difficult?

Maybe she's not ready to get married to him right now. It *is* kind of quick. They really only officially started dating about three months ago and now she's ready to marry this man. But she knows him and they've been talking on and off since some time after Bryan's death. She feels this is the right choice and *it is* really time to move on.

"Hold that thought Yolanda I'm going to go to the restroom and then we can pick right back up to where we were," he said getting out of his seat and walking off towards the back.

Finding one of the restrooms Steve walked in the small space and closed the door. Instantly he reached to his side, grabbed his cellphone, and activated a call.

"Yeah it's me…no the plane hasn't taken off yet there's a delay. Are you ready cause I ain't coming down there to go to jail. We need this to be as smooth as possible and not make it look like it was planned…. yeah she's cool, she's a little nervous but that's regular. There's no way she suspects that she won't be coming back to Maryland alive…"

****

"And who are you again," Erica asked as she opened the door to Tony's house even wider to hear what the woman is saying. She stood in the middle of the doorframe blocking the woman's advance.

"I'm his girlfriend, Sharnia Burkefield and who are you?"

Someone who is not Tony. You're not saying what you want, girlfriend."

"Who are you," Sharnia asked again.

"Girl, what do you want?" Erica asked impatiently.

This scatterbrain white chick is probably one of those random thots Tony seems to order as if he's ordering takeout. She has the nerve to come to this man's house knowing he has a woman and say that she's his girlfriend. This one's off the rocker. It's incredible how Valerie puts up with that shit Tony does she thought. That's why she hit it and quit it because she knows Tony is as dirty as they come. He makes a hell of a good ass friend and business partner but that's where it ends.

But this thot is not going to get on her nerves.

"Tony's maid," she said the maid part under her breath. "If he's busy…"

"Tony's not here but if you like I can give him the message that you stopped by, alright, thanks bye," she wasn't sure but she thought she heard her call her a maid.

No this thot didn't, she thought as she looked her. She had better be glad she's busy.

She started closing the door.

"Is Val here?" she asked as she stuck her hand out to block the door, looking pass Erica into the foyer.

"Excuse me, no," Erica, continued closing the door.

"Are you his sister or something?" Sharnia said beginning to get agitated.

"I'm a friend," she said in response smugly. "Well thanks for stopping by. I'll be sure to tell Tony and Val that you stopped by," she said again.

"Well can I used the powder room?"

"Huh. I don't know, um."

"It's not like I haven't been in there before. Its right there to the right am I correct?"

"Yeah. Well alright but I was sort of doing something when you came by so can you hurry up," she said as she backed out of the way to let Sharnia in.

Once Sharnia is through the door threshold, she went straight for the powder room like she said. Erica sat down on the stairs and waited until she finishes. She just shook her head because it's pathetic how this chick is so press to get into Tony's house like she thought he's hiding in the powder room. She'd better not try to go anywhere else or when Tony gets back here, he's going to see a crime scene. Bad enough she's bold enough to want to be lurking around and she probably knows that Valerie lives with him. She's trying to be cute with her wannabe coco tan. Pushy white chicks she thought as she shook her head again.

Who does she think she is Amber Rose?

Sharnia emerged from the powder room and looked into the rest of the house as she walked towards the door. She made sure that, she made a wide turn as she walked. Looking around she bumped into the table stand that sat against the foyer wall. The table responded and rocked a bit causing the lamp that sat on it to tip over. She caught the lamp that sat on it before it hit the floor.

"That wouldn't have happened if you were watching where you were going. I told you that Tony isn't here. Now it's time for you to leave," Erica said getting up off the stairs thanking God she didn't break that lamp.

If she had broken that lamp, Valerie would be all over Tony about it. She already noticed how Valerie looked at Tony when he agreed that she could stay at the house alone and print out the paper work. Hell, what do Val think is going to happen, that she's going to run around the house naked or rob Tony? That's another one that don't know when to roll the hell out when a man ain't about them. If Erica wanted to she could have Tony in a minute but she likes the way they are now, friends. There's not going to be no friends with benefits crap going on around here. So the uppity broad can relax and really so can this desperate thot.

"I'm going but Tony really needs to get better maids around this house. Not only are you not cleaning bathrooms right you're rude as hell," Sharnia laughed as she walked out the door giving Erica the finger.

"Bitch," Erica said to her as she closed the door.

Who the hell is she calling a maid? She must think because she's leaving that she can't get her ass whipped, but she can.

Don't let this fine businesswoman fool her ass.

She went to go back into the office. Then she stopped in her tracks and thought about it. She thought about what Sharnia said. She walked to the powder room and opened the door. That nasty hoe, she thought as she looked on the floor and there's urine all over the ceramic tile floor. Oh the next time she sees her she's going to slam dunk her ass because now she has to clean this up.

It's all she needs is for Val to see this.

****

"So she went to Las Vegas just like that?" Deron said to Sherry.

"I wasn't here when she left. Trina was here and she said that Yolanda and her got into it."

"About what?" Valerie asked.

"Steve asked her to go away with him and Yolanda called Trina to stay with Bryan. Trina didn't know she was going out of town. When she got here Yolanda told her that Steve asked her to marry him and that they were going to Las Vegas to do it. Well, all kinds of questions started coming out of Trina's mouth. You know out of all us sisters Trina is the most outspoken. So she asked Yolanda if she's pregnant and so one thing lead to another. I ended up coming over. Trina said that Yolanda didn't seem like herself, like he is controlling her. But when I spoke to

Yolanda she had a totally different story. She said they'll be back in two day."

"Sherry we got to call Yolanda," Tony said. "She can't marry Steve Powers because he ain't right. I can't tell you now but we got to stop them."

"They're already in the air. She won't get in touch with me until the land and get settled in. I understand why she seems like she's rushing because if anybody knows I know how many nights she laid awake crying through the night trying to get herself together. It took almost a year and Steve has always been around trying to lift up her spirits. So I can see why she feels like she wants to marry him."

"Trust us Sherry," Dawn said seriously. "Steve is a snake and Yolanda is in danger."

"What do mean?" Sherry said panicking.

"Valerie, you and Dawn talk to Sherry," Tony said. "Deron this is what we got to do. We got to get on a plane to Las Vegas right now. Let's book us some flights," he finished.

The two of them walked away from the women.

Moving away from Valerie will give him a chance to call Sharnia and shout out to Phaedra.

****

Hours later Tony, Valerie, Deron and Dawn are on a flight to Las Vegas. They were about an hour behind Yolanda and Steve on their flight according to the ticket agent. The trip through the airport terminal was a piece of cake because they didn't have any luggage. They also were flying nonstop which cut their time down. No one is really saying anything and Tony is asleep. Valerie sat back in the seat beside him thinking Dawn and her should have watched out for Yolanda a little more. Really, it's Dawn's fault she thought and she's not willing to take responsibility for it. All this time she was trying to get Yolanda to talk about her relationship with Steve because it didn't seem right that she is moving so fast; but no Dawn wanted to mind her own business. She has to realize that she doesn't know everything and that she's not always right.

"Do you think that Steve will hurt Yolanda?" Dawn asked Deron as they sat together in their adjoining seat.

"I don't know what I want to think," he answered. "This guy if we're to go with our theory is desperate for money, blood money."

"So you don't believe that he's responsible for Bryan's death?"

"I do. Tony showed me the texts. It appears that he set Bry up to be murdered and especially what Carl said. I keep going back to that. He sounded like he has made peace with God because he didn't have to tell us anything. It wasn't the same Carl that was at the trial."

"I remember how he was, evil."

"I have to go with what Tony thinks. It pieces together. So to answer your question, yes I do think Yolanda's in danger."

****

In Las Vegas with the 3-hour time difference, it's about dusk. Yolanda and Steve enter into the lobby of the hotel Steve chose. They decided to get a bite to eat before they went to the rooms he booked. He knew that Yolanda would give him the blues about spending the night together in one room so he avoided it; plus, giving himself more gentlemen points.

It won't be long before they're husband and wife anyway. It's only a few more hours before daybreak and they're going to the wedding minister. Once they finish at the minister he will take her back to the hotel and make love to her. Then he's going to asked Yolanda to take a drive to the outskirts of the Las Vegas strip. There Jerrell will be waiting at dusk to shoot her as they come out of some out of the way restaurant; an attempted robbery. Unfortunately, Jerrell and him changed the plans to this. They need fast money and being her beneficiary will get it.

He owes it to himself to sleep with her first for all that hard work he put in to get with her. It's a wonder he could put up with her 1990's thinking. Nobody's waiting these days to give up those panties. He should've taken it on their first date. No matter, now that she has signed the papers to sell her property and he was able to transfer her signature over on all the necessary paperwork; a new husband and wife would fill out together. He's got it. Not only the townhouse but the house she lives in now and all the bank accounts. Then she can join her weak-minded husband in the grave and he can enjoy the rest of his life. The kid can go live with her people.

"I need to call home to check on Bryan Jr," Yolanda said at the dinner table.

"Didn't we agree that the phones were to be used after we finish with ceremony?" Steve smiled as he asked her. "Beside nobody called check your phone."

She checked her phone and saw that nobody called.

"No, no one did."

Of course she's not going to get any calls he thought smirking to himself. Not when your phone's been set to airplane mode. He took the liberty of doing that when she left her phone with him on the plane and went to the restroom. She's so trusting she don't even have a passcode lock on her phone. How stupid can you be in this day and age to have a smartphone and not lock it?

****

After he saw Yolanda to her room, Steve went back to his and entered the room. When he walked in, his business partner in crime *sort to speak* Jerrell is there sitting in one of the two wing chairs near the window watching TV.

"Everything's okay Steve," Jerrell asked.

"Yeah I got it."

"Good we don't want to mess this one up like Bryan. Shit we'd better be glad that Carl took that hit or we'd be out of business. Don't lose your cool and make any changes to our plan unless you check with me. This has got to be clean."

It is man," Steve said plopping down across his bed agitated by Jerrell's constant checking.

Their plan this time only involves just the two of them. That alone will make this job easy. But this time it's different. He's never been involved this directly in something like this. Jerrell on the other hand was involved in three murders when he was just a teenager. It was a drug run gone bad and one of the customers was shot their boys came after Jerrell and he was lucky to get the drop on them first. He never served no time either. So he's happy to take care of Yolanda, but he says it's not for fun; this is business.

They need that property, all the properties in that neighborhood and more money.

"Alright then, I'm going to my room," he said as he got up and walked to the door. "I don't want nobody to see us together."

****

The next day after waking up in the hotel, they checked into the night before Deron and Dawn got ready to meet Tony and Val down in the hotel lobby. They didn't know what hotel Yolanda is staying at so Dawn tried all night long to reach Yolanda. Her phone kept going to voicemail like her phone is off. Of course, that upset her and Deron spent most of the night trying to calm her down. Eventually she must've been tired from the plane ride and fell off to sleep.

"How are we going to find Yolanda," Dawn asked Deron as they walked towards the elevator.

"I don't know," Deron, said shaking his head. "Hopefully God will give us the break we need. We should pray."

****

It didn't seem right to Yolanda as she looked at her phone. No one has called her all night and her phone is on. She should've tried to call Sherry and let her know that she touched down safely yesterday.

She picked up her cell phone to make the call and pressed her sister's cellphone number. A message box popped up. 'You must disable airplane mode to place a call' is what it displayed. Wow, she thought no wonder she isn't getting any calls. Airplane mode shuts the cellular connections down. When did, she chose that or did she select it unconsciously? Well it doesn't matter. She turned off airplane mode and made her call.

"Yolanda where have you been?" Sherry said excitedly as she answered the line. "I've been trying to call you."

Yolanda heard and felt the vibrations as her phone begin to receive all of the communications that started to download into her phone.

"My phone was turn to airplane mode. It must've happen automatically. What's going on is Bryan okay?"

"Oh yeah girl it's not that. Dawn, Valerie, Deron and Tony are looking for you. They say there's something wrong with Steve, but they wouldn't say what it was. They say he's dangerous and that you may be in danger."

"Huh? What are you talking about?"

"They're down there with you in Las Vegas right now trying to find you."

"What?" she said as she stared at her phone screen and saw Dawn's text message.

"They're down there looking for you."

"Oh okay Sherry. Look I'll call you back. Let me find out what's happening. Tell my little one I'll see him soon and I love him. Love you, girl bye," she said ending the call.

Instantly she went into the message area and read Dawn's text.

Where are you, girl? We're here in LV
looking for you. It's an emergency.

What is it she thought? Sherry said something about
Steve being dangerous. What is Val and Dawn doing now?
She shouldn't call them until after the wedding and that
way whatever they say won't matter either way; not that it
is going to matter anyway. Val has finally convinced Dawn
that Steve's the devil huh?

But she couldn't help but noticed that they've traveled
this far this quick. They have to be literally two hours
behind her. Not only is there this text but several more from
her and voicemails. Something has happened to get Dawn
and Deron to come to Las Vegas this frantic. Tony and Val
well they're predictable anyway, that's to be expected.

For about a minute Yolanda agonized over whether to
call Dawn or not. She did text that it is an emergency. She
has to trust in their friendship that it is what she says. She
pressed the Dawn's name on the recent calls list.

****

"Guys it's Yolanda," Dawn said excitedly as she looked
at her ringing phone. Dawn put the call on speakerphone.

Everyone gathered around her but Tony. His phone rung
as well and looking at his watch he saw that it's Sharnia
again. He decided that he's gonna to take the call so he hit
his Bluetooth and walked away. Valerie noticed his actions
but she didn't want to say anything that might avert
everyone's attention from Yolanda. As much as Tony is
going on about getting Yolanda to safety and 'f'ing up
Steve you would think he'd be right on this call too she
thought. Instead, he's going off to answer a call from one
of his thots.

"Yolanda where are you? We need to see you as soon as
possible. Where's Steve, is he there with you?"

"Dawn slow down, hello to you. I'm fine. What are you guys doing down here?" Yolanda asked her calmly.

"Is Steve there? What hotel are you at?"

"Dawn what's happening, now you're scaring me?"

"Oh Yolanda please get away from him as fast as you can. He had Bryan killed," Dawn said quickly and wished she hadn't.

Something like this should be, told to the person face to face, but Dawn got so excited that she panic.

"What are you saying?"

"It's true Yolanda."

"Why would you say something like that Dawn? I love Steve and I can't believe that you and the others are being this cruel. I...," she stopped talking and started to cry.

"You know I would never lie to you or purposely try to hurt you. Tell us where you are, Steve Powers is working with some guy to buy property in your old neighborhood where the townhouse is; some land deal. Didn't he try several times to buy the townhouse from you? You signed some documents recently, good faith seller/buyer agreement with him but what you actually did was give him your signature on a blank beneficiary deed. With that, he can claim your properties if something happens to you. Erica, Tony's friend has been digging up a lot of information that ties him to all of this. Please Yolanda let me know where you are. I need to tell it all to you."

"Dawn it doesn't make sense," she cried.

But Yolanda knows that some of what Dawn is saying has some merit and she knows that her friend would never deceive her.

CHAPTER 13

"No Dawn tell me now. I want to know all of it now."
An hour passed and Yolanda hurried around her hotel room
picking up her things and crying uncontrollably. She
shoved everything into her small luggage tote bag. Instead
of Dawn, Tony told her the story and now she knows the
truth. Steve Powers is a monster. He's planning something,
maybe to kill her. He's so adamant about taking that drive
to have dinner at this out of the way place outside the Las
Vegas strip. Because of that she knows that what Tony is
saying is the truth. She was about to make a mistake that
was going to cost her life. It's a good thing that her friends
are here to stop her.

They are on their way to pick her up from the hotel.

Her thoughts are interrupted when she heard the knock
on her door.

She didn't answer the door immediately.

She just looked at the door.

"Yolanda it's me Steve," his voice barely heard through
the door. "Are you up? It's time for the big day. I thought
we'd get some breakfast. Come on open the door."

The sound of his voice activated some sort of panic in
her mind like two icy hands choking her throat; cutting off
her breath. She couldn't have known that she's going to
feel this way at the sound of his voice. There's a rage that
started to build up in her that wants to confront him but she
knows if she opens that door and do that it could trigger
him violently. Even though Tony says that, he's a spineless
punk those types of people are unpredictable and could be
dangerous. He could lose it and try to kill her here.

"Go away Steve," she said nervously.

"What are you talking about?"

"I'm…I'm not marrying you," she said trying to remain
calm. "I've changed my mind," she said simply.

"Why baby?" he said again quietly knocking on the door. "Let me in so we can talk."

"Leave me alone Steve. I know everything go away before I call the police."

On the other side of the door, Steve paused.

What is it that she knows?

Does she really know *everything*?

He has to get in there to talk to her; if not she'll ruin the plan. He at least has to get her out of this hotel to marry her. If he doesn't this won't work.

"Okay obviously something's going on that I don't know about but we can work this out. I'll be back in a few."

Steve left the door. He decided he is going to go down to the front desk and get another keycard. He'll just walk in her room and find out what's going on so he won't draw any attention.

****

Five minutes later Yolanda opened the door to her room. She took the chance to be exposed because he could've been waiting for her to open it to grab her. When she saw the way is clear she bolted down the hallway to the stairs and ran down the steps.

At the bottom of the stairs, it cut off into two directions. One of the directions is through an alarmed door no doubt to the underground parking area. The other is an unalarmed to the lobby and that's the direction she headed to. She didn't want to miss the others when they come for her. She exited the stairwell and into the large fancy lobby. It appeared humongous to her this time because she didn't know where Steve could be. Also it's his partner that she feared; the one Tony talked about. She doesn't know what he looks. It confused her where she should go because she didn't want to run into Steve or the other guy.

Almost instantly, she spotted Steve at the front desk waiting for the woman that's speaking to guest services to finish. He isn't looking around probably arrogantly thinking that she's going to be that stupid to stay in her room and wait for him.

All she needs to do is slip pass him and duck into the dining room where she told Tony she would meet them. She started to walk towards her goal. It would only take a few seconds and she would be free. Still it didn't matter because she could always just start screaming in the middle of the lobby; if he threatened her. As she came up on him and walked passed, she swore her heart stopped.

"Yolanda wait," Steve called out to her.

It isn't like she imagined it would be, she's scared; too scared to scream. He's going to get her because she's too scared to scream. She looked back in his direction and saw him coming towards her. She turned towards the dining room, which is near the entrance and she felt herself moving but she felt faint, like she's going to pass out.

"Yolanda wait," he said catching up with her and as he grabbed her arm roughly; but he smiled. "Why did you run off like that?"

"Let go of me Steve. Let go of my arm."

Instead of obeying her order, he grabbed hold even tighter and began to pull her the opposite direction towards the elevator. People noticed but it appeared to them as if she isn't feeling well and that he's helping her.

He whispered in her ear.

"I have the keycard let go up and celebrate a little pre-marriage loving before the ceremony."

He held her tight.

She couldn't scream and she couldn't move.

Even though she wanted to, she couldn't do what she knows a woman in danger should do.

Then she saw Dawn and then Val, then Deron and finally Tony coming through the revolving doors. Simultaneously Steve saw them too and let go of Yolanda's arm. Once Tony got through the revolving door behind

Deron, they both began charging towards him through the large lobby and the large crowd. Steve shot off through the crowds of people that just happened to begin gathering that instance at the front desk to; check in or out the hotel. Deron and Tony stopped pursuing him, as he got lost into the crowds. Their focus turned to Yolanda who by this time is standing in between Dawn and Valerie as they held her tightly. They seemed to be holding her up and she relaxed in their combined embrace.

She just cried and cried.

****

A few minutes later outside the hotel in his car, Steve sat talking on the phone.

"I said we have got to get the hell out of here man before the police gets involved. Tony and Deron came charging at me like they wanted to kill me," he said nervously. "Yeah they're here. We need to get back to Maryland and lay low."

****

Just after the sun went down the girls and the guys arrived back to Maryland and split up. Yolanda, Dawn and Valerie went to Yolanda's house and Deron and Tony went to Deron's mother's house to drop off something for Deron Jr. Tony wanted to go wait at Steve's house for him to get home but Deron reminded him of what Yolanda requested. She simply asked them both not to get involved. She's going to handle it when she feels she's able to. She wants to talk to her cousin that's on the PG County police force first. That didn't sit well with Tony but he complied. He didn't want to upset her any further than she was already.

The girls settled down in the family room with Yolanda who is still visible upset. She is so out of it all she did is cry the whole time on the plane. To her this is like killing Bryan all over again. To, finally face the man that actually killed her husband, the real killer and it be a man that supposed to be his friend. When Tony explained the entire story to her, it reminded her of a Lifetime movie. Steve liked her all along and his wife knew about it, but Bryan never mention it. However, she did remember him asking her if he ever said anything out of the way to her. She thought he was talking about being rude because that's what people say Steve's known for; being snobbish and rude. Besides, he seemed to change around her and now she knows that it was all nothing but an act to get in good with her. Then he planned to marry her and kill her to get her property and her money to be killed for. It didn't make any sense. It's not a lot of money. He lured Bryan that night to the townhouse so Carl could kill him. This land deal must be a huge development.

She laid her head down on the arm of the sofa and snuggled as close to the cushions as she could and watched her son who laid sleeping near the opposite end of the sofa in a small playpen.

She's exhausted but at least now she can really start back healing.

Dawn walked over to her and placed the blanket that sat on the large wing chair nearby on Yolanda.

"You go on and rest as long as you want. We'll look after Bryan."

Yolanda just nodded in response to her without looking at her or opening her eyes.

It didn't take Yolanda long to fall off to sleep. The girls decided that they would go sit in the adjoining sitting room so they could talk but still keep an eye out on Bryan.

They sat down on the small sofa that along with one chair stood in that room.

"I have to say Val," Dawn silently. "You really out did yourself on this," she said smiling to her. "I really do apologize for shooting your concerns down in regards to Steve. I just didn't want to believe that he could be anything less than what Yolanda wanted him to be. I guess I was so caught up more with her moving on that I didn't see the flags he was sending her. I'm also sorry about anything I said about Tony…"

"No," Val said politely. "You didn't say anything that wasn't a true factor. You are absolutely, right. I have to value my own self-worth. That's what you said in a nutshell. Dawn I appreciate you, I really do. You're a great friend to me and to Yolanda. I'm not the easiest person to get through to and I'm glad you stuck by my side. I can't say that I'm jealous that you have such a great husband in Deron but I do see what I don't have in Tony. I'm frustrated and I believe I want to get married so badly to him to win the prize. But my own self-worth is what I have to focus on and everything else is going to fall into place," she said as a tear fell from her eyes.

"Well like you said we're great friends," Dawn said and hugged her. "I'll always be here if you need me."

****

Sharnia drove her car boldly into Tony's neighborhood and parked her car on the street in front of his house. She's tired of getting the short end of this stick. Why won't he pay any attention to her? He just told her over the phone that he's not with Valerie anymore but that rude woman that answered the door acted like Valerie still lives there.

Sharnia got out of her car and walked steadily to the front door as if she expected someone to be there. She already knows that Tony's not there and now she suspects that Valerie is with him.

He's a lair.

He's using her she thought.

Things will never change.

No matter how much she sleeps with him and how good she is to him, he always seems to choose someone else.

He always wants more.

They're going get this solved tonight, she can't keep going on like this; back and forth. But one thing is that, she's going to see for herself whether Valerie lives there or not.

At the front door, Sharnia reached into her tight blue jeans and produced a key from her front pocket. It is the key that Tony had sitting on the foyer table for Erica. She made that move seem like she's a secret agent. The way she managed to knock that lamp over distracting that stupid chick is priceless. She simply scooped the keys off in the fall. Now she has access to Tony's whenever she want's and that's going to come in handy.

Once she goes inside, she went straight to the basement. She went into the utility room and walked around searching for something. This room Tony uses as storage and it has all the utility and operating systems in the room as well. Sharnia walked over to something in the corner and turned the handle to the opposite direction. Please with what she's done she went back upstairs to the first level.

She went back outside through the front door to her car. She reached in and pulled out an overnight bag from the backseat. As she went back inside, she saw Marietta on the side of her house standing in the diming light. What's with that crazy chick she thought? There's no way she's ever doing another repeat performance of what went down a few months ago. Tony caught her off guard that night and she didn't want to rock the boat but if that woman ever comes within a foot of her again she's going to need a doctor.

Marietta waved to Sharnia. She just waved back slightly and went into Tony's house shutting the door.

Up the stairs, she went swinging her overnight bag like she's shopping at the mall.

She walked towards Tony's room and went in.

Inside Tony's master bedroom she looked around for any signs of Valerie, there is none. There are no bottles of perfume, no female lotions, nothing that even hint that a female was ever here. Happy with that she put her large bag down and pulled some garments from it; something she got from Victoria's Secret. She took off her jeans and the thin shirt she had on. Then she started to put on the Victoria's Secret Chantilly lace teddy. She brought this one especially for Tony because she knows he'll like to see her in this. He always likes to see her in Victoria's sexy lingerie and usually he rips them from her body after he had sex with her so he could have sex with her again naked.

She loves that about Tony.

Feeling herself getting excited, she walked over to the mini liquor bar that Tony has in his room and pull out the bottle of Patron that is chilling in the mini refrigerator. She poured a drink into one of the glasses that Tony keeps on top of the mini liquor bar. She brought it to her lips and closed her eyes. Opening her eyes, she instantly thought about music, walked over to the Bose system on the wall and turned it on. Sexy thug music filled the air. She got on Tony's bed and started to gyrate imagining he is there with her.

Lying there, she worked herself up and felt that wasn't satisfaction enough. She got up off the bed and went to the smallest closet in the bedroom. The one where he keeps all of the sex toy he likes to use on her and probably on Valerie too. She didn't want to think that but she knows they are having the same kinds of sex the two of them are, raunchy. But Tony likes vanilla not chocolate she can tell and he loves this vanilla she thought.

Opening the closet, she looked on the floor for the large box container that stores the toys. She looked up and she sees Valerie's clothes rows of them hanging in there. Then she sees female shoes. Then she sees a makeup case, perfume bottles, brushes, combs, lotions; all on the small counter to the left of the closet.

She lost it instantly and slammed the closet door shut, then ran back to the bag beside the bed. She reached into the bag again pulls out three candles. She brought them to use when Tony came home to make love to her. She began to place them around the bed, and then she lit them.

She went back to the bag and pulled out a can of lighter fluid that she started to squirt all around the room in the closets while she silently cursed Tony. Then she used the lighter that he has on his dresser, the fancy one he uses when he wants to smoke weed. She picked up each candle one by one and threw them in three corners of the room and the fire from the candles set the lighter fluid on fire. It became a chain reaction as the large bedroom slowly began to fill with a small fire and smoke.

Sharnia got back into the bed and laid down on the pillows. She watched the shadows of the flames dance on the ceiling.

****

Minutes later Tony pulled his Escalade truck onto his residential street. He is tired from the flight back from Las Vegas and didn't want to take any more time getting to his bed. The girls wanted to make sure that Yolanda is all right so they stayed with her. That is fine with him. Deron and he wanted to give them some time to themselves.

Once he turned the corner to his house, he noticed something funny.

"Damn D, look my house's on fire," he said hurriedly. "In my bedroom look at the big window, shit," Tony said speeding up his truck to get to his house.

Deron looked in the direction Tony indicated. There is indeed flickering fire light coming from that large window in Tony's bedroom. He got that window especially installed because he wants his house to be different from his neighbors. He wants house to be boss.

"Yeah I'll call the fire department," Deron said urgently.

On his cellphone, Deron waited for the call to 911 to connect. Tony parked the truck in front of his house in the street and saw Sharnia's car parked there. What the hell he thought? If she's here why isn't she out here or running down the street?

It took just a few seconds to realize that he'd better get into his house. Sharnia could be in there but how. He looked to his bedroom window again and the fire is building slowly.

Once Deron got off the phone, he heard the fire department sirens in the distant background. It's just as the 911 operator said that a call has already been placed for the address he's calling about. Deron didn't seem to notice Sharnia's car parked there, maybe he's distracted.

Not telling Deron about Sharnia, Tony ran into the house. Deron followed closely. The first thing they noticed was the sound of the fire alarm throughout the house. In the foyer, they saw the small amount of smoke flowing from the direction of the master bedroom. Faint visible smoke is everywhere on the first floor.

"Tony your sprinklers are not on," Deron said to him in a panic.

"Shit D I can't let that fire spread. I hear the fire department but the sprinklers should've came on by now."

"I'm going to the basement and take care of it. Do you have an extinguisher?"

"Yeah in the garage," Tony said running off to get it.

Deron ran down to the basement and went directly to the utility room. He knew just what to do because he remembers the diagram of instructions that he saw on Sharnia's computer.

Tony after grabbing the extinguisher shot upstairs to his bedroom to fight the fire. The house phones started to ring all around but he didn't stop to answer them. His cellphone rang next. He couldn't let all his shit get burned up as slamming as his bedroom is. Once he got to it, he stood to the side before he opened the door. He saw all those movies that when you open a door to a room or something, fire will explode on you in an instant. He touched the nob and it isn't hot, so he turned it and slightly jarred the door. Once back to the side of it again he back kicked it with his foot and the door flew open. No fire rushed out at him, which is a good sign.

He entered the room to assess the fire and found that it mostly gathered across the other side of the room near the big window. The desk that he has over there near the window is burning slowly. That's the reason why it seems like the whole room is on fire from the outside. He started over there with the fire extinguisher trying put out the fire as he back away from the window. It became too much. He then went to the other corner to try to put out that small fire.

Then Tony looked towards his bed and saw Sharnia laying on the bed. His heart dropped into his stomach and it isn't like he's panicking but seeing her on the bed, unconscious, probably dead; shocked him. The fire's out of control by now. He hoped the fire department hurried. All of a sudden, water started to flow from the sprinkler heads above him. He threw down the extinguisher and ran over to Sharnia.

"Sharnia," he said to her as he got a close up view of what she's wearing. What in the hell is she doing laying in lingerie? "Wake up," he yelled to her this time as he checked her neck to see if she has a pulse.

While he did that, he saw that her chest rose but her breaths are shallow. He picked her up off the bed and carried her through the showering water down the stairs as Deron came running up the stairs.

"Tony is that Sharnia?"

Before Tony could answer or even if he is going to answer the fire department charges through the open door. Deron motions the fire department towards the bedroom and Tony carries Sharnia outside to the ambulance.

CHAPTER 14

It is no way that Tony could hide the fire from Valerie and the next day she had many questions. He tried to give her a story that would register sanely in her mind but she is skeptical. Valerie is not stupid and Tony knows that for damn sure. As he went through his spiel Deron watched him as Dawn sat by him closely at their home. Tony stayed the night with them due to the smoke in his house. He'll probably be there for a bit until his house is restored.

Nobody went to work today and of course, Tony's still off.

Tony continued with his story of how the fire must have been smothering since they left overnight to go to Las Vegas. It is the dumbest thing that Deron has heard in a long time but he sat there quiet. Tony said that the fire department thinks that it took twenty-four hours or more for the fire to, finally take life. To make matters worse he added is that when the fire went full blast the sprinkler system malfunctioned and didn't activate to put out the fire at first. If it wasn't for the fact that the fire department arrived on the scene just at the right time his house would've burned down.

Deron couldn't believe that Tony has the nerve to tell that story. He knows that Deron ended up going down in the basement and turning the main water valve back on. It was, turned off manually. That's something Sharnia had done and why she was looking up how to disable sprinkler systems in house. She planned to set fire to Tony's house and possible die in the fire herself. What would make her do that? Although T has said he's not messing with her Deron knew all along that they are hot and heavy. Even last night Tony wouldn't admit why Sharnia happened to be at his house so Deron left it alone. He only asked him once and he said nothing. He's not going to pry in T's affairs because he has his own troubles.

The next custody hearing for DJ is in a few days and he can't imagine what new shenanigans Cheresse has planned for him. Anyone with any insight can clearly see that this custody battle is not about Audrey and Deron it's about Cheresse's revenge on Deron. He tried to get the mediator not to allow Cheresse to be a part of the case because they had a prior relationship. But the judge decided that it would violate Audrey's rights to choose her own representation.

She says that Cheresse is a part of her legal team.

What about his rights not to, be harass by his crazy ex-girlfriend?

Cheresse is smart.

She waited just over a year and a half, which is roughly the length of the restraining order. When that ran out here, she is again. This time with a force. Deron still can't get over how Audrey factors into this equation. What does Cheresse have over her that's making her do this? It has to be something because Audrey has never been afraid of her but it seems like she's not putting up no effort to be on Deron's side. Or could Audrey be doing this herself? She won't even return his calls. As good as he thought they are, he guesses they aren't. They could've worked this out by themselves and not have to go through this arbitration.

This court action is all Cheresse's idea, that's for sure.

He has to start seeing her for the enemy that she is and in God, he will see that his enemy becomes his footstool. He will bring peace to this conflict Deron is sure of it.

Finally, it appears as if Valerie is satisfied or has heard enough bull from Tony that she stood up. She decided that she's going to spend some time over at Yolanda's she thought. This will give her an opportunity to spend some time with Nathan. She needs a break from Tony and this is how she can get it without sending him in some other woman's bed. But it doesn't matter he'll take the downtime to do just that; that she knows. She can also keep an eye on Yolanda and make sure she's okay. She's just glad that she hadn't moved all her things into his house. All of her clothes would've been ruin like the ones in that closet.

****

"I just want to know why you would let a woman like that in my goddamn house Erica," Tony yelled into the phone.

It's the next day, Tuesday and Tony is up bright and early at his house with a crew of workers trying to clean up the mess the fire and the fire department made. He isn't going to wait for the insurance company to start repairs. He's going to pay for this shit himself. He's frustrated and he's taking his frustration out on Erica. He feels he has just cause. He trusted her and she just let this crazy thot walk into his house go upstairs and try to off herself in his bed. She probably wanted it to look like a cover up murder. Sharnia is a crazy ass bitch. It's a good thing they took her ass to the hospital and basically to the psyche floor.

At least all this came at a good time, at least work wise. He was due to go back to work but his supervisor called him and told him to remain off from work. It seems as if they're being audited at the corporate office branch where he works. His supervisor assured him that this is routine for their organization to do that. He said there's no need to come back and not be able to do anything. Since the audit is occurring, he won't have to do any of the telework; that has been recalled. So, basically Tony is beginning another month on free paid vacation.

"I didn't let your thot do anything but use the powder room. Then she took her nasty ass on her way. Oh yeah she's nasty peeing on the powder room floor. I don't know how she got in your house but it wasn't by me."

"She did that? Something ain't right. Did you leave a door unlocked or something?"

"No Tony damn it I told you, your house was locked tight when I left. I checked every door and I never had to use the keys you gave me because I never went outside."

"Keys. That reminds me can you come give me the keys?"

"I told you I didn't use the keys. It's on the foyer stand where you put it."

"It isn't."

"It is."

"Oh boy," he said blowing air out of his mouth. "Where did Sharnia go exactly when she came in here?"

"To the powder room and then the clumsy bitch almost turned over the stand in the foyer. She almost broke that lamp you got on it. I swear if she did that she would've gotten her ass beat because I don't need any drama with Val. She already don't like me and..."

"Erica," Tony yelled to get her attention. She is just going on and on talking. "Sharnia took those keys. She's sneaky as hell. That's how she got back in here."

"I don't know what you see in those trouble makers Tony? Most of them are nothing but trouble. I may not vibe with Val all like that but at least she's a deceit woman with some class and she loves you. Hell you see that the way she keeps her eyes on you. I guess I could be her friend if you act right. You may be driving her crazy with this trash you been parading around. I bet she don't even know that you slept with those nasty sisters next door does she. You're a mess."

He wasn't really paying any attention to what Erica is saying. He had long since fell off the conversation because his phone vibrated with a text; it's Phaedra.

Call me baby I need some bad.
09:34 today

He simply disconnected the call from Erica without telling her and found Phaedra's number. He then pushed the spot to connect the call.

"Hey baby," Phaedra said sweetly.

"Hey baby right back," Tony said slyly when she answered. "I need some bad too. Let's make it happen right now."

****

On Thursday, Deron and Dawn followed the instructions of the Prince Georges Police Officers that sat the entrance of the courthouse building. They went through the usual x-ray and magnetometer screening and then went in the direction of what the summons said to family court. Again, Deron couldn't believe that he's taking Dawn through this thing again but she's his wife, he couldn't possibly hide it from her. Days like this remind him of how he knows that he really doesn't deserve a good woman like her because he just keeps messing it up. He knows that some of these things are out of his control but that doesn't soften the blow the least bit. Looking at Dawn, he knows that one day she's going to wake up and realize that being with him is a mistake and bolt.

On that day, he hopes the Lord has mercy on him.

Walking into the courtroom Cheresse is the first person they see on the end of the table next to Deron's table. Audrey's sitting by her. Cheresse eyed the couple as they walked in and took their seats but Audrey does not. There's a man sitting on the other side of Audrey who must be her attorney. Deron's attorney is there too talking to him.

****

Thirty minutes later after the case had been, read and Deron's lawyer gave his side of why things should stay the way they are. Audrey's lawyer is about to present his case. To Deron, he thinks he did very well explaining to the judge that Dawn and he offer a stable home to Deron Jr; they are churchgoers. That Dawn is in the process of adopting him and it's just around the corner. It's that bond that the three of them have that makes them a family and that he has offered to Ms. Butler a chance to be a part or her son's life; even as recent as last year; but she adamantly refused. She wanted to stay away, so he didn't understand the change. He wanted to tell the judge that this is just a scheme by his ex-girlfriend to get back at him. But he knows that in this world it's hard to get people to see the obvious. The scenario here is that a man is trying to keep a child from his birth mother and that's all they see. They don't see the hateful ex-girlfriend trying everything she can to ruin him and hurt him.

He'd have to wait and see what the Lord will do for him.

"Mr. Casey are you ready to present your side of this hearing," the female judge asked.

"Yes your honor," he said. "Ms. Butler is seeking custody of her child from the father, Deron Stone. She feels that he is unfit to be a father, his wife as well…"

Mr. Casey went on to, talk about Audrey's desire to be a full time mother and how much so misses her son. He explains further that Audrey felt an embarrassment after she had a one-night encounter with the father. Mr. Stone, he said didn't make it easy on her and pressured her to give the child to him. She felt that she could do nothing but comply at the time and she gave him full custody out of fear that he would make it difficult for her to live in peace with her child.

Deron looked straight ahead not saying a thing or showing any expressions as he noticed the judge eyeing him suspiciously. Dawn is less in control as she shook her head to the accusations that the opposing attorney said out of his mouth. She wondered why Audrey isn't talking. She is as quiet as a church mouse. Dawn thought if that were her, she would be nodding her head to confirm what he's saying.

It's wrong Audrey thought in her mind. This is not right. Everything this man is saying about Deron isn't true and she wanted to say something about it but she couldn't. She promised Cheresse that she would help her to win Deron Jr so she could have a nephew even though she and Audrey are not sisters. They're just as close she thought. But the lawyer is basically destroying Deron and making her out to be a nun. She's the one who said she didn't want kids and Deron accepted full responsibility. Maybe one day he'll understand that she's only doing it because Cheresse is sick. Especially since she says, she'll probably die soon. As much as she knows, he hates Cheresse he would understand that's the kind of man he is.

She should've returned his calls so they could talk.

"And this is new evidence that we have uncovered to show you what kind of reckless father this man is. How this supposed church going, man is nothing but irresponsible behind closed doors. The evidence is on DVD your honor if I may?" Mr. Casey asked cutting off Audrey's thoughts. "I warn you it's disgusting."

This is new to her.

She doesn't know anything about any evidence.

Deron and Dawn are thinking the same thing that here comes the sex video. At least this may work in his favor because the judge will see Cheresse in the video with him and he can start in on that road. Although this is the first time Dawn will see this she braced herself for a view into Deron and Cheresse's sex life. She doesn't know how she will react once she sees it even though she knows he was drugged.

Mr. Casey placed the disc into the DVD tray and pushed play. Instantly the video played.

The video opened in Cheresse's bedroom from the apartment she no longer lives at and Deron is again nude laying on the bed. This is the part he thought that Cheresse is about to join him in the bed.

The video continued.

Then another woman enters into the picture not Cheresse. Immediately Deron recognizes who it is. It's Tammy, the girl that lived above Cheresse at her, old apartment building.

Deron literally stood up out of his chair.

"Mr. Stone be seated," the Bailiff commanded.

"I don't remember that. I was drugged," he said looking over at Cheresse and she simply smiled like crazy. He had no choice but deal with it. "I was drugged your honor and that was taken without my knowledge. That happened two years ago."

"Mr. Stone sit down. Mr. Bostwick control your client," the judge ordered. "If this happens again I'm going to rule in favor of Ms. Butler."

Everyone including Dawn watched as Tammy slipped a condom on Deron and climbed atop of him. The two of them grinded together and then he flipped her over and they went at it again. He looked to everyone like he's having the time of his life.

"I've seen enough," the judge said shaking her head unconsciously and fell silent.

Dawn sat in silence.

Through the whole viewing, she looked straight ahead and she kept swallowing hard. From her experience with Deron, she knows that he has always been active sexually but to, actually see it displayed in front of her is painful.

She didn't know about this one and it just made her numb. Audrey just shook her head.

She can't believe that Cheresse gave this to her lawyer to discredit Deron. She knows its Cheresse because she recognizes her bedroom of her old apartment. But who's the girl. What did Deron mean by saying that he was, drugged?

Deron couldn't believe that even Tammy is involved. When Cheresse drugged him that day with the 'roofies' he was out of it for over six hours anything could've happened during that time. He's sure that there's all kinds of pictures and video footage floating around now. When he was dating Cheresse he's never known for her to have a video camera. It must've been Tammy's. No wonder she appeared out of nowhere at the door when he was leaving. From her apartment, she couldn't have heard Cheresse and him or could she? She probably was in the apartment all along when Cheresse and he were arguing.

"I think we have all seen enough for today," the judge spoke again. "This hearing is adjourned. We will reconvene tomorrow."

The judge got up from behind the large bench she sat at watching Deron curiously. Deron couldn't discern what she's thinking as he stared back at her. He tried to smile but he couldn't. There's nothing to smile about. The judge then looked at Cheresse, not Audrey but at Cheresse. She saw her looking at Deron and smiling mischievously. Then she walked off to her chambers.

Jumping out of his chair Deron went straight for Audrey, not even looking at Cheresse.

"I can't believe you would do this Audrey. What have I done to you?"

Audrey didn't say anything.

She didn't even look at him.

"Deron please calm down. Don't do this," Dawn said grabbing his arm and rubbing it.

"My, my, your Mrs. is so nurturing," Cheresse said tauntingly moving in front of Audrey.

"This has nothing to do with you Cheresse, so can you mind your own business."

"I am one of Ms. Butler's legal representatives so I have much business here."

"Cheresse, I think we should be going," Mr. Casey said.

"Yes this court is adjourned, exit it now," the Bailiff said.

There is no getting a good night's sleep last night for Audrey. As she laid in bed in the second bedroom Cheresse has in her new apartment she couldn't help but still see Deron's face. Every time she closed her eyes she saw him like he was at the courthouse; angry as hell. It's mid-morning the next day and she isn't prepared mentally for another hearing again today. It's scheduled for two 'o' clock this afternoon and Audrey is just not ready to face Deron again.

Cheresse lied to her.

She said no one is going to be hurt. What's really going on with Cheresse because she's even crueler than she's ever been?

If Renita were here, she would get to the bottom of all of this in one conversation. Cheresse has always listened to her. The way she's going on these days it's hard to believe she's a woman with a terminal illness. Why won't she say what it is? She doesn't seem interested in her doctor appointments. She surely doesn't seem sick even though she's heard her throwing up a couple of times. She has lost a lot of weight, at least five dress sizes.

She doesn't dress like she used to. Though she's always wore designer clothes now she's wearing clothes that are weigh out of her price range; even with her Paralegal Specialist salary. Just seems like she riding a little too high. Maybe this sickness is making her take financial risks because Cheresse doesn't think she'll be alive soon. The law firm that she's with has taken care of her for her loyalty over the years but where is all this money coming really from.

A Louis Vuitton bag is over a grand; the cheapest ones and she has at least ten in her closet. Since Audrey's been in town both times she's seen Cheresse go to Niemen Marcus at least seven times and she always comes out of there with many outfits. All these bracelets, rings, earrings, real and expensive. Her sickness has done nothing to slow her down from her shopping. It doesn't make any sense.

Her thoughts are broken from her cellphone ringing on the nightstand beside her. She reached over, picked up her phone, and saw its Cheresse's number.

"Hello," she said as she answered it.

"Audrey the hearing is canceled for today. Next one is, scheduled for next week on Wednesday. So that gives us some more time to get more ammo."

"Yeah Cheresse about that. Are you sure this is about my reconnection with Deron Jr or is it about you and Deron?"

"No girl. I do have to admit that pissing Deron off does make me feel good while it's happening but it's all about us girls getting our family member back."

"You shouldn't be doing all this. You need to concentrate on you getting well. Don't you need to do some treatments or something?"

"Audrey let me worry about that. I need to keep my mind off all that," she said as she dropped her voice. "I got to go, bye."

Cheresse hung up the phone and to Audrey it seems as if she's upset. She didn't mean to upset her. She just wanted to make sure she's taking care of herself.

The cellphone rung again.

Hopefully it's Cheresse she thought so that she could ease her mind. This sickness is definitely messing with her.

"Hello."

"Audrey. Girl, hi," the female voice over the phone said.

"Renita, hi girl. What...?

"Do you know I had to call from North Carolina to California to get your correct number only to find out I had the right number all along," Renita said happily. "How are you, girl? Ooh it's great to hear your voice. Oh my, gosh it's good to hear from you."

The two of them excitedly started talking to each other and catching up. Audrey started crying and after the tears continued to talk and laugh. She listened to Renita tell her about her wonderful new job that has her making six figures. She patted herself on the shoulder the fact that she stayed in college even after she got pregnant with the twins. Audrey told her that she was sorry that she fell on hard times and that she wasn't there to help her.

"What are you talking about Audrey?" Renita said curiously.

"Well Cheresse said…"

"Che."

"Well yeah she said you lost your job."

"Why would she say that? When I talked to her last week…"

"Last week? She said she hasn't heard from you in a year and she didn't drive up to see you like she said she would when I went back to LA for a week."

"You're in D.C.?

"Yes I came to town to be with Cheresse for a bit while she goes through this sickness."

"What sickness?"

"Aw Renita I thought you at least knew that."

"What are you talking about, knew what?"

"Che has Cancer."

"What would make you say a thing like that?"

"Cheresse told me."

"Girl, Cheresse doesn't have Cancer."

"But she does she's so thin. She's lost all her weight."

"Audrey that bitch's lying. She gained all this weight after Deron stop messing with her; I mean over two hundred and twenty pounds up to a size 16. She went from Beyoncé to Jennifer Hudson back when she was fat. It was something. She kept wearing all these big clothes. Then she went on this crash diet last year sometime in April. I mean it was strict and in less than six months she loss all the weight. Went down to a size 2 or 3. Its pass what she weighed before, that. I didn't see her on a regular then, maybe once or twice."

"Why would she tell me something like that if she doesn't? She said that she is terminally ill."

"I don't know girl but you know how Che is when she's working on something she wants, she don't care what she does."

"That's the reason why I'm letting her help me get Deron Jr back."

"Why are you getting Deron Jr back, I thought you said you didn't want kids?"

"It's a long story and…Renita let me call you back in an hour, is that okay?"

"Sure baby, make sure you call me."

"Oh I'm going to call because I think I got something to tell you," Audrey said as she hung up the phone.

The anger built in Audrey so fast that she thought she is going to have an aneurysm.

That lying bitch she thought.

Audrey got up out of bed and ran to Cheresse's bedroom. She opened the door and headed straight to her dresser drawers. On any other occasion this wouldn't happen because she always respects someone else's privacy but Cheresse is trying to use her for something and she wants to know what. She started with the top dresser drawers first going to each one, then to the second row and finally the third.

The final drawer's where she found multiple paperwork.
She knelt down in front of it.

She shifted through the papers and found a check. It's in the amount of two thousand dollars from some man name Mondle Shaw. Then there's some other paper work with his name that's too wordy for Audrey to bother to reading. Then she found what she knew she would. There are statements from some weight doctor where Cheresse had multiple B-12 shots. There's also some other weight loss medicine, Phen-something Audrey didn't recognize the complete name. Right behind this paper work is a gym membership agreement.

Putting the papers back into the drawer, she closed it. Audrey got up and went back to her room. She didn't do anything but sit on the bed.

All of this is a sham she thought.

Cheresse is using her to get back at Deron and that's it.

Here Audrey is about to alter her life and do something that she never wanted to do in the first place. How selfish can you be to mess up peoples' lives as if they didn't matter?

This is so typical Cheresse.

This is the reason why Audrey is in this predicament with a baby son now playing these stupid games with Cheresse. Even though ultimately it's her responsibility to protect herself she let her own need for revenge cloud her judgment. She shouldn't have slept with Deron just to piss off Cheresse.

Who does that?

It's obvious her friendship with Cheresse is strained to where this woman can lie directly in her face and not crack a smile. Well this is the last time she is done.

She decided that quick that she will play one more game with Cheresse. Then she'll be done with her. Her friendship with Renita has nothing to do with this so she don't have to worry about that, they're good.

As she gathered her things and started placing items neatly in her suitcase and travel bag, she thought of the person who really suffered out of this game, Deron. How could she let a good friend like him down, because she doesn't have many men she can think of in that way; that's not a relative? If she wanted to, she could've had a relationship with him but she knew he wouldn't move to LA and she wasn't moving back to the Metropolitan Area.

That one thing made her choice for her and he was good about it. She'll have to make things right with him, that's the first thing she has to do once she gets out of this apartment.

She got on her Bluetooth and continued packing.

"Renita, girl I told you I would be calling you back. You won't believe what Cheresse has done now…"

****

Audrey waited patiently as the call she placed on her cellphone connected.

"Hello," the male voice said.

"Deron, don't hang up, please," she said to him hurriedly.

"Give me one good reason why I would want to talk to you Audrey."

"Please just let me explain."

"Exactly whose side are you really on?"

"I know you're angry and you have every right to be. I've done you wrong."

"Like fighting me for my full rights to my son. You think this is one of yours and Cheresse's games. This is this boy's life."

"I know I was tricked."

"Tricked huh, that's a laugh?"

"Yes tricked," she said sternly. "Cheresse lied and told me that she was dying. I thought it might've been Cancer. Really, I thought those damn cigarettes had finally caught up with her even if she had quit. That left me wide open to try making amends with her by trying to get Deron Jr back in her life as she wanted. I didn't know that it was all about trying to get you back. If I would've known that I wouldn't have gone along with her."

"Dying huh?" Deron said in disgust. "What kind of lowdown, devious, trashy person would pretend to have a terminal disease to try to get a man? Don't she know how many people have suffered with terminal diseases and how it effects the people in that person's life? It's not a joke."

"My thoughts exactly. That's why I moved out of her apartment today and came to stay at this hotel. I'm done with Cheresse, she's nothing but trouble and every time I connect with her I end up with crap in my face. I also end of hurting innocent people, like you. I'm really sorry for all of this."

Deron breathed a sigh of relief.

"I knew something had to be going on because it just didn't seem like you. Not the, you that I've come to know. You and I have always been able to talk no matter what. That's what I like about you. You don't hold no grudges when things don't pan out the way you want them to. It don't make sense what that woman does."

"She's been like this since we were kids. I guess Renita and I just got used to it; and ignores it. I should have known she isn't sick. Renita told me all that happened is that she gained all this weight real fast. She overdid her weight lost. She said she had really gotten up there in her weight the one or two times she saw her."

"No wonder I hadn't seen her for months until now. I mean we had a restraining order against her but now I know why she didn't want me to see her. Too, busy messing up other people lives I guess. That's why I'm glad Jesus is in my life, Audrey. I was heading in a trick bag with Cheresse. For some reason she likes to play games with me and you never know what to expect from her because she's always lying about something."

"Well you better watch out because she's on you. She's not trying to let you go that easy."

"I'm good. I got my wife and my son, I'm good."

"By the way I never got a chance to say congratulations to you on your marriage. Dawn seems like the kind of woman you need in your life. I always said that. Always stick close to her and don't let Cheresse get in y'all's way."

"You sound like you're saying goodbye, again."

"I am, you know me I'm LA bound tomorrow morning and I'm definitely not coming back here unless my son needs me for something. Thanks for everything Deron you are one of a kind. Dawn is really lucky."

"I'm nothing special, I'm the bless one. I got an angel watching out for me," he said strongly. "Well what about the custody hearing."

"Trust me Deron one more time, will you do that? I have seen for my own eyes what's going on. I don't need no more bricks falling on my head. Just sit back and watch."

"Okay I'll trust you."

"Good. Really, I am so sorry this is my mistake. It's on me. I should've talked to you first. I shouldn't have let Cheresse get in my head like that. I'll see ya' the next time, baby," she said as she hung up the phone.

Deron hung up the phone and settle back into his chair in his office. He put his feet up on his desk and laid back. For the first time in a long time after all this started, he felt like he's going to get a good night sleep tonight.

Thank you Jesus.

CHAPTER 15

Walking into the courtroom or rather the hearing room Dawn felt a little apprehensive. She's always going to support her husband but it's starting up again all this drama with Cheresse. Maybe it's wrong to think this but is it worth all this trouble. She couldn't help imagine what went on between those two that has Cheresse so hell bent on being with him or getting revenge on him. She really couldn't figure out which one. Sometimes she seems like she loves him and wants to be with him then other times she'd be his worse adversary. Maybe she is bipolar and hasn't been diagnosed. Whatever the reason Dawn wonders which personality is she going to bring to court today.

She just hopes it's not another shocker like the last hearing. What was Deron thinking when he went back to Cheresse after she broke the two of them up?

Watching that scene with now some, other woman he slept with is another hard blow. It's like being hurt all over again but she has to remember that they weren't together then. At that time during the break up it was a clear fact that they weren't going to get back together and she guessed that Deron must have thought the same thing. So what do most junkies do when they think that their life is not going to get any better? They go back to the old reliable and as much as it sickened Dawn, Cheresse was Deron's reliability. Another factor she has to weigh in is that it is true that Cheresse slipped Deron a 'roofies'. She really didn't believe it then no she found it hard to believe.

Never had she ever heard of this happening to a man.

She thought he was lying like the rest of the lies.

Whoosh, momma never said there would be days like this she thought. She held her head down and said a silent prayer and Deron who sat quietly beside her took the cue and did the same.

"I know you're a good man," she said to Deron without looking at him and squeezing his hand.

He didn't look up or open his eyes; he just smiled.

During this Cheresse entered with one of the lawyers from her firm. Both Dawn and Deron looked up and eyed Cheresse. Cheresse returned the stare by mushing her face at the two of them. It wasn't as elaborate as some of the other things she has done so the judge who sat facing in front them didn't notice her.

It's been hard trying to get the judge to see who Deron is now rather than who he was when he was with Cheresse. Also the two of them aren't playing dirty, but Cheresse has her plan well played out as if Audrey is a victim, rather than a woman who slept with a man one night and got pregnant. A man she slept with to piss off a friend. Then she gave the man full custody of their child because she didn't want the child. She wasn't coerced as Cheresse would want the judge to believe. The worst part is that Audrey's been sitting there and saying absolutely nothing other than one-word answers. Cheresse is leading her. It's as if Cheresse *is* the mother who's seeking restoration of her parental rights.

Let's see what Audrey does this time Dawn thought.

It is a good thing that their mothers weren't in the courtroom the other times to see and hear all the things Cheresse tried to use to discredit Deron. It's one thing for her to hear this trash but no mother wants to hear negative stuff about their child and especially negative sexual stuff.

Dawn watched Cheresse as she kept looking back at the door watching for Audrey. Then she whispered something to Mr. Casey and he looked at his watch.

In that, moment the judge walked out of her chambers and the bailiff did his usual court procedures. When everyone settled down the judge spoke.

"Mr. Casey and Mr. Bostwick I will not hold this case up any further than its necessary," the Judge said.

"Your honor we have not finished presenting and Ms. Butler isn't here yet," Mr. Casey said quickly and then he stopped. "Unless you have decided your ruling."

"There's no need. I received a communication from Ms. Audrey Butler late last night requesting an immediate dismissal of this case."

Immediately Cheresse and the lawyer reacted to the news.

"But your honor," Mr. Casey said.

"That's impossible," Cheresse yelled out.

The Judge simply looked at Cheresse and said nothing. She just hammered her gavel and everyone got quiet. To her there's more to this story than what's being told here, her career instincts tells her this. It seems like a woman's scorn but not the mother it's this woman the attorney's assistant.

Cheresse wanted to explode right there as she sat fidgeting in her chair and staring right at the Judge.

When she last talked to Audrey, she said that she was leaving her apartment because she wanted to reconnect with a guy she knows that lives downtown. Far be it for Cheresse to interfere with a bitch wanting to get a ride on the magic stick.

That trick lied.

See that's why she doesn't like to fuck with Audrey and Renita. Those hoes don't have any backbone to do anything and those tricks ain't loyal.

Ugh, she thought *I can't wait to see that trick and cuss her ass out. How could she do this to me?*

"In the communication to our office, Ms. Butler reveal that she doesn't want to be involved in any further disruptions in the life of her birth son regarding parental rights. It is her wish that Deron Alexander Stone Sr and his wife Dawn Lauren Stone become the sole parents of Deron Alexander Stone Jr. Well," the Judge said looking at Cheresse. "It seems as if Ms. Butler has had a change of heart and so this case is dismissed. It is so ordered that the child remains with his father and his wife without prejudice, *okay*," she said directly to Cheresse.

Cheresse wanted to give the Judge the finger.

She's a trick too.

Deron and Dawn got out of their seats and didn't even look in Cheresse direction. They just celebrated to themselves praising the Lord as they exited the hearing room.

Cheresse just stared at them with hate in her eyes.

****

Sitting at the dinner table at Outback Steakhouse in Largo, Md. Deron, Dawn, Deron Jr and the couples' mothers are celebrating. Everyone is laughing at the table and having a good time. Deron's especially happy because he realizes that once again God has shown him mercy. Just when he thought his world was going to, be turned upside down, the Lord arrives at the final moment with a right solution. That's why he wants to serve him for reasons like this. Cheresse tried to destroy him again and stopped dead in her tracks.

Will this woman ever get enough?

"Deron excuse me I'm going to the restroom," Dawn said getting up and walking off.

Deron got up because he thought that's what he should do as a gentleman.

"You two are so blessed," Deron's mother said. "I know that God has anointed you."

Deron smiled, nodding and grabbing her hand.

"Gladys you haven't said nothing but the God's truth," Dawn's mother agreed. "So do you know when Dawn's going to get the final results of the adoption?"

"Ma Sylvia, I don't know but I think it's soon. Then we'll have something else to celebrate. Dawn really needs this because she loves this little boy so much," he said tickling Deron Jr in his high chair.

Everything is great.

****

"I'm back bitch."

"What are you following us again, Cheresse?" Dawn said to her standing in front of the sinks in the restroom.

This again she thought.

It just seemed like Cheresse appeared out of nowhere when she exited the stall. She thought the last time at Olive Garden would've taught her a lesson.

She should be surprised but really, she's not. It isn't as if she was expecting her but she *is* getting used to it.

"I don't follow people I take care of business," Cheresse said blocking the door. "You put your hands on me and I'm here to put my hands back on you."

"I believe you're here because you lost the court case. I'm here to have a good time with my husband, my son and our parents. I don't want to talk to you. I don't want any trouble. All I want is for you to leave us alone."

"*I don't want any trouble, I don't want to talk, leave me alone*," she said tauntingly to Dawn. "All I want to do is put my foot in your ass."

"Cheresse please move from the door."

"Or what, what are you going to do Dawn if I don't move?"

"I'm asking nicely. What's wrong with you? Deron has made it clear that he doesn't want to be with you. You don't share children, you weren't marry, nothing. It was all about sex. He doesn't want that with you anymore, can't you see that. Now please move," Dawn said raising her voice.

"You don't know what Deron and I have together. If you had stayed off him, we wouldn't be having this problem right now."

"You mean if you weren't such a…a whore is your problem."

"Bitch," Cheresse yelled as she lunged at Dawn.

Grabbing Dawn, she held her tight and Dawn had no choice but to punch at her with her free hand. This time she realized Cheresse is trying to take this to another level and she'll have no choice but to fight her back to protect herself.

As the two of them fought the other lady who was in one of the stall all along opened her stall door. She watched the two women exchange blows as Dawn smack Cheresse several times and Cheresse fell back against the sink. When she got herself together quickly, she went for Dawn again. She tried to interlock her arm around Dawn's head but she counteracted it and pulled Cheresse to the floor, getting on top of her. Once Dawn was in that position she felt herself lose it and she literally let loose on Cheresse with punches drawing blood from her nose.

"Miss, stop," the woman yelled to Dawn. "Stop don't do it."

That plea from the woman seem to stop Dawn in her tracks. She's simply just tired of Cheresse and all the trouble. She felt she didn't have any choice but make this statement to her that she won't keep going on like this.

Instantly the door to the restroom burst open and in came two PG police. They were eating in the restaurant when one of the servers heard what was going down and alerted them. They pulled Dawn off Cheresse even though she wasn't hitting her when they rushed in.

Cheresse just laid on the restroom floor dazed.

"Help me," Cheresse said weakly when she realized who they were.

"You know you two are in trouble, right?" the police officer said.

****

Outside in the parking lot Dawn is, sent to one squad car and Cheresse to the other. They both stood on the side of each car. Each police officer is interviewing them.

"I'm telling you the truth, it's just like you saw for yourself, she just attacked me out of nowhere," Cheresse said crying to the officer and trying to look sexy.

"She said you started it."

"No I was walking in and bump into her by accident and she just let loose on me. Is she on drugs or something?"

Across to the other police car the officer is talking to Dawn and Deron is standing nearby.

"I tried to leave the restroom and she lunged at me," Dawn said calmly. "She's tried this once before at Olive Garden but I was able to get away from her then without getting into a fight. This time I couldn't get out of the restroom because she was blocking the door. There's an expired restraining order against her in the system."

The other police officer walked up just to hear Dawn's last words.

"But that doesn't mean that she attacked you in the restroom. It just means that the two of you know each other."

"Officer she's telling the truth," the lady that was in the restroom when the two of them were fighting said as she walked up. "I'm Mrs. Mayna Blake and I was the woman that was in the restroom the whole time remember? This young lady right here had no other choice but to fight her. That one over there," she said pointing to Cheresse. "She was blocking the door and wouldn't move. This young lady kept asking her to move several times and she wouldn't. She just kept talking very nasty to her like she wanted a confrontation. Then she grabbed her and this young lady didn't have no choice but to hit her to get her off. She probably would have pound her to the floor. This young lady was lucky enough to get on top of her to stop her from moving."

Dawn looked at the woman and knew that the woman purposely omitted the fact that she lost complete control and beat Cheresse while she was on top of her.

She started to say something but the officer cut her off.

"Mrs. Blake I'm going to need your statement in its entirety and for you to sign it if you will."

"Of course officer," she said looking at Dawn and Deron. "It's a shame a young lady can't enjoy dinner with her husband, her child and their mothers and not have to worry about crazy people…it's a shame," Mrs. Blake said shaking her head.

"Mommy, mommy, mommy," Dawn heard Deron Jr cry out.

Dawn's mother cradled him in her arms and when Dawn and Deron looked over to him, he reached out to Dawn.

Dawn's mother brought him over to her.

Dawn took him from her and he hugged her so tight she couldn't believe the little two-year-old had that much strength in him. This isn't the first time she's heard him call her mommy but this is the first time he's called after her. He called to her like he wanted her to know, that he wants the world to know who she is to him.

"My mommy," he said to her and kept right on hugging her.

In that moment, Dawn closed her eyes and smiled. When she opened them, again, she saw Cheresse staring directly at her and the two exchanged no expressions.

What's going through each other's mind is a mystery but something is exchanged.

Maybe Dawn is saying to her no matter what you do this is all that matters. She kept right on hugging Jr and tears filled her eyes.

Maybe Cheresse is asking why not her?

Whatever the message it's clear that as far as Cheresse is concern this is far from being over. This is just the beginning.

****

The next night Cheresse having been released earlier from her stay at the jail overnight, she's still angry. All of her hard work down the drain and she is embarrassed at her office. That attorney's never going to work with her again no matter how much she flirts with him. Not that she has to do that because she knows her shit but these little amateurs piss her off when they don't do what she tells them to.

When the bail posted this morning for her, the judge told her this is her second strike. The next one's going give her some lengthy jail time. She don't care about that because she knows the law. She knows that Outback can't press charges without really pressing charges on Dawn. Also, the statement from that nosey ass old lady wasn't enough because she never really saw Cheresse hit Dawn first. So, she don't know for sure who threw the first punch. Another thing an amateur lawyer could punch a hole through. Then there's the fact that the old bitch and dumb ass Dawn said that she was on top of her. That alone could be, flipped. All it would take is the right kind of ruthless lawyer and we've got a lawsuit against Outback.

She made sure the manager understood that or rather her friend did when he posts the bail. He makes sure she's all right when she needs him because he don't have no choice.

Her cellphone rang, as she got lost in her thoughts. This better be Audrey calling she thought. She's been ignoring her phone calls sending her straight to voicemail.

She has a lot to explain with that move she made.

"Hello Renita," she said rolling her eyes to the ceiling once she saw the number on the phone screen when she picked it up to answer it.

"Hello, Che," she said not really hiding her disappointment. "You sure have been busy."

"What do you mean?"

"No sense in trying to play innocent with me Audrey told me everything the two of you were doing. Why did you do that, telling her that you have Cancer?"

"I don't recall telling her that. She must have misunderstood. You know how animated Audrey can be. I only told her that I was losing weight real fast and didn't know why."

"Che, you know why. You went on a crash diet. I don't know what's been going on with you these past few years but this has to stop. Girl you're twenty-eight years old..."

"Twenty-seven," Cheresse corrected her.

"Twenty-eight liar and you're running around like a teenager, doing childish shit. Why don't you stop and leave Deron alone?"

"Why don't you mind your own business, Nita?"

"I know you not talking to me like that. You might talk to Audrey like that but I'm not but two hours away and I'll come down there. I'm not pregnant no more."

"You're always going overboard with something. I just want you to stop getting in my business. All I did is ask little Audrey to help me with something that I knew up front she wouldn't. I had to tell her something to convince her to do it."

"That was some low petty shit. Real people die of that every day and you're playing with it. Where's your heart Che?"

"Where was y'all's heart fourteen years ago, when y'all left me there?"

"Che you know we told you to come with us but you wouldn't; you stayed. That was on you. Besides we've been with you ever since."

"Still..."

"So this is a get back, especially with Audrey? You know she don't want any children. What if she, did get him back then what? She would've gone back to LA with him and have to take care of him while you run around living your single life. That's some foul shit. I thought you two were closer than that. So this *is* get back?"

"I want what I want and she shouldn't have slept with my man."

"Oh that's it. You want Audrey to pay for sleeping with Deron. You know that having to be a mother full time would straight mess her up."

"Next time she'll keep her legs together instead of spreading them for my man."

"You didn't say that when you were spreading your legs for her fiancée and Deron is not your man Cheresse. He's married to that other one. You need to stop living in an illusion. Besides you got a man in your life Audrey says. Who's Mondle Shaw and why is he giving you large amounts of money?"

"I forgot how nosey and bossy you can be Renita; all at the same time. Always taking Audrey's side in everything. Sometime I don't even know if you're my friend or not."

"Oh please stop the drama sounding like a reality star," Renita said brushing her statement aside. "What about this guy?"

"Mondle Shaw is a friend of mine," Cheresse answered figuring that Renita isn't going to listen to anything else but the answer to her question. "He owns this pub called the Roasted Almond. He likes to take me out from time to time and he likes to spend money on this booty every chance he gets. We have a little arrangement. I keep to my bargain and he keeps to his. You know how these men can't resist this, what I got."

"An arrangement? He's married isn't he?"

"So?"

Renita laughed in her mind.

For as nosey as these girls like to call her they equally like to rubbed their flashy boyfriends in her face. Both Cheresse and Audrey knows she don't like to do that and she doesn't like it when they do it. She keeps her quiet little life to herself and raises her children. She can only manage to keep her one man away from all those women who's degrading themselves to be with professional football players. There's nothing fun in telling people that you're opening your hole to every penis that has legs that can walk just to get some cash. These chicks know these players are married but yet in still they be trying to run them down anyway just to get on. Stick with the single ones who like to be out there she thought.

She already had her problems with her husband, Jeremiah when they were in college. Those girls used to be all over the field trying to shake their ass for him. Some may have got through but he learned his lesson when he wasn't drafted straight out of college. After having to play semi-pro, which is really a death wish to the majority of hopefuls he was, blessed. He got his contract here in Philly. She showed him that she isn't in it for the good times but for the bad as well; they're a real family now.

"Am I going to meet Mr. Money Pockets," Renita said mockingly wondering why she's even still on the line talking to her about this nonsense.

"I don't think Mondle's wife will allow that," she said with a laugh. "I keep, having to deal with those you know."

"No you put yourself in those deals by messing with their husbands. I know you knew that man was married before you dealt with him."

"Is that a question or do you know that for a fact?"

"Cheresse, I love you because you're like my sister but you do some do raunchy shit and the way you carry yourself like a…"

"I know you're not about to call me a hoe? You think about me like that?"

"No not as harsh as all that but you set it off. Every time I talk to you, I'm hearing about a new guy. So don't think about what I think about you, what do you think of yourself?"

"I'm a bad bitch."

"It time to stop Che," she found herself yelling to her. "You need to stop running these guys and messing over their money *and* especially you need to leave Deron alone. It don't make sense, you have another man."

"You don't know nothing about Deron and me, Renita Combs-Martel," she said spatting back at her. "Deron needs me in his life to make him relevant."

"Relevant?"

"You don't know what that man told me when we laid together in his bed and mine's. How much he wants to be better than the next man is. I made him what he is. He was in love with me and your girl, Audrey and that other one the Christian bitch Dawn interfered in it. They made it seem like it was me…"

"It was you. You always try to be the victim but you're not."

"Renita are you trying to throw a dig at me?"

"No Che I'm trying to get you to admit that you were the cause of why Deron and you didn't work. You were out there on that man doing some ratchet ass stuff and it backfired. You do remember Philly don't you when he had to call me to track you down? How mad you got with me about it but you were foul. I only let you get away with that because I was pregnant and I didn't want to get upset. You know you shouldn't have brought him to Philly if you were going to hook up with your old boo, Kavon. Now you want him back and he don't want you. Ain't no man going to keep on letting you use them for, their money. You're lucky you got away with it that long. He must've like you a lot. It ain't right what you did."

"To you. He don't know what he wants but I do. I have some more stuff I'm going to do to get my man back. He's the one that I'm gonna marry. Like I said I make him relevant. I make all men that I give the pleasure of being in my company feel relevant. You see I make these niggas feel like they're boss niggas. I make them think yeah I banged that broad but I can take her or leave her; but they can't leave me. They want to spoil me. They are fighting to get to this pussy."

"Humph," Renita said deciding to take another approach. "You have a good career why play these games?"

"It's fun, I like to play. You should try it."

"Girl you're a trip," Renita said knowing she isn't going to get to Cheresse like all the other times they've talked on this level.

"No I'm real and you better start recognizing it. Because when your husband start making some real NFL money, somebody like me is gonna be there to do what you won't, so beware."

"Just make sure it ain't you," Renita said with all the seriousness she could muster in her voice. "And Che, those others like you better beware. Cause a bitch will go postal for her man, believe that."

CHAPTER 16

The next day early Saturday morning Tony and Deron were hanging out at Home Depot. Deron wanted to buy a Power Washer so he could clean his deck. He's decided that in light of his blessings he's going to keep on focusing on the Lord even harder. The hearing could've gone another way and he truly believe that the Lord put every possible step in place to shut Cheresse down.

"So PG took Cheresse down to Glenarden police station," Deron said shrugging his shoulders. "I guess they might charge her for disorderly conduct if they haven't already. I know that Dawn hasn't pressed any charges for assault. I think because she got the best of Cheresse in that fight."

"I still can't believe that thot did that to you D.," Tony said. "She's worse than that crazy ass Sharnia. You know coming back in your life when you don't even be checking for them."

"Really man, are you still trying to act like you're not messing around with Sharnia willingly?"

He could tell Deron no but what's the big deal. No shame in his game and D's his boy.

So what's the problem he thought?

"You know how I do D. Sharnia wanted to take a bite of the apple so I let her. I didn't expect her ass to be off da chain behind it. I didn't promise her shit."

These conversations with Tony is beginning to bring to light what the Pastor was saying months ago. Sometimes you just get tired of the same old thing and this is one of those times. Driving women crazy so they try anything to be with him ain't his style no more. Tony's always going to be his boy but they're lifestyles are changing; moving in different directions. The constant need to get turnt up every five minutes doesn't strike a chord with Deron anymore.

Maybe it works for T to be at the strip clubs and latest bar clubs every week and weekend but that's not for him he thought. That don't mean they can't be friends but he doesn't think that's going to sit too well with Tony.

"I don't see why you felt like you had to hide it from me. It's on you but the problem is that when you do stuff to her she acts out at the office."

"It ain't the only place she acts out at. I didn't tell you this either but she's the reason why I got suspended."

"What did she do?"

"Went through my office like tornado. Security had to escort her out."

"And you got suspended behind that?"

"Yeah, but I don't know why I'm still being casted out. I mean the supervisor's saying now there's an audit going on. I don't even have to do the telework no more. It's sweet but this thing is going on too long it's beginning to look fishy."

"All this because of Sharnia?"

Tony nodded his head.

"You know T, I got to say this to you because you need to hear this," he said stopping in the aisle they were going through. "Maybe this is a sign that you need to slow down a bit. You know we've been wrecking up the streets for a long time; all through our twenties. But it may be time to start leaving that wild life to the twenty-something's."

"Look D, I'm still young and so are you, ain't nothing changed. You don't just stop having fun just because you reach a certain age," Tony said getting a little agitated. "See this is what the church does to you; make you feel bad about doing things that makes you feel good."

"Man I'm not saying that. No one said anything about not having no fun. I'm having fun, now that I really got myself out of that slump I was in. The Lord did that. Dawn, Jr and I have a good time together..."

"But that's your deal Deron that ain't what I want. I don't want no family, that don't work for me."

"I know and you have a point. A family is what makes me happy," he responded reasonably. "But if your side girl is trying to burn down your house with herself in it, that don't seem like fun to me. If you about to lose your job because your side girl comes on your job and acts a fool that ain't fun. What's next?"

"And your ex tried to take your son from you, what's your next point?"

"You're going to go through a storm, if you're trying to say that Christian's shouldn't have no issues. The point is how you go through the storm and do you still praise Him while you're going through it. Another point is that Cheresse tried but didn't succeed. I prayed for a relief from it all and I got it. I didn't even have to do anything but show up. She tried to get me but she didn't."

"Yeah at what cost? It didn't stop your woman from seeing another nasty video with you and some new hoe?"

"Oh you think it's easy when you give your life over to Christ, man it's worse. The enemy ain't going to leave you alone; he will reach down in the lower bowel of your discarded past to find something to destroy you with. In my case, it's Cheresse. But the trick is that you got a cover in the name of Jesus. Each time Cheresse came after me it got shot down and it's going to keep on getting shot down as long as I stay ready in my faith."

"I ain't joining the church D."

"I'm not saying that. All I'm saying is slow down man before you self-destruct. I know you Tony there's a whole other world your leading when we're not hanging; one you try to keep on the low. You like to get revved up and I'm saying to you put it in perspective before you lose it all."

"Shit I ain't losing shit," Tony said defensively. "Tony Parker's always gonna be on top of his game. I live and adapt to my circumstances so I ain't gotta worry. D you know I'm a solider and I'm always armed."

"You can always arm up with a little Christ."

"I thought you said you weren't trying to get me to join the church?"

"You can always pick up that bible we got you for Christmas, engraved with your name on it."

"Yeah," he laughed. "That bible, it's the only thing to survive on that desk that caught fire at the house."

"That's my point, He's real man. He can help."

"D, I hate to say this to you but you're wasting your time I'm good. Hard work and beating these fools at their own games is gonna keep me rolling. That's all the help I need. I'm on top man," he said, as he turned serious with Deron. "And what's the big deal with heaven and hell? We're all gonna die anyway right," he finished saying staring at Deron.

It wasn't anything more Deron could say right now. Just like all the other times he's tried to get through to his buddy it just seems to roll off him like water. Tony's running from something, something that even he can't get a handle on.

Something that messed him up about settling down.

Something that makes him not take life too serious.

Something that makes him don't want to trust the Lord.

It has to be, his parents or does it have something to do with Bryan's death or both.

"So D before I forget," Tony said deciding not to stay on the subject anymore. "Aijon's having a party next Saturday and you got to roll with me man. This way in advance man so you got to go."

"No, I'm good, I'm not going. Have a good time *or* you can come shoot some pool with me down at Bart's."

"Let me see, a house, backyard and a swimming pool full of half-naked thots or playing pool with you? Something I can do anytime. No brainer or better yet one of those thots gonna give me some brains at the party, ha, ha, ha."

Deron just shook his head.

In his mind he said a silent prayer for his brother and then as he turned away from Tony. He then whispered it silently to put it out in the universe. Speak it and it will be, done he thought. He knows that the Lord will watch out for T. But He may have to break him down like He did him so T can see where his help really comes from.

****

The following Saturday around six in the evening Tony pulled up in Aijon's large circular driveway. The party is already in full swing and you can tell that the happenings are occurring on blast in the backyard. Up front, the help staff is all around parking cars or directing them where to park. Different event staff are everywhere even down to the caterers. It's wild to Tony how he has a straight shot to park right in front of the house with all the party guest parking in the cluttered area over to the right of the property. This is where he was, directed to go by security at the gate. He has to hand it to Aijon he's a loyal dude to look out for Tony with that.

Aijon sure knows how to buy some property. It's in a newly built community where the houses start upwards to the high eight hundred thousand. Not only did he buy one lot he brought three altogether. The one lot is already two and a half acres. Then he built this huge ass house on the three adjoining land something like six thousand square feet. He got it what would have been a cul-de-sac with three lots but he got them all.

How did he get that pass PG County strict as their ass is? They let him put that mansion up with these other estate homes.

Hell in some neighborhoods you can't even put a shed on your property without big brother PG in yo' business.

Tony gave his truck keys to the valet because the valet said he might have to move his truck. Maybe they are just there to make sure crash-bangs don't happen in the lot and the culprit gets off.

Bet not one damn thing better happen to his ride.

Of course, Aijon has security there and they're deep. That must be the football celebrity side of him coming out. Always looking out to prevent some trouble.

Won't be no shit tonight he thought.

Tony entered through the front door and the whole first floor is full of people. There's a lot of dudes talking to women with nothing on but low tops, short mini dresses and booty shorts on. As he walked around he started to notice that these, women Aijon got up in here, wall to wall, are strippers and they are too fine. All the women in the place look like dime pieces. He even has some fine heavyset, thick ones up in here. Booty's twerking everywhere yeah man Tony thought.

Hell Aijon has a broad up in here for every dude's taste.

Tony rubbed his hands together cause he sees a long hot time tonight. He just needs a place to himself and a bucket list.

Deron's gonna be mad he missed this. He ain't gonna admit it but he's gonna feel it. He thinks he's having fun denying himself all this pleasure but it'll get to him real soon.

If he wasn't sure Tony swears that Aijon got this crib imported from off the shores of one of those islands. When he walked into the joint, it was something foreign. Just then, an Asian broad walked pass Tony and he thought '*you know I got to cop that, foreign*'.

"That ain't the only one up in here T," he heard a dude say standing beside him. He turned to see who it is.

"Cert what up man?"

"Nothing. Aijon's out did himself this time didn't, he?"

"Yeah this is off the chain. Where is he?"

"Out by the pool with some chicks. Man he's revved up."

"Oh yeah well what about you, why you ain't revved up?"

"I got something on my plate and I want a clear head to do it; not even a smoke."

"Well damn she must be fine for you not to wanna drink or do some weed. I got to see this one."

"Naw dude you ain't invited to this party not this time," Cert said shaking his head at Tony's boldness.

He remembers the last time he let Tony in on one of his tricks he went right after her. Even though she was some thot he'd been smashing she was his at the moment. Cert doesn't like to share his women with the dudes he knows. Now if she's out, there hoe banging behind his back; on her own well then that's another story altogether.

Shit's not complicated.

It's just a natural order to the way things should flow and that's how niggas stay alive by staying out of each other's way.

"Man Cheresse ain't worth mentioning. One bad move on a friend and now I got a bad rep with you."

"Yeah well next time don't be putting yo' hands on a chick and she won't have to threaten to lock your ass up."

"Man you know I was high and she started it. I didn't think she would try to clip my money like that after she got me for the first ten G's."

"I thought it was five? Damn it was ten?"

"Yeah nigga," Tony said not wanting to hear it anymore.

"Hookers got to be paid T, you know what the deal is. And they'll get what they want no matter what."

It isn't that T isn't listening to Cert his mind is on Cheresse. She's some trouble and he really has to admit she's a pro with the things she does. Deron didn't stand a chance and he let him walk blindly in it. Hell thinking back on that night him and Cert double-teamed Cheresse; he remembered how that shit backfired.

At first she was all in and willing.

It went down in a hotel in Philly.

Cert hook it up cause he could always get her to do the nasty with just about anybody he wanted her too. For some reason she was all in on him and Tony couldn't see why. Cert's an average looking dude a little shorter than Tony with no big cash flow. He ain't got no flow. Hell he just got himself out of debt. Back then, he drove a used Denali truck, white, custom-up but not enough to pull a high-end hoe like Cheresse; but he did.

After Tony found out how she like to get down with two niggas at a time, he was all in cause he wanted a return on his money.

It just so happened that Tony and Cert were in Philly at a bachelor party that one of their co-workers at the bank threw cause; he was getting married the next day. Cheresse just happened to be visiting some girlfriend of hers that lives in Philly. The girlfriend knew the fiancée of the guy Tony and Cert knew.

So they all met up by chance at this wedding reception. Cert and her reconnected and when she saw Tony it was like it always is damn war; like it is every time.

But Cert convinced her to get down with the two of them and like putty in his hands she went for it. He didn't tell Tony that he had promised her that she would get paid. So when it came time for Tony and her to get down after Cert smashed her first; she held her hand out.

She had this sly ass grin on her face and it looked like she was playing games with him, again.

Tony went ballistic, calling her all kinds of whores and telling her she'd better give him some.

The bitch had nerve cause she jumped up and slapped the hell out of him. He had no choice but to grab her around her neck and start choking her. Well it wasn't his only choice but that's what he wanted to do. That bitch stole money from him and trying to clip him again.

Once the yelling started, it was looking like Tony might catch a charge, so again Cert got her to calm down. She really was gonna get Tony arrested up in Philly.

She likes to do that to dudes to control them.

"So who's this freak and does she got a friend?" Tony said interrupting his own thoughts.

It wasn't no use crying over spilt booty it's best to do something here and now to make up for any bad regrets. Besides he's gonna get some of Cheresse one of these days.

You can bet on that.

That hoe owes him.

"This chick I met name Tiasha," Cert said not really caring about whether Tony knows or not.

"What? Man that's Aijon's girl."

"She said she's here alone."

"I'm telling you that's Aijon's girl."

"Well what?"

Tony didn't say a thing. He just looked at Cert and before he could speak, Tiasha walked up.

"Cert you ready baby," Tiasha asked and then she saw Tony. "Hey Tony what's up?"

"Hey Tiasha what's up with you?"

"Nothing, me and Cert about to go for a ride."

"Oh yeah y'all going to pick up something to drink, where's Aijon?" he said trying to make sense of this.

"He's in the pool with some tricks. I'll be back before the party gets popping. I got sumethin' I gotta do," she said laughing and looking at Cert. "But if he asked you, you don't know nothing right."

Tony looked at Cert before he answered. Cert just lifted his eyebrows. Ain't this some shit he thought? How's this nigga gonna be uptight about dudes rolling up on his women but he's at this man's party about to go screw his woman? Cert is a fucking trip.

"I ain't getting in it," Tony said.

The two of them walked off and Tony decided to get his hunt on before all the prime property goes off the market. This is one more thing that reminds him of why he needs his boy Deron back on the streets with him.

Shit like this would get you messed up.

Cert don't have no discretion just wildling out for everybody to see.

****

It's about an hour before Tony actually caught up with Aijon and he seems like he's drunk. Tony had a few drinks himself but it isn't enough to stop him from getting it in with that Asian chick he saw earlier. As Aijon promised all these chicks that attended this party were open game brought and paid for by the host.

Aijon's the man on this one.

He had asked Tony what he thought about that VIP service he gave him on the parking, door-to-door action. He says that he only does that for his friends. Tony didn't consider them friends just running partners to get drunk and smoke weed with sometimes. His real friend is Deron; a nigga he can trust. He don't think he can trust Aijon or even Cert as a matter of fact. But he went along with Aijon cause at least dude thought enough to look out for him on the parking.

Thinking back on the Asian chick; come to find out little shorty has a bit of black in her and when Tony got to her, he put some more in her too.

Deron's correct on what he said when he said that Tony's got a whole other world that he lives in. But he likes this world cause it's a big ass world of fun. What should he be doing playing husband and wife with Valerie?

Hell's no.

Since they've been taking a break she's been doing her thing with the girls; probably shopping and shit he don't want to do.

This is just how it would be if they were together anyway, spending time apart.

CHAPTER 17

A few minutes later somewhere in D.C. as they sat real close to each other on the same side of the table, Valerie and Nathan clinked their glasses. They sat at a table in the corner of the Ruth's Chris Steak House and Valerie is having the time of her life. Nathan's everything, he makes himself out to be every time they got together. He always finds the nicest restaurants to take her to and the most romantic. If they're not doing that they're traveling to other cities just for the day to take in the décor of wherever they would be. Its good Tony and she are not on top of each other so she can get this chance to spend more time with Nathan.

Why is she so difficult with her choice of who she wants to be with?

Obviously, Nathan is her perfect choice.

Why is it so hard to choose?

Maybe she doesn't want to choose. Maybe she likes it that she has a man on the side to cater to her as she slowly makes Tony jealous. But, the jokes on her, he's not the least bit jealous.

He could care less whether or not she is even around.

That's why they're on this break.

"So have you thought about what I asked you Val?" Nathan asked her.

"You mean about going to Tampa with you?" she responded knowing absolutely what he's asked her before.

"Yes Val, you know what I mean. What's going on, you're not responding to me?"

"I am talking to you."

"No that's not what I mean. You seem like you're miles away from me, like you don't really want to be with me."

"It's not that. You know when you came to town I already had a life going on and I'm not done with that life."

"You mean that hood wannabe boyfriend you've been dating for the last past few years?"

"So you know about Tony huh?" she said letting out a deep breath. "And he's not a hood wannabe. He's a professional just like you."

"I've always known about him and I know he's not your type. Professional maybe but hood mentality. I don't know why you're with him."

"Are you asking me?"

"No. Yes."

"He has his good qualities and well I don't know. I guess I've just gotten use to him. You're not my second choice."

"I'm not? Are you sure?"

"Nathan I have feelings for you; that I know you know."

"But you're not in love with me and you know that's the bottom line. Got to have that or you don't have nothing."

"Well what do you expect me to do when you keep moving around the country all the time? Besides I don't really know that much about you and your past affairs."

"True but you should take the time to know me," he said as he reached into his suit jacket pocket. "And to prove it I have something for you," he finished saying as he laid down the envelope in front of her.

Valerie didn't need to pick up the envelope to see that the envelope has an airline ticket inside.

"You really do want me to go to Tampa with you don't you?"

"I want my woman to go to Tampa with me," he said grabbing her hand with his and pulling her to him.

As Nathan kissed, her Valerie thought in her mind that he called her his woman. This is something that she told Dawn that she wanted a man to declare to her, those very words.

"Nathan, I…"

"Shh, don't answer me now, let's just enjoyed the rest of our dinner without the tension, without other people on our minds, just let it be you and me and this bottle of wine. I want to see that red wine, pass those sweet lips of yours and savor every drop."

****

"Where the hell's she at Tony," Aijon yelled at the top of his lungs in his bedroom.

Tony had to take him up there because he was getting a little violent toward some of the folks, downstairs. He was already high as a damn kite and just as drunk.

Tiasha said that her and Cert were only going to be gone a minute; it's been over three hours. It's a good thing that Aijon's got all this help at the party or it would've turned up. Security and the girl that helped him put all this together Ikiera, Tony found out about her later, they helped cap the shit up and keep the party's flowing on.

Hell to most of the people there's nothing going on.

Ikiera made sure she cleared out the bottom level of the house first thing and everyone is either in the basement or outside in back unaware. After it turned dark, they were limiting the new folks that are coming in but those that did went straight from their cars to the backyard outside. Wasn't no reason for them to, draw PGP back there arresting folks they know will be drunk.

"I don't know where Tiasha is man, that's yo' lady," Tony said trying to stay out of the drama.

Shit he was trying to get in another round with another chick, making that move until this dumb ass Aijon started rolling through the house like a charging bull. Yelling and hollering like somebody shot him. Man should have some damn dignity. Can't be hard-up on some young broad not with all these *fineries* walking around here.

Tony guess after he got finish playing with those thots outside at the pool he decides he wants to look up his girl and see what she's doing. If you ain't keeping a fine ass looking woman like Tiasha, company or at least leaving her something that she'll never forget then this is what you get. Some other dude's digging out your lady.

Tony can't say he wasn't thinking about hittin' it either.

"Ikiera said she saw you talking to her and Cert."

"Shit that was almost five hours ago when I first got here."

"Ask Cert see if he knows."

"Man why don't you relax. This is a big ass spot; she could be anywhere joking with her girlfriends."

"Ask Cert man. Call that nigga. See if he knows where she is."

That is the last thing Tony wanted to do is to call Cert. Right now he's probably going three rounds with Tiasha ass up and he ain't gonna answer no phone.

He's not gonna do it.

He's not gonna get involved.

As a matter of fact, he's about to dust out cause this thing can get dirty and he ain't trying to spend the rest of the weekend being a witness or better yet outlined out in chalk.

"Well let me know what happens, I got to bounce," Tony said walking toward the door to Aijon's bedroom to leave.

As he was opening it, Ikiera rushed in.

"Aijon she's back," Ikiera said to him somewhat strange like to Tony.

It's almost as if she's disappointed that Tiasha's back.

"I'm going down there to see where she's been," Aijon said brushing pass Tony.

Tony didn't stop him either.

Just as soon as he hits the bottom step, he's out of here.

Walking pass the hall bathroom Tony thought he should take a leak before he hit the road. He's definitely leaving he confirmed in his mind as he walked into the bathroom. He done already scored, had some good weed and some drink, now it's time to get going.

Maybe he can stop over at Phaedra's before it turns midnight.

He sure, as hell ain't gonna go back over Deron's house this late, even though he knows him or Dawn won't mind. Like he told Deron, he'll go back to his house and sleep in the guess room in the basement if push comes to shove.

The construction at his house is almost complete and he's thinking about moving back in the house permanently anyway. At least he don't have to smell the dust that settling over there. After tonight if he doesn't end up over Phaedra, he'll moved back at his place a week before he planned.

****

Downstairs in the great room Aijon and Tiasha are getting into it while Cert and Ikiera look on.

"You don't seem to understand shit nicca, Ti-Ti do what she wants to do," Tiasha screamed. "And she wanted to take a fucking ride."

"Keep yo' voice down, I got people here."

"Nobody's gonna hear us up in here Aijon with that damn music blasting out there. You a dumbass."

"Don't everybody feel like you do. I'm glad of that."

"I know that baby. I saw those two hookers you were out there with at the pool. They were all up in yo' face. That's why I told you I'm no needy chick. I gets what I need," she said looking at Cert.

Aijon didn't say anything he just looked at her then to Cert. So this is what this nigga do come up in his pad and fuck his woman after he allowed that dude in his place. That's some foul shit and he's gonna deal with him some other time when that busta nigga ain't waiting' for it. And when he ain't on his property. He ain't gonna give him nothing to collect on.

It's gonna be clean.

"You owe me a damn apology, Tiasha."

"For what?"

"Why you think? You don't go off and not tell your man you leaving."

"You might as well forget that. I'm not lowering myself down to do that for your psycho ego. I keep telling you I got my own thing."

"Oh yeah you gonna apologize."

"You crazy. No never gonna apologize comma, never gonna apologize semicolon; never gonna apologize explanation point!" Tiasha said with a smirk. "I'm not gonna do it."

From Ikiera's standpoint, it is funny what she said even though she thinks that Tiasha is a slick ass trick. She knows that Aijon's unstable and weak with women and definitely that he's on her hard. One of these days he's gonna snap under her streetwise, reality show, talk and do something crazy.

It didn't take too long for Ikiera to see that because Aijon hauled off and smack the hell out of Tiasha.

"Son-of-a-bitch," Tiasha lashed back at him and they swung at each other right there in the great room.

Cert got in between the two of them pushing Aijon back. He went back on Cert and started swinging on him. The other man had no choice but to swing back. As they fell to the floor Ikiera ran to get the security and Cert had Aijon in a chokehold.

"Stop that shit, Cert let him go," Tiasha screamed. "Stop it, stop it," she started hitting him in the back of his head.

When he did, Aijon got up a little on him and forced him onto the floor. Cert thought damn I was just all up in that chick and she's taking that nigga's side. That's some messed up shit.

"I'm getting the hell out of here," Tiasha screamed at the two of them and ran pass security as they came rushing in.

They rushed up on Cert who is now back on top of Aijon and forcefully pulled him off him; throwing him to the floor then putting a knee in his back. The other whipped out his plastic nylon handcuffs and wrestled with Cert to put his hands in the small of his back. Then he cuffed him.

"Tiasha wait," Aijon called out to her but she was gone out the great room and out the front door by now. He followed her.

He ran to the cabinet that is on the side of the wall out of the way, unlocked it with a key and opened it. He reached in and grabbed a bag out of it. He shut and locked it then headed for the front door.

Outside Aijon went to one of the valets and asked him quickly where Tiasha went, whether she drove off he said. The valet told him that she took her car and drove off the property screeching her tires.

He needed to follow her Aijon thought.

Looking around remembered, his cars and his truck are in his garage. The garage door is block with trucks from the caterers to the DJ. He has to get a vehicle. Then he saw a truck parked in the circle and he knows it is Tony's. He got the keys from the valet and instantly hopped into the truck, started it and drove off.

****

"What the hell y'all doing," Tony said as he walked casually into the great room.

There on the floor two big security guys has got Cert lying face down on the floor with a strong plastic tie bounding his hands together on his back. Ikiera's there too saying nothing and talking to the third security officer that's standing by her.

"Get back sir this don't have nothing to do with you," one security guy said.

"Ikiera what's going on? Where's Aijon," Tony asked.

"Gone after that Baltimore hood rat. They must be outside. I hope he ain't out there fighting her," she said to him plainly like this is all business. Then she turned to the security guy again. "It's time to shut this party down before the police come here. Somebody might call them."

Tony ran outside after he heard her say that.

When he got out there, it is quiet except for the music coming from around back and the speakers that are, installed up front. He hadn't noticed it before. Boy Aijon sure spent a lot of money on this place and you would think he'd have that style to go with his place.

Instead, he's just a crazy lunatic with money.

PG might be here in a minute if they have Cert down on the floor like that. Somebody done called them he knows it; even if everybody's outside and don't have a clue what's going on.

He's about to be ghost.

Out of instinct, Tony then looked over to his truck.

It's like a blow to his head when he looked over there and it is gone. He instantly ran to the valet and asked him about where it is now.

"That truck that was parked there? Yeah the owner Aijon took it."

"What the hell I'm the owner. Did he tell you that was his truck?"

"Yeah. I wasn't here when you pulled up so I didn't know."

Tony wanted to punch the valet in his mouth. How you gonna let anybody just tell you that a truck belongs to them and you give them the damn keys no question asked? Who does something stupid like that Tony fumed in his mind. He'd better be glad it's Aijon that took his truck but that fool is high and drunk he might scratch his shit up.

****

On the road Aijon, manage to follow Tiasha directly onto I95 south only because he got a tracker put on her car. His IPhone 6Plus is tracking her car's every move on the google map. She had a few minutes on him but he was catching up with her. He dodged in and out of traffic weaving into the other vehicles a little, as he passed them. When he does catch up with her they're gonna have it out. He wasn't smashing those chicks at that pool just entertaining them. She had no right messing with one of his friends and that son-of-a-bitch is, done when he gets things settled with Tiasha. She just don't know how much he cares for her and she went and did something like that. Now he's gonna have to cut her off because he don't share pussy with dudes and know about it. She wanta be out there then she can do it.

But he's gonna have it out with her first.

Tony's Escalade moved faster than it should be going down I95 in the darkness. It is a good thing that southbound traffic wasn't that heavy or Aijon would have ran in the back of somebody. His reaction is already a little slow and his anger is making him reckless. He picked up his phone and pushed Tiasha number on his phone. In between that call, he saw Tony's number pop up but he ignored it as Tiasha call connected.

"What is it Aijon," Tiasha said flatly over the speaker on the phone.

"You know you ain't right. You let that dude smash you."

"You don't know what I did; you just accused me of the shit."

"Yeah I know you did. You ain't wifey material."

"I ain't trying to marry you Aijon, you crazy. I'm too young and hot for that."

Aijon noticed a text come across his phone.

> **Bring my fuckin truck back now man!!!!!**
>
> **11:56 PM**

It is Tony and Aijon just deleted the text and went back to talking to Tiasha.

"I want you to pull over," he demanded to her.

"Leave me alone Aijon. I know you put a trace on my car. You keep following me and I'm going right to the police."

"You don't stop I'm gonna shoot myself," he said to her patting the bag he had in the other front seat.

"That's not funny Aijon," she said with a little concern in her voice. "You need to turn around and head back to your house. You forgot you have people there," she said.

"I ain't doing nothing. Just pull over and wait for me," he said pressing the gas pedal a little harder.

Aijon droved about fifteen minutes more and suddenly, he saw it in the rearview mirror and on the two side mirrors.

The first light blue.

The next light red.

Then the lights mixed as they rotated and he knew what that meant. Looking at the police lights flashing caused an anger in Aijon and he flashed back to some other time he stopped for the police.

Well he ain't stopping for these county cops.

He's gonna outrun them.

He pushed the pedal to the floor and the Escalade kicked into its full power. He's got to hand it to Tony he's got a bad ass truck. He started to pull away from the police but just slightly. He heard Tiasha on the other end telling him to turnaround and head back to his house but it's too late now he's in the chase now.

Five Prince Georges County Police's cars chased Aijon down the beltway across Allentown Road and then pass the exit to turn onto it. Aijon is getting it and the Escalade is handling the speed excellently.

A few minutes later just before he could get pass the National Harbor to get to the Woodrow Wilson Bridge,

Aijon saw four police cars pull onto I95 from the shoulders. Two on the thruway and on the other side of the divided interstate also heading south two are on the local side to block him. The police and probably news helicopters that are following him are swirling around in the distance behind the blockade. He didn't see a way to go except to push right through them. He didn't think that it would work to do that. Then he looked over, saw the exit sign for D.C. and drove towards it. He saw the cop car that is halfway blocking the off ramp and felt he could go around it. Then he could lose himself in southeast somewhere. All he has to do is abandon the truck when he gets there. Once he pays that money to everyone who knows he's behind the wheel to be quiet the police will just think that it was a stolen truck from his party. Then they'll think the truck was abandon.

The police car is partially on the road and Aijon thought he could maneuver the truck around it and keep up the speed. Just when he approached the car, the officer pulled his car up slightly forcing Aijon to compensate. He had no choice but to drive towards the embankment to the left and over it the truck went. It is going too fast for him to really slowdown and compensate. He ended up rolling it several times down the embankment before it went into the small pond off to the left side. The truck stopped resting in the murky water. The entire vehicle is, banged up pretty badly. Aijon isn't moving as the police got to the vehicle with their guns drawn and shining flashlights. Some of them actually treading the murky water to get to Aijon in the vehicle.

Somewhere on the ground, Aijon's cellphone laid. Tiasha's voice could be, heard on the cellphone screaming his name repeatedly.

****

Back at Aijon's house Ikiera has shut down the party and the people are all leaving slowly. No one is in the house but Ikiera, Tony, Cert, a few security guys and the hired wait staff.

Tony and Cert are off by themselves talking. More like Tony is getting into Cert's shit.

"It's yo' fault Cert. You had to push up on Tiasha today at this dude's party. You know how much of a damn loose cannon he is."

"Man that's her fault. She wanted to ride so I took her for a ride. Why that shit on me?"

"I just said it nigga, he's a fool. Now he's running around in my damn truck, probably scratching it up hitting parked cars."

"Well I was just sticking around to see if Tiasha okay. If she ain't coming back no time soon I'm out. She ain't returning my calls or my text. You don't think he's caught up with her do you?"

"Oh now you worried about her? Naw don't be worried. Don't be worried he might be strangling her ass in the backseat of my damn truck. He's got my truck," Tony yelled getting security's attention.

He waved them off.

"That ain't my fault," Aijon said hitting his chest with his open hand.

"Nigga it's all yo' fault. Smashing hoes and ain't doing the background check. I told you she's Aijon's girl from the jump. You ain't care. Then you gonna fight the man in his own home after he invited you."

"Man look T that wasn't my fault. Aijon went in on me, I was defending myself."

"Y'all guys got to go," Ikiera said walking up to them. "The party's over and all guest got to exit."

"Trick Aijon got my truck," Tony said angrily. "Did he tell you when he gonna return it?"

"First of all no trick's here. Second, I know you don't want security to put you down like they did your friend. Y'all ain't no friends of AJ anyway screwing his woman."

"I didn't have nothing to do with that," Tony said back to her. "And security ain't doing shit to me."

"Oh yeah," she said waving the security over to her.

"How am I supposed to get home," he demanded.

"You can ride with him. I know he got a car because him and the real trick Tiasha was riding in it."

"You got a point. I'm gonna leave. But when AJ comes back with my truck make sure it's clean and there better not be a scratch on it or I'm gonna sue somebody. You his personal assistant get it done, press ass wanna be yo' boss' side chick," he said exiting the great room and then the front door.

Cert just stood there until Ikiera looked at him and tilted her head curiously. Then she motioned her head to the door as if to tell him to follow his boy out the door.

Cert gave her the finger and did just that.

****

Outside all the vehicles are gone all but Cert's car. They walked over to it and Cert unlocked his driver side door to get in. Tony tried his side and found it still locked.

"Man open the door."

"You got gas money T?" Cert joked. "You live on the other side of Bowie all out the way."

"Nigga I oughta hit you right in yo' face for playing with me. Open the damn door."

****

She couldn't believe it.

She actually did it.

She came here with him and now they're lying snug in his bed and she loves it.

He is easily just as good a lover as Tony, Valerie thought just like she remembered.

But did she play her hand too quick? She still deeply loves Tony and it's amazing how she can even be thinking about him at this time. Nathan squeezed her a little tighter as if to agree with her thought.

This is what she is trying to avoid her heart being pulled into two separate directions. Dawn is right. She heard what Dawn was trying to tell her she just didn't want to listen because her pride was hurt. She didn't think that after all that she's done to show Tony that she's in love with him that he just won't be good to her.

Now what?

What does she do now that she's just complicated things and now that she has reacquainted herself again with Nathan?

And she has no regrets.

"I take it that the answer is yes?" Nathan asked her.

"Yes to what?"

"To everything that I'm going to ask you."

"I don't get what you mean."

"That's because your guards are up. Let them down Val like you just did earlier. I've always loved you since college and I was a fool to let you slide by me. I don't plan on making that mistake again."

"Really," she responded caught up in the euphoria of his words.

Again, he found the right words to say and she knows he means every word of it right down to the letter.

"Come to Tampa with me Val," he begged and kissed her neck.

"I don't know Nathan," she sighed trying to lose her sanity in his romance.

CHAPTER 18

By Monday morning, Tony is still mad as hell. He's gotten no sleep on Sunday. He had to talk to his insurance company all day once that broad Ikiera called him to tell him Aijon crashed his truck. How the hell did that happen? Useless question because Tony already knows the answer. Aijon tried to run a police blockade and ended up flipping the truck.

My badass truck he thought, gone.

That fool stole my truck and crashed it.

The insurance company's probably gonna give him some bullshit disbursement check with an amount that ain't even gonna be close to what that truck is worth.

It's a total lost; body frame, motor and all the circuitries, everything.

Oh yeah and miraculously that fool Aijon lived.

Guess he was more, juiced up than anybody thought. He just broke both his legs, an arm and crack some ribs. Maybe the accident knocked some sense in his head about messing with them young ass girls and not turning them out instead of falling in love with one. Clearly, he's in love with Tiasha or he wouldn't had gone after her taking on the police while he was doing it.

He's in big trouble.

He hasn't told Deron yet cause he didn't want to hear his mouth telling him he told him so. He'll just go on and on about how he should have just gone with him to shoot pool. He'll definitely start in on him about God and Tony definitely don't want to hear about that; not all the time. Even after he's showed how much fun he's been missing staying out the night life. All it is all the time is Dawn and his son. The man acts like he's in his fifties or something. All Tony want to do is turn up like they used to.

Sometimes he feels like going to church with D just to shut him up about it.

Now he has to go and lease a vehicle until he can get his money for his truck.

Damn Aijon.

****

Sitting at his desk, Deron made every effort to make sure he knocks out his work for the next two days. Usually when he did that, he didn't have anything to do for the rest of the week but oversee the operations. Before Dawn, he used to take that downtime to go to an early happy hour with Tony and Bryan. Then after Dawn and him got together he started meeting her for lunch. Now he tries to be productive taking some online classes at Maryland to up his game.

It's good to see Sharnia back on the job after being off for the last week and a half. She doesn't seem to have any burns and no smoke damage. She's blessed and don't know it. She of course don't know that Deron was there at the house when she laid in Tony's bed near death. Since she's probably not spoken to Tony at all she thinks he didn't tell him; which he probably wouldn't have done if Deron wasn't there that night. It's a lot of that these days.

Even though she's back in full swing she still isn't talking to anyone and not being herself. That she hasn't been for a long time. Deron thought that with this fire she would have learned her lesson but she don't look like she has. She may need professional help. Deron really doesn't know her like that other than working with her. He's never hung out with her and they certainly don't know each other on a personal level. So he doesn't know how she is really. He really thought she was cool and that they were friendly. She could have real deep issues and no one would know it. He does know that she purposely tried to burn Tony's house down. Now whether she meant to kill herself is another thing. That's stupid to want to kill yourself over somebody he thought. He remembers when Cheresse asked him if he was going to do that over her, she must be nuts. Not trying to be self-involved but out all his mother's kids he loves himself the most.

He wants to talk to Sharnia bad but he doesn't want to set her off. She seems like she would go there if he did say something to her and he doesn't need the headaches.

Getting out of his chair, Deron walked over to the large window that viewed the parking lot. This is where he usually goes when he has a lot on his mind. As he was standing there, he saw two PG county police cars pull up in the parking lot and parked. The two officers got out and headed for the entrance. He can't imagine what they would want unless they had more to talk about dealing with that fight Dawn and Cheresse had. He thought they had settled that with Cheresse getting probation and another year restraining order for her to stay away from the two of them that long. Maybe this time she'll get Deron out of her system. That would be fantastic.

He decided he isn't going to cow tail like he did a few years ago thinking he's going to get arrested. This time he knows he hasn't done anything wrong and he certainly isn't going to do or say anything to get his wife in trouble.

He opened the door to his office in just enough time to hear the officers addressing Sharnia at her desk.

"Ms. Sharnia Burkefield, you are to come with us. You're under arrest for arson," the one officer said.

She didn't say anything she just got up from the desk and turned her back to them. As the officer put her in handcuffs, the other one read her rights to her. She remained quiet and said nothing still except to nod when he asked her if she understood her rights. When they turned her, around she saw Deron, she stared at him and said nothing; but she smiled. What's going through her mind he wondered but he smiled back at her and nodded.

It is an awkward moment. Deron didn't say anything to them. The officer took her out as quiet as they came in.

He went back to his office and walked over to the window. He watched as the police put Sharnia in the back seat and closed the door. She looked out of the window defeated. To him it is lucky that nobody at the plant saw this happening at least to his knowledge. He went back over to his desk and pulled up the number to the Temp agency that he's been using off and on since he hasn't had a permanent reception. Now he's going need someone to replace Sharnia's job because he don't think she's coming back anytime soon. He tried to warn her about messing with Tony but she just wouldn't listen.

****

At the end of the week by Friday, Tony moved back into his house. Everything is done and he's slowly but surely getting his life back to normal. He is beginning to enjoy the brand new Suburban he's been leasing and thought he just might buy a new one when he gets his papers. A few days this week, he's been getting with Phaedra and she's been turning him out. She seems to be enjoying that account at the bank maybe that's the reason why he's been getting all this sex action.

It's been a while since he's heard from Valerie and he can't understand why. She said this is only a break, but did she break up with him? He noticed that things about the wedding are still coming to the house like their invitations, an appointment with some caterer and an appointment to see the Pastor that's going to marry them. That latter appointment is the one he don't want to do. They have a month session with him once a week and he don't feel like sitting up in no office talking about their life together.

He should go head and tell Valerie that he don't want to get married.

Why don't he want to let her go?

He knows he loves her but not enough to get married.

If he didn't he would be worried about where she is he'd be enjoying this time smashing Phaedra when he wanted.

No word from Sharnia either.

He's been calling her cell but she ain't been picking up. He wants her to explain that dumb ass episode at the house and what she's planning on doing. He's still a little pissed with Erica being so careless with his keys. She acts like she's mad with him but she's the one that fucked up.

It was strange that he got that call from that police Detective Hayden earlier today. But then again he is the one that suggested that Steve Powers is, connected to Bryan's death. Detective Hayden told him that after he brought him in on suspicion they couldn't put nothing on him, so they had to let him go after 24 hours. Even though Carl said he got his marching orders from someone, they couldn't pinpoint Steve. Even the texts were out there and meant something but not enough. They may have been compelling but wouldn't stand up in court. They couldn't even use the trip to Las Vegas and his attempt on Yolanda's life. That couldn't be proven in front of a grand jury either. What's gonna need to happen is that Steve trips himself up somehow. Once they get a foot in that will open up a can of whoop ass on Steve and they'll finally get him.

His thoughts were, cut off by his cellphone.

He looked at the number and pushed the green call accepted button on his phone.

"What's up Nick, you taken my calls now?" Tony said to the caller.

"What's up Tone?" Nick said.

Nick Sanderson is Tony's running partner on the job. They became fast friends when Tony started there and always keeps each other on notice to anything coming the other's way. Tony don't have too many white male friends but he likes Nick cause he's real. He don't have that kind of ego when you fear somebody you don't know; that's a different race. They click because they both know their shit and don't intimidate each other. Not like that other dude in his office name Walter. This dude must be going through a middle-age crisis or something because he's always talking about all the stuff he does around his house; and what he's buys. Especially that damn RV he's trying to sell. He's been after this one dude to buy the damn RV and it looks like the guy's backing out of the deal. So every day the office has to hear about this RV and how he's waiting on the dude to make a decision. How much he could actually get on Craigslist. He gets on Tony's nerves so damn bad that sometimes he feels like taking a loan out just to buy the damn thing, so the dude can shut the hell up.

"Where you been I've been calling your office."

"Man I had to check to see if my phones aren't tapped. You have got the bank on edge dude."

"What do you mean on edge?"

"I don't know too much but they're going through your accounts like crazy. You doing business with somebody criminal?"

"Hell no. I don't do shit like that Nick, you know that."

"I do. Well if I hear something else I'll call you."

"Yeah and thanks Nick, I appreciate that."

****

The next day around four o'clock Tony decided to go over to Phaedra's house. She claims she had customers at the shop late today but she canceled all her evening clients to lay in bed with him. Tony knows he has her where he wants her when she gives up that dollar to be with him. He hopes she's just falling for the pipe and not falling in love.

He already experienced what a stalker can do when Sharnia started that fire.

They spent most of the afternoon having sex all over her townhouse. They are lying in the living room on the sofa about to go for another round when the doorbell to her townhouse rang. Phaedra got up and put on her robe that barely covered anything and then went to the window.

When she looked outside the window, she saw it is Jerrell and Steve and panicked.

"Oh shit. Tony you got to go. Um I mean I got to answer that door because they know I'm…," she said almost losing it in front of him.

"Phaedra what the hell," Tony said just lying back on the sofa naked.

Then she heard the top lock to her front door unlock.

"Get up, get up, get in the backroom back there and don't say nothing no matter what," she said in a panic hurrying around trying to pick up the liquor glasses that are on the coffee table and the torn condom wrappers lying about. She quickly threw it in the kitchen trash.

Fortunately, Tony's pants and shirt are upstairs in the bedroom and out of the way. He hopes that whoever it is, isn't gonna want to go up there or to this other room in the back.

They unlocked the bottom lock and came in just when Phaedra is returning from taking the glasses to the kitchen sink. She stood awkwardly in the middle of the living room as both Jerrell and Steve mounted the stairs.

"You didn't hear the doorbell, Phaedra?" Jerrell said to her.

Tony heard the one male voice but he also heard the other dude with him. He could tell by the sounds of the footsteps as they ran up the stairs.

"I heard the door I was just about to come down after I put something on but you didn't give me a chance," Phaedra said smartly to him.

"What's the point in waiting when you got a key?" he said dangling a set of keys up to her. "Don't be shy."

He walked over to her and noticed she didn't have nothing on underneath her robe. He opened her robe and then ran his hand down her stomach between her legs. Steve just looked on nodding and smiling. Treat her like a prostitute he thought. She's always trying to act like she's this tough business woman. As it stands when it came down to doing business with this chick the only thing she could use as a bargaining chip is her body. He should have got on her first before she became Jerrell's trick.

Jerrell don't like to share though.

Jerrell pulled his fingers from between her legs and put one in his mouth.

"Don't taste right. Taste like a condom. You been fucking this morning?"

"Maybe, it's not any of your business dirty old freak."

He just did one swift backhand move and smacked her so hard across the face, it shocked Steve. This fool is crazy. They may already be in trouble now because he let him convince him in trying to kill Yolanda for her money and property; and that shit backfired. Now he's in here manhandling her like she's stupid.

They don't need her calling the police.

He collaborated with him because he has that shrew business sense almost ruthless. At forty-eight, he's seen a lot of real estate deals go down above and below the table and can teach him some things. Steve wanted to be on the fast and he's keeping him there. So when that day comes for him to branch off on his own independently he'll be good to go.

Phaedra cried aloud which made Tony perked up in the backroom. He wanted to know what's going on out there but he's not going out there. He don't know what mess Phaedra's mixed up in but she didn't say that she has a boyfriend. Now Tony's gonna have to fight these dudes buck ass naked to get out of here.

Damn, his clothes, is upstairs.

"What the hell you hit me like that for Jerrell? What I do with my hole is my business," she said as she backed away from him and shut her robe; tying it tightly in a knot.

"That ain't the reason why I hit your ass. You, dumb ass bitch. You don't steal from us," Jerrell said. "You make money *for* us. We own the mortgage on that salon. I put money in this townhouse. When we funnel extra money to you, it goes in your account not to your financial advisor. You don't skim shit off. Who is he?"

"I don't know who you're talking about," Tony heard Phaedra say. "I got that money in another account. I didn't know you needed it that fast. Dag I was only borrowing a little of it. It's a lot of money. I was trying to flip it to make a profit."

Whew, Tony thought. He's not afraid of them punks but he don't want no dealing with them because this thing has gotten heavy. Dudes like those will try to get you on the sly if you don't keep an eye on them. Best for T to be out of sight for this unless things start to get a little rougher.

Phaedra's lying. She didn't invest in anything that seems like it's going to flip her a profit real fast. She only invested in these local businesses around here and he told her that was stupid.

So this is Jerrell.

What's Phaedra doing messing with these guys and she used their money in the account Tony authorized at his bank? Their shit is illegal and that could spell trouble for him.

"We need you to drain all our money out of that account and hand it over. You might as well make arrangements and we'll get back to you in a couple hours. I don't care if the bank is closed," he said as he turned to leave and Steve followed him silently. "Don't think that body of yours can get you out of everything, remember that."

The two of them walked down the stairs and out the door, slamming it. Tony came back out into the living room and got in Phaedra's face, as she stood there shocked from her encounter with Jerrell and Steve.

"So you smashing with that guy? Don't you know he's bad news?"

"Don't talk to me like I'm some empty headed trick Tony, I got this," she said nervously looking around for something.

"All you got is trouble coming your way and you ain't getting me mixed in this shit with you. Let this be the last time you contact me and yeah get yo' money out of my bank. I'm already getting investigated because of you."

"You ain't nothing but a punk Tony. I thought you was a man, you ain't hard. You can't handle a little bit of pressure from a couple of punk businessmen."

"Look cut that shit. I ain't got no low self-esteem. These guys are trouble. Jerrell has realtor companies trying to buy land and property and the way they go about it is criminal and shady. Their ass and you gonna get locked up," he said and she turned to look him in the face. "He's got a partner Steve Powers and he's already set somebody up who was killed and one to be killed, so don't tell me what I know. Keep messing with them and they'll stunt you."

That's right Phaedra thought Steve never said anything so Tony couldn't have known he was there. How did he know Steve and is what he's saying about him true? There's no sense in telling him that Steve was just there.

"You're always so dramatic nigga. You're not in the fucking mafia Tony so you need to cut that shit. As a matter of fact, get the hell out of here, I've got things to do."

"Ain't nothing but an easy request to me," he said heading up the steps to her bedroom to get his clothes. After a minute, he came back downstairs fully dressed. "Hell I'm with that punk Jerrell that body ain't poison enough," he finished opening the door and storming out angrily.

All Phaedra did is look on.

She really didn't have time to get into it with Tony like this. She already knew anyway that the two of them were ending. It's because he's the kind of dude that'll get on your nerves quick and she's there right now.

Like she said she's got other things to do like find out where she's going to get this money she took from them. She spent what she took from them and there's nothing left.

****

While Jerrell and Steve rode in the car together, they discussed an alternative to their plans.

"We got to cut our losses on that trick Jerrell," Steve said as he drove his car heading back to their office.

"I know what we got to do but it's got to be done now," he responded. "Turn around."

****

Tony drove the leased truck towards home. He may just get a Suburban when Aijon pays him for his truck. Wasn't no sense in trying to, get a new one until he got his money. Right now he doesn't want to spend any more money because of the money he spent on his house waiting for the insurance company to cut him a check. Once inside his house he went upstairs to his bedroom to relax. As he threw the keys onto his dresser, he reached to his back pocket to pull out his wallet and it isn't there. Immediately he started looking around for it because he has over six hundred dollars and his credit cards in it.

He backtracked all the way back to the truck and realized he must have left his wallet over Phaedra's townhouse. Well he thought he ain't leaving his shit in her hands or most definitely it will be empty when it's returned to him.

With her money problems.

He got back into the truck and drove off heading for Phaedra's house.

****

This is just how he likes his Saturdays, quiet and productive Deron thought. Dawn and Deron Jr are over Yolanda, which gives him time to work on some more, home projects. He's on his way home from his third trip to Home Depot now after picking up some shelving this time; for his garage. Something's he can do but the bigger projects need Tony's contractor connections.

They're cheap but they're good at what they do, really good.

Wow, he thought as he looked at the gas gauge. He's almost empty on gas. How did he not realize that? Something must be wrong with the indicator chime not letting him know he's almost out of gas. He can't let the BMW truck run completely out of gas at least he don't think he should. He pulled over and decided to give Tony a call.

****

"Yeah D I can scoop you up but we can't go directly to your house. I got to slide by to this chick's house and get my wallet I left there," he said thinking it'll be best not to say anything to D about it being Phaedra.

"Well Tony then that's alright I don't want to take you from where you gotta go. I'll just call the emergency service and get them to bring some gas."

"D if big brother can't help you then you short. Besides if that service of yours brings you gas it's gonna hurt you in the end for when you really need 'em."

"That's what they're there for."

"I got you man five minutes, out,"

****

It didn't take Tony but five minutes like he said to pick up Deron. Then it was off to Phaedra's before she finds his wallet and go buck wild with his cash and cards. He don't trust her in this state when she broke and she's mad with him too. She'd probably do it out of spite.

"I'm serious T, I like this new truck," Deron said after they went a little way.

"Yeah big brother wanted to change up a little. I'm thinking about trading my truck in for one like this."

He still didn't want to tell Deron that Aijon crashed his truck. He don't think he'll every tell him. This will be just one more thing he would feel like he's gonna judge him on. Especially since its Aijon cause Deron did jive like warn him about that nut case.

"So where are we heading T," Deron asked him making conversation.

"Just to a little freak I know townhouse. You don't know her," he said lying to Deron and wondering why he keeps doing that.

"You know I wasn't going to say anything about this," Deron said before he paused. "The police came to the job and they arrested Sharnia on Monday for arson, did you know that?"

"Naw D, why didn't you call me man?"

"I didn't want to put you on the spot. I mean we never really talked about that night and I figured you wanted to keep it that way."

"I guess you got a point man. I just didn't feel like hearing another lecture from you on how foul I'm living."

"Man I'm not doing that. I'm trying to get you to be aware of your salvation."

"I get it but let me choose like you did D if that's what I want to do. Just like Bryan did for you. But I tell you that's not what I want right now."

"I got it."

"You know Valerie ain't been talking to me lately."

"Oh yeah," Deron said realizing that Tony just skipped right passed the Sharnia thing.

It didn't matter.

No need to talk about it, he was there.

The fire and the arrest speaks for itself.

But he sure would like to know if she meant to kill herself or was it something else.

"Yeah."

"What's going on there? You know she's over at Yolanda's still, so why don't you call?"

"I know but I'm not running Valerie down. She knows where I am. Where I live."

"Is that the way you want to play it T."

"I ain't playing no games she is. She acts like she don't want to get married."

"Well give her some time and you at least got to speak to her before you assume what's on her mind."

"I'm not used to begging D. You know that's hard for me."

"If you compromised it wouldn't look like you were begging. You know Valerie's on your every word. All you got to do is talk to her and be honest with yourself and then to her."

Deron didn't want to sound like a broken record but this is something serious. Years ago, when Tony first proposed to Val he quickly called it off. He just started messing with Sharnia and other women like running water. He never gave Val a chance and she stuck by him probably thinking he would change but he's gotten worse. It's time for Tony to let Val go so she can find her own happiness apart from him or she's going to hate him soon. Then she'll leave anyway. What would be the use?

****

Once he got to Phaedra's neighborhood, Tony parked in the guest parking instead of in front of her house. He wanted Deron as far away from the house as he could get without being too obvious. It's funny even though he don't bother too much with Deron's religion, for some reason he wanted to keep his antics away from him. He got out of the truck and walked steadily to the front door. He rang the doorbell and then he noticed the smell.

There is no answer.

It's faint but it's something he couldn't ignore.

Its gas he thought.

He banged on the door repeatedly and still no response.

Instinctively he tried the doorknob and found it unlocked. Once he opened the door the gas rushed at him and he turned away coughing.

"D, D," he yelled to him in the truck.

Deron jumped out of the truck to see what Tony wanted and when he got to the door, he smelled the gas as well.

"What going on Tony?"

"Phaedra's in there in the townhouse," he said that as the gas got to him more and he started coughing repeatedly.

Deron knows he heard him right but he can't react to it right now. T didn't look like he's able to go in there so he's got to do it, he thought. He has to get in there and see if Phaedra's all right. He took in a deep breath and ran into the townhouse right up the stairs. He didn't know where to look but he didn't have to look far because Phaedra sat, tied to a chair; slumped over unconscious.

Running to the gas stove he turned off the burners that were on and then to the windows opening them fast. He let out his breath. He went back to Phaedra as the gas started to get to him too. Lord please let her be all right he thought. He didn't think about where to grab her he just did pulling her and the chair with him down the stairs. He couldn't take it as he got down to the bottom of the steps and saw that he was at the front door. Fresh air filled his lungs as he pulled himself, Phaedra and the chair she was tied to outside. He saw Tony still coughing on the side of the townhouse stoop.

Untying Phaedra from the chair Deron checked her to see if she was breathing.

"Tony call 911," he said as he started to perform CPR on Phaedra.

****

When Dawn got to Doctor's Hospital Deron and Tony was just coming down from the emergency room. She ran up and hugged Deron but still didn't understand why he's here. When he called her to tell her he's at the hospital, he was vague. He told her that Tony is with him but she couldn't get in touch with Val to tell her.

She guesses he was able to get in touch with her himself.

"Why are you here?" she asked him curiously.

"A girl we know was in trouble," Deron answered reluctantly.

He really didn't want to tell Dawn anything because Phaedra's somebody that before today he hasn't seen or heard from in almost two years.

"Dawn," Tony interrupted. "Deron didn't have anything to do with this. I know the girl, well we both know her but I took Deron with me to go over to her house. It's on me. I mean he was just…I picked Deron up because he almost ran out of gas. He didn't know I had to go by this girl's house and he got involved accidently. I'm glad he came because I had a reaction from that gas fumes. I might've gone in and passed out too. Thanks for being there bruh," Tony said slapping Deron on the back.

"So my baby's a hero?" Dawn said proudly thinking that she has seen it all. Tony Parker is finally speaking the truth, right out taking responsibility. "What about the girl?"

"She's still unconscious but she'll live," Tony said.

"Umm Dawn before we leave I need to holler at Tony for a minute."

She nodded and walked off.

"T now that we've got a chance to talk…"

"Deron I don't know."

"Damn it Tony, Phaedra was almost killed and you just so happened to be sleeping with her. What's going on?"

"Steve Powers and Jerrell again man."

"I don't get it."

"Phaedra is in with them. They fund a business for her."

"What kind of business?"

"A hair salon."

He's not gonna tell him that he opened up an account for Phaedra's business that he's probably going to get in trouble behind; because she's stealing money from them. She said she spent that money in the account. So she probably over drafted it and that's what trouble he's in at work. He pulled strings to get her that business loan and account. She didn't have the juice to back her to get all that. Now she's done burned him royally.

So he only told him that she stole money from them.

"So they tried to kill her and you're messing with her? Man Tony this is serious. You need to go back to the police."

"See D. this is the reason why I don't tell you shit. You blow things way up. I'm just diggin' her out not involved with her no other way," he said confidently.

"You knew this when Yolanda was dating Steve?"

"Hell no, I just found out earlier today. I told her I was leaving her ass alone. Only reason for going back over there was that I left my wallet. I don't know all that they had going down. Once she told me I warned her that they would try something like this."

"And I warned you."

EPILOGUE

It is late in the afternoon and Dawn is preparing to go over Yolanda with Deron Jr in tow. She's had the day of all days and it's a day that is the best.

She has the most fantastic news to share. It's funny how she found out about it and will be a story to tell all her kids in the future. Dawn chipped a nail during that stupid fight with Cheresse and at first, it didn't bother her but it must've chipped into the skin. It didn't bother her before but eventually it did. So she went to the nail salon and got it repaired about two weeks later because it was uneven as it was growing back. Well many times, they warn you about nail salons and how you sometimes pick up bacteria. The nail bed under the repaired nail became infected. After a week of trying to doc it up herself, she had no choice but to go to her doctor.

The pain started to be intense.

It was pretty routine. As she sat there, she thought how silly it was for her to go all in and fight this woman. A woman who has taunted her from everything about having a sexual relationship with her man to the fact that she hasn't given him children yet. But that didn't matter to her because her son gave her confirmation right there in front of Cheresse.

And if that didn't show her how powerful Jesus is this sure will.

The jokes on Cheresse.

She can still hear the doctor tell her, "Before I give you an antibiotic for this affection I need to run a pregnancy test to make sure you're not pregnant…"

Then he came back later and said, "Guess what, you're pregnant."

She couldn't believe how fast the Lord moved even though she's seen it happen like this before. Months ago she has been thinking, even worrying about the fact that she couldn't give Deron any children and the possibility that it may be permanent. She let that wicked woman get in her head. Now wham, out of nowhere she's pregnant.

Father you are so good to me, Dawn thought.

It's one of the best gifts she could receive. Things were finally turning around now and she's so happy. This is what they wanted, to start having more kids.

Deron Jr's about to have a brother or sister.

Hope this one's a girl she thought.

She can't wait to tell Deron.

****

She pulled up in the driveway of parking lot and parked her car in two spaces on an angle. She did that on purpose because she didn't feel like moving it to properly park. To hell with other cars she thought, they don't get visitors like that out here at this dump anyway.

As she turned off her car, she looked up to the big bay window and hoped she can catch him off guard.

This is going to be good, she thought.

Getting out of the car, she walked boldly into the office building entrance. With the three-story climb up the stairs, she reached her destination. These little office spaces out here in Maryland made her laugh. It isn't like where she worked at downtown, with its twelve or so floors and fancy décor. The older woman temp who sat at the desk looked at her puzzlingly as she walked into the office space.

The temp watched her steadily as she walked toward her desk. She noticed that she's dress in the perfect business attire with the shoes and purse to match; even though the skirt seems a little bit too high, she thought. Clearly the wrong type of woman. She didn't know if she belonged here or not and went to address the unknown woman.

"Don't worry, he's always not expecting me; but he won't be mad. You go on and have a seat," she said rudely with a laugh. "Just sit your old ass down," she added just in earshot of the receptionist.

She didn't give the woman a chance to protest as she just headed to the back office; down the hall.

Without knocking on the door, she opened it and walked straight in letting the door swing back hard against the doorstop that's mounted on the floor.

Standing over at the opposite window the one in the newly built conference portion of his office, Deron turned quickly to face the unannounced visitor.

"You just don't call do you? You're just gonna barge in here unannounced? And it don't seem like you obey the law either. Remember the restraining order," he said to her.

"Damn that, I do what I want remember?" she said slamming the door and taking a seat in one of the chairs; that sat in front of his desk.

"What do you want Cheresse, what's left?" he said deciding to sit down at his desk because there's no point in trying to put her out physically.

Boy did he want to though.

Suddenly his office door opened again and in ran the temp.

"Don't worry about it Mrs. Parring, I was expecting Ms. Bennett."

Giving Cheresse a dirty look Mrs. Parring nodded and then left.

He didn't want to make this scene get turnt up as Tony would say; he just wanted her to leave.

"What's her old ass gonna do? It's not like she's going to put her hands on me, cause I'll fuc…," Cheresse said to him rolling her eyes.

"Okay, okay, now that's not even necessary. What do you want?"

"Deron I didn't come here to cause no scene. I came to tell you that I missed you, really. These past few months, these restraining orders and all these lawsuits have ruin what I set out to show you; that I really do love you. Dawn has really drove a wedge between us."

"Aw come on Cheresse, I don't have time for this anymore, I have a new life. I'm married to Dawn now you know that. You and I had our time, it was wrong and now it's done, the end. I don't want to keep going on for the next twenty years telling you this."

"So you're saying that you never loved me," she said a bit agitated.

"Not the way I love Dawn. That's my wife," he paused as he thought that he should back up before the conversation gets off track. "What you and I had was just sex, that's all."

"I don't believe you just said that."

"Believe it."

"So you think that you can hide behind the church and be holier than thou? All those nights you used to beg me to let, you come over so you could pour that champagne on my body and lick it off, especially between my legs. That's not love? Then you turn around and smash me like you a virgin getting his first piece. You couldn't resist me then and now you say you don't have no feelings for me," she said smirking at him. "That's some bullshit and you know it. You have and you will always be hooked on this pussy. You know all I got to do is get up on this desk and drop these panties; you will throw all that halo crap out the window just to lick on this again. I'm getting wet just talking about it. As a matter of fact…"

She got up out of her chair.

When she did, Deron did as well.

He immediately ran to the door and opened it.

"LOL Deron, you think because you opened a door; that would stop me? You *have* been with that Christian bitch too long."

She stepped around the chair and reached into her purse. However, she didn't take her hand out of it.

"You think you're so in control, don't you? You're the altogether man. You think you can screw me and throw me away like trash without consequences."

"I don't think about nothing that should concern you right now Cheresse. No I take that back," he said as he slammed the door shut. His patience has worn through. "I wonder all this time why you are on me so much? I'm no different from all the other countless men you have messed over or messed with. When we were together all you did was mess with other men like you didn't want me. Even when I was trying to tell you how I felt about you. That really worked out for me in the end, though in my favor. God is good. Once you showed me how you really felt about me, I saw the light. I was able to find a woman who wouldn't try to get me to fight other men over her and who wouldn't take me for my money, blowing it up for nothing. A woman who told me and show me that she's in love with me. Oh yeah and not film us as well as a girl I didn't even know like that having sex and selling it on the internet while I'm drugged. That one's the top kicker right there. You risked my health to do all that. What could you do that could top any of that?"

"It is what it is *baby*," she said humorously and shrugging her shoulders.

"Ever since I met you I've been in nothing but chaos and I've been glad these past few years to be rid of you. You were the wrong woman at the wrong time no you're the wrong woman at any time. So if you're going to pull mace out that mighty expensive purse you got, spray me and try to make it seem like I'm attacking you or something; go right ahead. I'm done, I'm done."

He walked back past her and sat at his desk.

While she quietly looked at him she took in every word he said to her and she didn't like it one damn bit.

That son-of-a-bitch she thought to herself.

Where did she lose her hold?

No, he's not going to put her down like some vicious pit-bull bitch on the street; use her and make a fool out of her.

"You're done when I say *I'm* done damn it," she said as she pulled her hand from inside her purse and produced a folded 8 x 10 piece of paper. "And oh yeah, I'm the wrong woman at the wrong time…turnt up, remember that *baby*."

She tossed it in his direction as he sat behind his desk.

"What's this a GIF from our porn movie. You're really trying to wear that one out aren't you?"

"Maybe you should open it and see how far I'm willing to go, *baby*."

"No I'm not. As long as Dawn knows who you are and what you're capable of I'm fine, clean and simple."

"Deron, I'm going to get you back you just don't know it yet. We are always going to be together, connected."

"Uh, uh," he said shaking his head with confidence.

"I'm the smartest one in our little story and do you know why?"

He just moved his eyebrows upwards in a curious thinking look and shrugged his shoulders.

"It's because I don't lose my patience that often. Not when it counts. I tend to leave something back just for the right time. You remember how I do that, right. You remember when I played cat and mouse with you and Dawn for weeks until I got the two of you in the right place at the right time. I dropped that bomb on her ass right. That hurt puppy look on her face was priceless. I really thought I got that little bitch out of your life for good. Then I was gonna get us back. I got to say she's got some big ass balls but she's not gonna get pass this," she paused as she sat down in the chair again. "I think you better open that paper. I tried to show it to Dawn but that bitch punched me and I tried to kill her ass. Go on take a look."

Every alarm that Deron has ever heard in his life is going off now. This is Cheresse after all and with Cheresse there's always something life shaking laying in the cut. What can it be now because she's sitting here like she's about to win the lottery.

"I'm not interested in anything you got to show me Cheresse. It's time you leave and of course if you don't mind don't come back…please."

"No *baby*, I'm not going away not for a long time. That piece a paper's going to ensure me of that and I'm not going to be as generous as Audrey," she paused and stared at him with a wicked smirk.

What the…no he thought. Deron felt the blood draining from his face. It's almost as if he now realizes that he's looking at a ghost. But it isn't a real ghost it's a ghost from his past, his not too distance past.

How could this be happening again?

It can't be happening again.

He reached down to the desk and picked up the folded paper. He opened it and sure enough, it's a copy of a photo.

It's a photo of a little girl, a toddler.

She looks to be about a year old. His experience with DJ has made him very aware of ages, especially when sent to pick up pampers and other age related baby items from the store.

"This isn't going to work; you know that right."

"Yes, yes, yes, it is baby," she got up and walked around to him. He is still in shock looking at the picture. When she got around to him, she stood in front of him and pulled down her skirt and panties. They hit the floor. "You think you can keep going raw up in this pussy, as juicy as it is and not get nothing back? I'm always hot for you. At least you know you're potent, right. You get every woman you screw pregnant don't you?" she said rubbing her hand on her vagina. Then she brushed that hand across his face. "Oh I'm sorry every woman except Dawn. Smells good don't it baby? Don't you want some more right here, right now?"

At first Deron is, caught off guard from the euphoria of her familiar scent. It filled the room it seems. The memories of how they used to go at each other came crashing at him fast and he felt himself stirring in his pants. He leaned his face into her stomach and caught another scent of her. Quickly he grabbed her hand and pushed it away, and then he backed away from her in his chair.

Then he stood up.

"I know you do cause you're hard up now. Let's get this thing popping Deron right here on your desk, I know you want to get inside me. You want to bend me over like this…," she said leaning forward on the side of his desk.

When she was on her stomach, she lifted one leg up straddling the desk with it. Then she reached around from behind and showed herself to him to see. He saw that familiar place that he was so fixated with years ago; that almost cost him the woman he loves.

"Cheresse it's time for you to go for real," he said throaty with lust as he walked again to his door and opened it. He shook his head and breathed hard. "You think I believe anything about this photo you're out of your mind."

"You're pitiful," she said patting her ass then pulling her leg down off the desk. "I was going to give you some."

Once she stood, Cheresse kept her back turned to him and bent over so he could see her from behind. He saw what she wanted him to see.

He's determined to resist going for it again.

She pulled up her panties slowly looking behind her to make sure he's watching her.

He knows he wants this she thought.

Then the pulled up the skirt in the same fashion.

He's going miss this and come looking for it one day.

She began to fix herself up, smoothing down her clothing.

How many times has she done this Deron thought trying to keep the lust back that's just a blink away from overtaking him? How many times before has she tempted him and he didn't resist. He simply dived right in and he knows what's there is worth, what he's feeling.

He can't let her win, not this time.

If he lets her in there will be no resisting her ever again.

I know you're a good man, he heard Dawn's voice in his thoughts. That helped him keep his mind steady.

She pulled out a compact from her purse and then lipstick. She put some on and smacked her lips with a big pucker sound. She then walked over to him at the door and stood with him face to face.

"You remember we conceived her at your apartment. You know that last time you tasted this. The last time you were all up in this," she said bumping him a little. He pushed her back gently. "Well that must've been a big load. She's about a year and five months old and her birthday is April 5. Our daughter's name is Chenae Imari Stone. You're going to need to remember that for your records not for my check though that'll be in my name."

"I don't believe it. If this baby girl exists, then where has she been all this time? You been out and about too much to be a full time mother."

"Damn Deron you've been watching me or something? I know you can't get enough of me can you?"

"Where is she?"

"Right now she's at my parents' house in North Carolina. My aunt is helping watch her until I get, situated with her deadbeat father, so I can move back to North Carolina. At least that's what they know."

"I'm not going to waste any time with this. I'm going to tell Dawn as soon as I get home. You'd better get her up here for the paternity test and I mean now. Now get outta here."

"Yeah tell that bitch, she needs to know. I'm leaving *baby* but you know my cell number's still the same, and I already know you know it. You're gonna need it when you tell that bitch. You can come stay with me. She's gonna kick your ass out once she finds out that you were fucking me right up to the minute you got back with her. I tried to tell her that too but she wouldn't listen," she turned to leave. "I'm a bad bitch ain't I Deron? Fuck with me will you," she said as she walked down the hall laughing.

Deron slammed the door so hard that he could've sworn it shook the entire building.

Every time he steps out of favor, something like this happens. He's trying but what's with all these trials. He trusts in the Lord but the devil is riding his back bad and at every turn.

How could Cheresse have his baby, it's impossible? They used condoms every time they had sex when he went back to her that last time.

Something's not right.

He never went raw on her again after all that stuff happened that year at Christmas. That is the only time she probably could've gotten him to not wear a condom. That can't be when she got pregnant because that was too long ago.

Before he got back with Dawn two years ago he was with Cheresse, in June or July. He was still messed up in his head from his breakup with Dawn that he doesn't know what went on those nights without her sometimes.

There's no way Cheresse could have drugged him again. She did it to make that movie but not again.

It was easy then because he still blindly trusted her. He trusted her until finally he allowed Jesus to break him and called on him to face his path. That got him on the road to his salvation.

Maybe this is a sign that he doesn't deserve to be with Dawn. All the pain that he's caused her, maybe God just wanted him to see what he could've had if he allowed Jesus Christ fully in his life. He allowed himself to be out there and got in too deep; now there's no turning back. All of his past troubles are coming in now to put him back on blast again.

He tried to change from his past.

He's going to lose Dawn behind this for sure.

He can't lose his woman not now, not this careless way. Not because some other woman wants revenge on him, because Cheresse don't have no love for him.

He's going to need Jesus now more than ever as he faces this thing.

Dawn is going to kill me he thought and shook his head.

What's going to happen between the two of them?

But he's got to trust in the Lord; he has to. Like Dawn has once said it's who you praise through the storm that's the blessing. He once told Tony the same thing. He can't go back on his own words now.

He got down on his knees, on the floor in his office and started to pray.

****

What's she supposed to do now Yolanda thought? It was later on in the evening as she sat on her sofa in her home. She sat with the TV on while Bryan Jr and Deron Jr played around her and Dawn's in the kitchen cooking.

Just when she is putting herself back out on the market this happens. Steve Powers hurt her so much and not just because he deceived her. By finding out that, he's the reason why Bryan was murdered and the reasoning behind it made her sick. She was just getting over her grief enough to enjoy her life. Now she finds out that this was all because this selfish wicked man wanted *her* and her husband's property for himself for some big housing scheme. It was personal and he disgusts her every time she thinks that he touched her. The only saving-grace is that she stuck to her guns and didn't enter in premarital sex with him; and also that the promise of God will bring her peace. She knows that she will never see him come to justice for the murder of her husband but he will have to face the Lord; if he doesn't repent in his heart what he's done.

She wants restitution for the devastation she's had to endure and for the pain of her son not having his father to raise him. Bryan was a good man and he deserves to be here, here with her.

It's too much to think about.

The noise from the kitchen jarred her from her thoughts. After she heard the movements, she reminded herself that Dawn had gone into the kitchen about an hour ago to cook something for the both of them. She's being a really good friend to her and she values their friendship.

Val the same way.

She's glad that the two of them have gotten what was bothering them out of the way. At least that's what Dawn told her. Their sisterhood must remain intact no matter what.

Regarding Val, she told Yolanda and Dawn that she is going to see Tony to make plans for their wedding. It's in two months and there's too much to do but Val swears it can happen. That's not the problem. The problem is whether she wants to marry Tony. She told Yolanda she didn't know what it is but she seems to be waiting for the other shoe to drop and so is Nathan. The confusion was going on so much that she had to tell Nathan that they had to cool it for a bit and he decided to take a three-month business trip to Tampa, Florida. He sent Val an open plane ticket if she changes her mind.

Whatever her choice they will definitely stand by her.

Picking up the universal remote Yolanda turned up the volume on the TV. The evening news is on and she thought that bad news is one more thing that she doesn't need in life her now. She was about to switch the channel when she saw something that caught her attention.

Breaking news...this is Barry Cabot with breaking news. Local PG County Police department made several arrest today resulting from a long time sting operation involving what sources are saying is a conglomerate of money laundering, phony land developing and housing deals; most importantly indictments on drug trafficking charges stemming from operating out of several local businesses; mainly the dispensing of the banned synthetic marijuana. Police arrested local business owner Jerrell Lewis, land developers Moore Penny and Morales Vatineo of MPM&M Land Developers, Hair Salon Owner Phaedra McCoy and business owner Steven Powers on multiple counts to include indictments on money laundering to synthetic drug trafficking. No word yet but there's talk of other arrests before the week is out a total of twelve persons involved. This story-unfolded a few months ago when an informant that works at the Washington Federal Security Bank discovered a substantial amount of funds being deposit in an account own by McCoy....

Instantly Yolanda let out a scream.

Dawn ran out of the kitchen when she heard Yolanda scream. The boys stopped playing and looked at her. Yolanda isn't saying anything but she's crying, smiling and pointing at the TV.

Dawn turned to the TV just in time to see Steve Powers being; hauled by the police into a police station. She didn't need any words, the look on her friend's face is priceless.

She sat down by her friend and held her while they watched the rest of the news together.

All the phones at Yolanda's house started to ring simultaneously.

****

When Tony came home later that evening, he walked into his house and saw Valerie sitting at the dining room table. What's on her damn mind he thought in his head? Is it going to be another gotta make him do right conversation? With this wedding he's still trying to get out of approaching with each month, everyday she's experiencing some new thought. She's trying to take control of him. She's making it pretty, damn hard to play this new devoted fiancée role.

It's a good balance though.

He's able to still sleep around and she still believes everything he says.

Sometimes though he still felt like saying fuck it.

"Hey baby what's up, you look serious?" he said to Valerie walking into the dining room and bending down to kiss her where she sat.

She turned her head.

That message wasn't lost on her efforts. Tony left her alone and sat down in the chair at the end of the table.

What is it now not enough time spent together before they're husband and wife? If he could do anything about it besides her leaving him, he would rather not get married.

"The insurance company called my cellphone looking for you," she said not really raising her voice or even looking at him.

He was going to ask her how did they get her number, but he remembered that he had added her as an emergency contact recently. One more thing to show in good faith.

"Yeah about my truck?" he said trying to joke with her.

"No the home insurance company. They just wanted some more information about the *arson* fire that happened here," she answered him quietly and calmly. "You didn't say the fire was caused by arson. You said a damn candle and that the sprinkler system malfunctioned. So I did some investigating on my own and convinced the insurance adjustor that I was there that night and got the story. Some woman tried to burn this house down with lighter fluid. They said the sprinkler had been, disabled at the source, not malfunctioning. I guess she did that too. They're not paying for the renovations," she paused some. She took a breath and then continued because she started to get, heated. "I don't think I ever stop to tell you all about my childhood growing up. Probably because I don't like to talk about it much and I was always a little embarrass then. My mother suffered from some sort of depression from my father leaving her and my father well he wasn't. Do you know how it is to grow up as a little child in that kind of environment? One parent off somewhere and another, well just away. You long for something for a long time and you don't even know what it is. You do crazy things to compensate for what really is pain. They dimmed my light a little and took me off my game. I mean I've known for a longtime that I could achieve greatness, but I just couldn't stop trying to get their attention. For the longest time I just couldn't see *me*. I was always their child. My grandparents though, they were my light at the end of the tunnel. I loved them so much and I didn't have to guess whether they loved me, especially my grandmother. They gave me that sense of stability to where I know the difference when life is, screwed up around me. They made me want to be that one, the best. But after they were gone I was left with those two again and it was back to feeling unwanted. The two of them couldn't look pass what they wanted to even consider how I was doing and of course I struggled. But I did what I was supposed to do. I got on top of this thing and I made a way for me. I made my own way. I *am* a success. Somewhere along the way, my heart hardened and I got stubborn. You tried to dim my light too. I couldn't see real love anymore. I passed up a man who really loves me waiting for the next best thing, but the next best thing never came. I'm hoping he's still out there. I knew I couldn't trust you. I mean I felt it deep in my heart that I couldn't trust you to do what you said you would do," she said as she slid the engagement ring across the table. More like she flicked it. "You know, I'm not the least bit upset. You can't do it. You just can't do it and you know there's no need for me to come back to this fucked up house anymore. So I just wanted to tell you that I'm done…and oh I'll send my itemized list for my things that your whore burned up. I need those things replaced."

"Val look it wasn't…," Tony attempted to say.

She got up; that interrupted him and walked to the door. She opened it and slammed it shut, hard behind her as she walked through it.

Even after she left, Tony didn't say another thing, he couldn't. He didn't know what to think. He didn't even try to stop Valerie this time because he knows she's right.

He can't do it.

He can't be that man she needs and not feel like he's choking.

Does he love Valerie?

Of course he does.

But he loves being out there in the streets, more. He loves all the new women that he meets and what they do to satisfy him. Hell he's only thirty-two years old; no more playing house. Being married before made him hard about relationships and especially marriage. Of course his parents ain't help the situation too much either. Their kind of love was cold. He knows that but knowing didn't change who he really is.

So she's been on some other dude huh?

So be it.

Valerie doesn't even know how much alike they really are coming from the same kind of fucked up situation. But he ain't gonna let those folks mess him up no more; he's gonna enjoy himself. It's best that Valerie isn't around for all this; he likes women with no drama. He likes them on their backs with their legs spread wide or on their knees, whatever.

He told Deron that he was wasting his holy words on him. He likes being bad and he doesn't worry too much cause he wants to live for now. He's not going to waste his life praying and not doing natural stuff like smashing different women every night.

Ain't nothing gonna happen to him, he's the golden boy.

Now he's living raw like he wants to. He should call Aijon and see if his girl Tiasha can't turn him up with one of her freak nasty girlfriends. She can turn him on to a whole new crop of thots, young and dumb ones. Maybe she might want to do something risky like getting with him. Hell Aijon ain't stable to keep her why waste her time. It's not like they're friends like him and D. He needs to call Aijon before his trial starts cause Tony don't know which way it's gonna flow. Reckless driving, excessive speeding and ramming Tony's badass Escalade into a police car on the side of a road on I95 is gonna draw some attention; from the police. Good thing there wasn't anybody in that other vehicle. But if you doing that shit you don't need to have an unregistered weapon in your possession. It's messed up though that his truck is totaled as bad as that Escalade was. All those custom alterations he made to that damn truck is well over fifteen grand.

Damn truck is mashed and flooded.

Aijon gonna pay him for that.

Walking over to where he keeps some liquor on a tray in his dining room he pours a drink and slings it back. It wasn't down his throat clear enough before he poured the next one.

His cell phone rang on his side.

He picked it up, looked at the screen and saw a blocked number. He chuckled to himself because he thought why in the hell did Valerie block her number. She can't stay off this magic stick.

He did like what they have together; it is what it is.

It's like clockwork; she got halfway down the road and got that Tony vibe again.

So he answered it.

"What's up girl, you wanta come back?"

"...collect call from the Prince Georges County Correctional Facility...Sharnia Burkefield calling. Will you accept the call?"

What the hell she wants, he thought? She damn near burn down his house and she expects him to talk to her. He didn't know she is this damn crazy. All he does is mess with crazy ass women, everyone except Valerie, she's perfect. Phaedra, she turned out to be a damn crook running with thieves and killers, what was she thinking? She wasn't thinking they would turn around and try to kill her ass. She better be glad he and Deron got to her ass before the gas did.

He thought Sharnia had class but she turned out to be one big old thot that he can use over and over. Tony now knows that, she didn't just want to hurt him by setting his house on fire. She was trying to off herself and him. That police detective, Hayden told him that Sharnia was really going to set that fire after he got home and fell asleep. Said she said, she was going to hide in the spare bedroom and light the fire then crawl in the bed with him and the two of them would go up in smoke. It is something in her juvenile records that is similar to this.

Maybe he laid on her too much he thought. Sometimes he knew he was saying too much hard shit to her and that probably broke her. The time in jail should straighten her up and knock some sense into her. When she gets out he's gonna have to have a long talk with her if she thinks she's gonna be hanging around. She gonna work of this money she cost him.

What the hell could she want with this call, money? Well pretty soon he ain't gonna have to give another hoe broad no more money just as soon as Tony Jr turns the big 1-8. And that's real soon.

Damn he's about to be free like a real G.

He started to hang up the phone.

"Will you accept the call?" the automated voice repeated.

He paused as he thought about it and curiosity took over. What does the psycho want? She can't give him no booty cause she got herself locked up.

Reluctantly he accepted the call.

"Yeah."

"That selection is not valid. Will you accept the call?" The automated voice repeated again.

"Yes, damn it."

"Tony it's me Sharnia. I love you…do you hear me I love you…you got to be there for me please…I won't be in here that long."

He has to admit that he like the way that Sharnia gets turnt up with him. It's the only way he really likes to live now; on the edge and punishing them. She'll be right when she gets out willing to do anything for him to keep him. She won't do that wild shit no more, like trying to burn down his house, that's guaranteed. She ain't gonna want to do no more jail time. Her lawyer's already pleading for a criminal mischief charge and some psych counseling. This way she'll only do a year or less, maybe nothing, probation. He ain't marrying her or nothing like that but yeah he'll be there for her. Just as long as she keeps giving him the business. Deron's gonna to give her job back to her too. He's gonna make sure of that.

"Yeah Nia baby I hear you…I got you."

"Good cause I got a surprise for you."

"Oh yeah what's that?" he laughed.

"I'm pregnant, isn't that great?"

"Naw I don't want no more kids," Tony said shocked with anger in his voice.

What the hell's this chick doing?

It was all right keeping her on because she has that hot body to use up whenever he wanted to but now, a baby.

Uh, uh she done fucked up now.

"Well it's too late," she said edgily.

"It's never too late," Tony said to her sounding like the devil.

Is he trying to tell her to get an abortion she thought? *Why*?

She thought he would be happy with the news.

The last time they were in the truck together, he told her to ride him like she wanted to make a baby.

Well she did what she was, told.

She always does what he tells her to do.

That seems to be her problem.

"I'll get out early before the baby comes and we'll see the doctor together. It'll be good you'll see."

"You can see the doc in there and do what you gotta do."

"I don't want to do that."

"I don't want another kid."

"I thought you wanted this."

"I don't even want you," he said as he hung up the phone abruptly.

This is gonna be harder than he thought.

This crazy ass girl done gone and got knocked up. She was supposed to be taking a pill or something cause they ain't used a rubber in a minute.

Stupid, stupid chick.

Ain't no problem though.

All it takes is to get the right chick to get lockdown for the weekend or so, punch the bitch a couple of times in her gut and the problem's solved.

He'll pay good money for that.

If she don't want to do it his way, he'll get it done his way next weekend.

The doorbell interrupted his thoughts.

He walked to the door laughing actually, as he really thought about what he planned for that thot Sharnia. She thinks she's gonna pin him down for the next eighteen years paying child support, that ain't happening.

Naw not this time.

Big Tony's gots a single life to live and bitches to buy. Hell with Valerie gone he might have some of those thot parties like the one Aijon had. Except he ain't gonna have no broad keep him from getting it turnt up the way he likes to turn it up.

When Tony got to the door, he opened it without looking out of it first. First thought who it could be is, Valerie. Instead of calling him she is gonna crawl back to him and this time he's gonna make her get down on her knees and really crawl to him naked.

When he saw two men in suits at his door, his shock must have been all over his face.

"Tony Parker?"

"Yep," Tony said trying to sound bold and wishing he had brought his Glock 43 to the door with him. Can't be too sure these days. It wasn't too many days ago that he blocked Steve Powers from killing Yolanda and even Phaedra too. So you never know. Criminals dress all kinds of ways these days. "Y'all want something?"

"Yes Sir," one of the men said.

"Federal Officers. Need you to come with us on suspicion of money laundering and drug trafficking," the other man said showing his federal badge with his left hand and motioning his right hand to the air pointing towards Tony and the house. "Move in," he commanded.

"Nah man, you can't come…," Tony said backing up.

Then he started thinking about Phaedra, Steve and Jerrell.

This is their mess.

He's not involved in any criminal acts with them.

Then he thought about the money Phaedra got him to deposit through his bank for her. About how he helped her invest it back into some local clubs and other local businesses she chose.

Where did she get that money?

Damn that was stupid.

He should've of listen to his instinct.

No maybe he should've listened to Deron.

Then he thought about his manager telling him not to come back to work. He told him that the company was doing an audit. He was trying to keep him away while they investigated Tony's transactions.

He's gonna need a lawyer.

Damn he cursed in his thoughts.

I ain't do nothing.

"Oh yeah we also have this search warrant to search your premises."

THE END

PLEASE POST A
REVIEW
ABOUT THE NOVELS @
www.dharveyrawlings.com

AUTHOR'S ADDITIONAL WORKS

Urban Drama
Wrong Woman at the Wrong Time

Suspense Thrillers
Lies Hidden in Darkness
Unforgivable Lies